# FRENCH RURAL HISTORY

*By the same Author*

FEUDAL SOCIETY

# FRENCH RURAL HISTORY

*An Essay on its
Basic Characteristics*

## MARC BLOCH

*Foreword by*
BRYCE LYON

*Translated from the French by*
JANET SONDHEIMER

UNIVERSITY OF CALIFORNIA PRESS

*Berkeley and Los Angeles*

*Translated from the French*
LES CARACTÈRES ORIGINAUX DE
L'HISTOIRE RURALE FRANÇAISE

*University of California Press
Berkeley and Los Angeles
California*

*Second Printing, 1973
ISBN: 0–520–01660–2
Library of Congress Catalog
Card Number 66–15483*

*Printed in the United States of America*

# Contents

## Contents

# Plates

*Between pages 142 and 143*

# Foreword*

BY BRYCE LYON

DURING that June of 1944 when the allied armies were chewing their way into Normandy towards Paris men dedicated to freedom and human dignity anxiously watched and began to hope and to plan for a time when western Europe would again be guided by those values that it had done so much to create. This was certainly the sentiment of many Frenchmen in the *Résistance*, especially of Marc Bloch who had joined the *Résistance* after fighting earlier in the French army and was at this time a prisoner of the Germans. Perhaps no man had pondered more the reasons for the French débâcle and no intellectual had thought more about how to improve the French system of education so as to build a better France than Marc Bloch. For him and his comrades of the *Résistance* the liberation of Paris would be the reward for their heroic sacrifice and would symbolize the reconstruction of France. It would unite him

---

* Those who would like to know more about the life and work of Marc Bloch should consult the following publications. In 1945 Volumes I and II of *Les Annales d'Histoire Sociale* were issued as *Hommages à Marc Bloch*. Of the various articles one should especially consult those of Lucien Febvre, Henri Baulig, and Georges Altman (Chabot). Here also are printed the spiritual testament of Marc Bloch and some of his correspondence. In 1947 Volume CIII of the *Publications de la Faculté des Lettres de l'Université de Strasbourg* appeared as a memorial to those members of the faculty who died between 1939 and 1945. Here Lucien Febvre writes of Marc Bloch as a colleague and Robert Boutruche writes of him as a teacher. Of the numerous evaluations of Marc Bloch's work the best are Charles-E. Perrin, 'L'Œuvre historique de Marc Bloch,' *Revue Historique*, CXCIX (1948), 161–188, and Lucien Febvre, 'Marc Bloch,' in *Architects and Craftsmen on History. Festschrift für Abbott Payson Usher* (Tübingen, 1956), pp. 75–84. For the chief articles of Marc Bloch see his *Mélanges historiques* (Paris, 1963), Vols. I–II. Charles-E. Perrin has written a fine preface on Marc Bloch as a historian and there is a complete bibliography of Bloch's writings.

with his wife and six children and permit him to resume his *métier* of historian.[1]

While most Frenchmen were soon to have these hopes fulfilled, the realities of history, as Marc Bloch was so fond of calling historical facts, were to deprive him of the same joy. Having been captured shortly before the allied landing in Normandy, and having been imprisoned and tortured for his part in the *Résistance*, he along with twenty-six others was shot by the Gestapo in a field not far from Lyons on 16 June 1944. Thus at the age of fifty-eight Marc Bloch died for the France that he loved, the France of which he had said that he had drunk from the sources of her culture and could only breathe under her sky.

Marc Bloch lived life as he wrote history: he always chose the difficult and spurned the easy. Like some historians, he could have effortlessly described simple events and dodged issues, but such history disgusted him. Like many men, he could have survived the war by taking no risks, but such was not his way. He need not have been mobilised when war came in 1939. He had seen four years of action at the front in the war of 1914–1918; he was married; he was a father. When France fell he need not have remained there; he could have escaped and gone to England or America where distinguished universities had invited him to join their faculties. But, seeing neither life nor history in simple or expedient terms, Marc Bloch shunned escape and chose to fight in whatever way he could for his ideals and his country.

Realistic, shrewd, and observant, Marc Bloch was bent by temperament towards economic and social history. Yet neither history nor life were narrow for him; he was broadly cultured and he hated compartmentalisation. To understand history and life one had to look at both in the broadest and deepest sense. Each nourished the other and both were so intertwined that only a fool could divorce them. Between life and history was a natural and essential bond. Perhaps the easy problems of both

---

[1] For Marc Bloch's reflections on the causes of the defeat of France see his *L'étrange défait. Témoignage écrit en 1940* (new ed.; Paris, 1957). In a moving foreword Georges Altman (Chabot), who had known Marc Bloch as a member of the *Résistance*, gives his impressions of Marc Bloch and describes his last days. Also included are some writings of Marc Bloch done after he had gone underground. This book was translated into English as *Strange Defeat*.

could be glossed over, and perhaps even serious problems could be ignored for short periods, but ultimately they had to be faced and solved. For Marc Bloch there was no world of make-believe; he was too intelligent to pretend that life and history are simple and easy. His greatest challenge was to be the true historian, to face directly the realities of history, and to divest himself of preconceived ideas.[2]

Marc Bloch wrote much social and economic history of the Middle Ages and stimulated others to do likewise by his perceptive remarks in the review *Les Annales: Économies, Sociétés, Civilisations* founded by Lucien Febvre and himself in 1929. Most of what he wrote concerned the land and how man lived on it. His first book published just before World War I was a geographical and historical study entitled *L'Île de France (Les Pays autour de Paris)*.[3] His *thèse*, which appeared just after the war, concerned the emancipation of serfs on Capetian land. Here, already, is evident that compulsion towards knowing the 'what' of history. He wrote that if historians had sufficiently known what serfdom was and what were the relations of serfs on the royal domain with the Capetians they would not have constructed the reigns of Louis X and Philip V as the period when serfdom ended on Capetian land.[4] These early studies confirmed his proclivity for agrarian history. His acute sensitivity to his surroundings, his love of tramping the country-side, and his delight in talking with local people and antiquarians dictated the historical route he was to travel. He needed only to broaden his knowledge and develop a methodology.

The scholarly achievements of Marc Bloch between 1920 and 1939 are indeed remarkable when one realizes that within this span of nineteen years he not only wrote most of what he published but also learned the techniques essential for his kind of research. He expanded his knowledge of all the relevant languages, even of Russian. He studied archaeology, agronomy, cartography, philology, and folk-lore. He began to see the implications of

[2] Marc Bloch expressed some of his ideas on history in his book *Apologie pour l'histoire ou métier d'historien* (Paris, 1949). This book, written during the first months of World War II, could only be published after the war. See also the English translation *The Historian's Craft* (New York, 1953).

[3] This book appeared in 1913 as a volume in the series *Les régions de la France* under the auspices of *La Revue de Synthèse Historique*.

[4] *Rois et serfs. Un chapitre d'histoire capétienne* (Paris, 1920).

aerial photography for the study of field arrangements. He read further in economics and geography. Though no Marxist, he willingly turned to Marx for insights on economics. He explored the working concepts of social anthropology, social psychology, and sociology. Intrigued with the sociological doctrines of Durkheim, he collected and analysed the phenomena which produced collective beliefs, attitudes, and behaviour. Although *Les rois thaumaturges* published in 1924 did not concern economic and social history, it asked how and why men came to believe in the miraculous curative powers of the Capetian kings. What was there in medieval Christian doctrine, pagan practice, custom, and superstition that contributed to this collective belief? What did the Capetians do to encourage such belief? These were questions typical of Marc Bloch.[5]

The early twenties saw him become completely disenchanted with facts *per se* and with the descriptive history written by most members of his craft. He lost patience with minute investigations of no relevance and with local studies unrelated to broader historical problems. Influenced in this attitude by a growing interest in sociology which whetted his appetite for the broad and basic problems, he was further inspired by the broad approach of articles published in the *Revue de Synthèse Historique* edited by Henri Berr and was captivated by the address of Henri Pirenne at the International Congress of Historians at Brussels in 1923 on the value of comparative history.[6] Though never to forget his early belief that history was a discipline of change or that it was 'une matière fluide', by the middle twenties Marc Bloch had formed his basic historical attitude and methodology and had perfected his erudition. He was ready now to write that book on French rural history which many scholars acknowledge to be his most original and distinguished work.

When Marc Bloch delivered his lectures on *Les caractères originaux de l'histoire rurale française* before the Institute for the Comparative Study of Civilisations at Oslo in 1929 and when he recast them in the book which appeared in 1931, he frankly

[5] *Les rois thaumaturges. Étude sur le caractère surnaturel attribué à la puissance royale; particulièrement en France et en Angleterre* (Paris, 1924).

[6] Pirenne, 'De la méthode comparative en histoire,' in *Compte Rendu du Cinquième Congrès International des Sciences Historiques* (Brussels, 1923). See also Bloch, 'Pour une histoire comparée des sociétés européennes,' *Revue de Synthèse Historique*, XLVI (1928), 15–50.

admitted that this synthesis was not intended to be definitive.[7] He predicted that it would be superseded, that it would be revised and corrected, but he hoped that it would stimulate vigorous research on agrarian history. He wanted to focus upon the fundamental problems of French agrarian history and place them in true perspective, to investigate them in their total complexity and deal with them realistically as would a man who was both a good historian and farmer. He was convinced that agrarian history could no longer be discussed principally in legal and institutional terms. It made no sense to speak of peasants, animals, crops, fields, and ploughs as though they were only items of revenue and terms at law. He felt that the armchair historian of Paris writing about seignorialism could never come to grips with the subject. What did such a historian know about rural mentality, the daily routine of farming, the smells of hay, manure, and pigs? On the other hand, the local antiquarian who knew much about such matters was deficient in historical erudition and perspective, and the farmer who knew even more lacked the intelligence to describe and conceptualise. Marc Bloch never believed that he could completely unite historical perspective, local knowledge, and experience; he knew this was an ideal, but he knew also that in so approaching agrarian history he would achieve truer pictures and answers.

Marc Bloch read all the pertinent primary and secondary sources. He read deeply in the literature of all the disciplines related to the land and its exploitation. He did even more: he observed and constantly asked 'why'. Why were there hamlets here and nucleated villages there? Why were fields open and regular here, open and irregular there, and enclosed in other regions? Why were certain crops produced here and others there and what relation did this have to the arrangement of the fields, the agrarian routine, and the habitation of the peasants? Why were some regions of France cultivated so early in her history and so constantly while others were put under the plough late and remained marginal? Why and when was land reclamation carried out and what impact did it have upon the social,

[7] In 1956 was published a supplementary volume by Robert Dauvergne, a former student of Bloch. The purpose of this volume is to bring Bloch's *Caractères* up to date by summarising his research done between 1931 and 1944 and by noting that of other scholars produced between 1931 and 1956.

economic, and legal condition of the peasant? How much manure did scrawny cows and pigs produce and how did the supply influence crop rotation and the two- and three-field systems? What do farmers of our age think and how bound are they by custom and tradition? How was it with the peasant of the Middle Ages? Such observations and questions were always in the mind and on the lips of Marc Bloch as he roamed over rural France, as he talked with local men, and as he got the feel of the land; they are the subjects of his book.

With what exhilaration did he push his quest! With what enthusiasm did he describe his work to his friend Henri Pirenne! How delighted he was to discuss the book with his colleagues. Did it make sense to start one's investigations with the known, as for example with seventeenth- and eighteenth-century maps of fields and villages, and work back to the distant medieval and thence to the unknown? Maitland had done so years before with his *Domesday Book and Beyond*.[8] Would not such an approach be even more fruitful with less attention to legal problems? Had not previous historians been too engrossed in the origins of institutions and too ignorant of how the present impinges upon the past? Yes, certainly, this method must have some merit.

Marc Bloch lived long enough to know that he was right, that his imagination and his courage to break with tradition and routine did have merit. He lived to see his students and other young historians embrace his methods and push forward. He knew, as do all historians who have worked in his field, that his book revolutionized the study of agrarian history and transformed many previous studies into museum pieces. From this book came the nourishment to write a broad synthesis of feudal society.[9] Although this second study is known to more historians and perhaps appreciated more, Marc Bloch knew even at the time of its writing that it would never equal his *Caractères*. He knew that his soundings had not been pushed as deeply, that his knowledge of local feudal peculiarities was not

[8] F. W. Maitland, *Domesday Book and Beyond* (Cambridge, 1897).

[9] *La société féodale* (Paris, 1939–1940), Vols. I–II. See the English translation by L. A. Manyon, *Feudal Society* (London, 1961). For an evaluation of this work see Bryce Lyon, 'The Feudalism of Marc Bloch,' *Tijdschrift voor Geschiedenis*, LXXVI (1963), 275–283.

as certain, and that occasionally his zeal flagged; he said this in his letters to Henri Pirenne. But when a man has written two superb studies, their relative value is of little importance. What is interesting is to know that Marc Bloch had a greater zest for the first book and knew that it was the better work.

In that spring of 1944 when Marc Bloch must have known death to be his fate he undoubtedly thought about life and how sweet it could be when the war was over and he was united with his family and his books. One of his hopes certainly was that young scholars would return to their work and write books that would not only reinforce some of his suggestions and conclusions but would completely revise others. How he would like to have seen his *Caractères* revised! Constituted as he was, he could never forget that history was a fluid in constant change and that his book was a part of this history.

It is now thirty-five years since Marc Bloch wrote his *Caractères*. Young historians around the world have devoured its rich pages, taken something for themselves, and proceeded on. Though revised by the work of such scholars as Boutruche, Déléage, Dollinger, and Duby,[10] unlike other books so revised, it will never cease being vital. Its timeless vibrance derives from Marc Bloch's conviction that history and life are inseparable and that the supreme values of both are worth a man's supreme sacrifice.

BRYCE LYON

*Brown University*

[10] Robert Boutruche, *La crise d'une société; seigneurs et paysans du Bordelais pendant la guerre de cent ans* (Paris, 1947), *Une société provinciale en lutte contre le régime féodal; l'alleu en Bordelais et en Bazadais du onzième aux dix-huitième siècle* (Paris, 1947), *Seigneurie et féodalité* (Paris, 1959); A. Déléage, *La vie rurale en Bourgogne jusqu'au début du XIᵉ siècle* (Paris, 1940), Vols. I–III; Philippe Dollinger, *L'évolution des classes sociales en Bravière depuis la fin de l'époque carolingienne jusqu'au milieu du treizième siècle* (Paris, 1949); Georges Duby, *La société aux onzième et douzième siècles dans la région mâconnaise* (Paris, 1953), *L'économie rurale et la vie des campagnes dans l'Occident médiéval (France, Angleterre, Empire), neuvième-quinzième siècles* (Paris, 1962), Vols, I–II.

# Preface

BY LUCIEN FEBVRE

MARC BLOCH'S *Caractères originaux de l'histoire rurale française,*
which was originally published at Oslo in 1931 and appeared
simultaneously at Paris under the imprint *Belles Lettres,* has
long been out of print. As he told me on more than one
occasion, he had every intention of bringing out another edition.
In Marc Bloch's own mind this was not simply a matter of
reissuing the original text. He knew, none better, that time
stops for no historian, that every good piece of historical
writing needs to be rewritten after twenty years: otherwise the
writer has failed in his objective, failed to goad others into
testing his foundations and improving on his rasher hypotheses
by subjecting them to greater precision. Marc Bloch was not
given time to refashion his great book as he would have wished.
One wonders whether he would in fact ever have brought
himself to do it. I have the impression that the prospect of this
somewhat dreary and certainly difficult task (however one
may try to avoid it, revision of an earlier work is always
hampered by the original design, which offers few easy loop-
holes for escape) held less appeal than the excitement of con-
ceiving and executing an entirely new book. However this
may be, our friend has carried this secret, with so many others,
to his grave. The fact remains that one of our historical classics,
now more than twenty years old, is due for republication and is
here presented to the reader.

This edition is made up of two elements. First, it reproduces
word for word the original text of 1931, the text which owes its
origin to the happy inspiration which descended on the
*Institut pour l'Etude des Civilisations* of Oslo. As we all know, in
1929 this important foundation, which had already called on
the services of men such as Meillet, Vinogradoff, Jespersen,

Karlgren, Magnus Olsen and Alfons Dopsch amongst others, was bold enough to step outside its usual field by inviting Marc Bloch, still quite a young man on the threshold of his career and uncertain of his direction, to lecture on *Les caractères originaux de l'histoire rurale française*. The success of the course gave Marc Bloch the first intimation of his burgeoning magisterial power; the lectures themselves, after some rearrangement and amplification, became the book to which we all owe so much: the truly remarkable book, as I said in the *Revue Historique* at the time, of a man untroubled by the bogy of upholding a 'scholarly reputation'—pedantic criticism of bibliographical omissions which left one or two books in deserved oblivion thus passed him by—but with a sure touch in striking a balance and setting out a programme.

His undertaking was arduous. France is a country whose provinces are very diverse, both geographically and in other ways; it has been settled at various times by an unusually large number of different peoples, who have left their mark and intermingled; lastly, the lands we call French have felt the influence of a number of rival agrarian civilisations, each with its distinctive material attributes and moral codes. In view of all this, it can have been no easy matter to lay bare the essential features of an agrarian history which was necessarily so complex. The undertaking was also vital. France has been an agricultural country from time immemorial; if we treat her rural history with undeserved neglect we run the risk of misunderstanding not merely the past but also perhaps the present of a land where revolutions have so often taken the form of resurrections. Bloch showed his daring by venturing into this field as a pioneer. But he had a further quality, and it was this that made *Les caractères originaux* a great book.

It is true that there had been men before 1931 with enough knowledge of agricultural practices to write with tolerable competence on 'the evolution of agricultural France'—a book with this title was actually produced by Augé-Laribé, and in its time performed a useful service. And as we all know, there were already a number of major historical works of quite formidable erudition: for example, *L'Alleu* from the pen of Fustel de Coulanges and the more debatable but lively and stimulating book of Jacques Flach, *Les Origines de l'ancienne*

*France*, which has perhaps been too much neglected. There were also some weighty text-books: which of us does not still turn on occasion to Henri Sée's *Les classes rurales et le regime domanial en France au moyen âge*, despite the legalism and aridity of its approach? The one drawback was that these historians— all of them, without exception—knew nothing at all about agriculture as it is practised. In 1932 I was forced to say of them 'their peasants always plough with cartularies, using charters for ploughshares'. In particular, the idea that the masters of *seigneuries* could have been faced with problems of a strictly economic order was entirely foreign to them. Nor did it occur to them, though the idea seems obvious enough, that agrarian problems could not be studied merely within the framework of a particular commune or even of a particular province. These are in fact questions which at the very least must be treated on a European scale—fair game, in fact, for the comparative historian.

Marc Bloch was at pains not to be the kind of historian who writes about agriculture in ignorance of what is an ox, a wheeled plough or a crop rotation; further, he had at his command a whole battery of qualities he could deploy simultan-eously—profound understanding of the texts and documents, a sense of living economic realities, insight into the way of life of past generations, immense and detailed knowledge of what had been accomplished in Germany, England, Belgium and else-where by scholars engaged with the great questions of rural history, in a line descending from Meitzen to Des Marez by way of Seebohm and Vinogradoff. It was because he could muster so many talents and cross-fertilise so many different fields of knowledge that this young teacher at the French Uni-versity of Strasbourg was the only scholar who at that precise juncture was capable of writing the book we so badly needed, and of enticing so many still younger men, happy to find a leader, into following the trail he so confidently blazed.

But, and none knew this better than Bloch himself, the fruit-fulness of his book could only be measured by the speed with which it was recognised as provisional and tentative. He must have hoped for it to be scrutinised line by line (why else should scholars write their books?), for its substance to become com-mon property and lead to exhaustive and unending debates, disagreements, corrections and revisions. Bloch himself was second to none in the enthusiasm, authority and skill he brought to the task of renovation. There is no need to make this a moral virtue. Anyone who believes himself to be infallible must be a fool. Anyone who believes that books can be 'definitive' is the opposite of an historian. Only the most sadly blinkered could fail to appreciate how important is the ceaseless labour of expanding, refining and adding depth and precision to the most brilliant hypotheses and most apparently impregnable constructions. One could say that all Bloch's contributions to the *Annales* between 1931 and 1941 were made with the single object of coming more closely to grips with the facts covered by this book in its original form, with verifying its basic propositions and enlarging its scope. When the time came to think of a new edition (the 1931 volume was by now quite unobtainable) we were thus faced with an additional obligation. Since Bloch was no longer with us, we had to do what we could to take his place. Our thoughts were no substitute for his. Nothing he himself had written could be safely neglected, so our task was to collect together all the suggestions, corrections and revisions which had occurred to him in the course of ten years' incessant activity between 1931 and 1941. This was a difficult undertaking which demanded a high degree of self-abnegation and tact, not to mention competence, on the part of its executor. The man to whom it was entrusted was Robert Dauvergne, a disciple of Marc Bloch, an historian with an inventive and enquiring turn of mind, and an expert in agrarian problems (he has been engaged for several years in preparing an important book on the Beauce). It is not for us to eulogise the spirit of devotion he has brought to bear on his task. We must, however, express our regret that it was not possible for this delicate mission to be completed in time to coincide with the publication of Bloch's original text, which we have decided to issue on its own as Volume I; Volume II when it appears[1] will bring before the reader the material contained in articles, discussions and reviews published by Marc Bloch after 1931, and so bring new life and interest to the original text.

[1] It should be noted that Volume II of *Les caractères originaux* containing additional writings of Marc Bloch was published by Librairie Armand Colin in 1956 under the editorship of Robert Dauvergne.

*Preface*

One thing further needs to be said. The book now reissued possesses one great and lasting virtue, the plan on which it is executed. As I wrote in 1932, *Les caractères originaux* 'marks the advent of a rural history which, because it holds the ring between histories devoted to agricultural techniques, the seigneurial regime and the comparative development of the peoples of Europe, must long remain one of the most fruitful of all fields of historical enquiry, one of the most accessible meeting-grounds for the collaboration of historians with a concern for realities and of geographers interested in origins'. I have had no reason to regret the soundness of my prophecies, made at a time when the newly published book was still awaiting its hoped-for success.

LUCIEN FEBVRE

I must not lay down my pen without some mention of the disinterested assistance this new impression has received, even before leaving the presses. The *Institut pour l'Etude Comparative des Civilisations* of Oslo has been kind enough to authorise reproduction of a text which is their property. And once again the children of Marc Bloch have displayed every conceivable understanding and generosity. It is only fitting that these benefactors should be thanked here, in the name of all those who will have reason to be grateful for this new edition.

xxi

# Introduction

IT would be churlish to saddle generous hosts with a responsibility which should rest with the author alone. But it is only fair to say that had the *Institut pour l'Etude Comparative des Civilisations* not honoured me with their invitation to deliver a course of lectures last autumn this book would probably never have been written. Any historian alive to the difficulties of his trade—Fustel de Coulanges thought it the most difficult trade of all—is reluctant to compress his account of a long drawn out and inherently obscure process, still imperfectly understood, into a couple of hundred pages. If I now yield to temptation by acquainting a wider public than my sympathetic audience in Oslo with certain theories which I still lack leisure to develop in the necessary supporting detail, it is in the belief that publication at this juncture may be useful to other scholars as a pointer to further investigation. Before embarking on the body of the subject it may be helpful to give some account of the spirit in which I approach it. As will be seen, however, some of the problems of method reach beyond and indeed far exceed the bounds of this little book.

There are moments in the development of a subject when a synthesis, however, premature it may appear, can contribute more than a host of analytical studies; in other words, there are times when for once the formulation of problems is more urgent than their solution. It seems to me we have reached this point in French agrarian history. I could liken myself to an explorer making a rapid survey of the horizon before plunging into thickets from which the wider view is no longer possible. The gaps in my account are naturally enormous. I have done my best not to conceal any deficiencies, whether in the state of our knowledge in general or in my own documentation, which is based partly on first-hand research but to a much greater extent on soundings taken at random.[1] Anxious to prevent this account from becoming unreadable, I have not allowed the question-marks to multiply as freely as they ought. It should, after all, be common ground that in a scientific subject every positive statement is simply a hypothesis. When the time comes for my own work to be superseded by studies of deeper penetration, I shall feel well rewarded if confrontation with my false conjectures has made history learn the truth about herself.

Factual data capable of definitive interpretation are to be expected only from a field of research prudently tailored to a topographical setting. But this scale is too small to allow the major questions to be posed. For that we need wider perspectives, where there is no danger of losing sight of the main promontories among a confused mass of accidental detail. Even a horizon whose sweep includes a whole nation may sometimes be too small. Unless we first cast our eye over France as whole, we cannot expect to grasp what is singular in the development of the various regions. And what was happening in France can only be properly appreciated when seen in the context of Europe. This is not a question of straining after forced comparisons but of making proper distinctions; we are not engaged in some kind of trick photography, which would produce a fuzzy conventional image, deceptively generalised; what we are looking for are characteristics held in common, which will make whatever is original stand out by contrast. Although the subject treated here is part of our national history, it also impinges on the type of comparative studies I have tried to define elsewhere, to which the Institute sponsoring my lectures has already contributed so much.

The simplification imposed by my chosen form entails certain distortions which it is only fair to point out. The expression 'the agrarian history of France' may at first sight appear quite straightforward, but when looked at closely presents a number of difficulties. In their basic agrarian structure the various regions which make up modern France differ more widely from each other than from their immediate political neighbours;

---

[1] I should mention that I have not been able to give as many precise figures as I should have liked (far from it, in fact), particularly for the dimensions of parcels of land—the instruments needed for work on ancient measurements are at present almost non-existent.

in the past this trait was more óbvious still. It is true that what might be described as 'a French rural society' has gradually been superimposed on these original differences, but its evolution has been slow, entailing the absorption of a number of other societies or social fragments which were originally part of a different system. It would obviously be absurd to treat data relating to the eleventh century (and where Provence is concerned of the thirteenth century) as 'French': absurd, that is, unless we agree in advance that all we mean by the description is that such material, derived from a wide variety of milieus, is indispensable to our understanding of a modern France descended generation by generation from ancestral diversity. In short, our definition is determined by the end-product rather than the raw material or the actual process of development: an admissible convention, perhaps, so long as we recognise it for what it is.

Rural France is a large and complex country whose frontiers embrace the tenacious survivals of a number of different agrarian civilisations, now reduced to a single social scale. The varying pictures we each conjure up in our mind's eye—the villages of Lorraine surrounded by their long open-fields, the closes and hamlets of Brittany, a Provençal village like an ancient acropolis, the irregular plots of Languedoc and Berry—speak also of very profound human differences. I have tried to deal faithfully with these and other contrasts. But in what is necessarily a brief account, in which my chief concern has been to stress the importance of certain universal phenomena all too often ignored and whose local deviations must be left for others to trace, I have often felt obliged to insist on the general at the expense of the particular. The chief drawback to this plan is that it partially obscures the importance of geographical factors. Although the limitations on human activity imposed by physical environment can hardly be held wholly responsible for the basic features of our agrarian history, they certainly deserve to be considered when reasons for regional differences are in question. The balance on this score is patently in need of adjustment, and we must look to further research to supply the correction.

History is above all the science of change. In my examination of the different problems I have always tried to keep this truth in mind. There are moments, however, when I have had to use evidence from periods close to our own to shed light on the very remote past, especially when dealing with agrarian regimes. When Durkheim was embarking on a course of lectures on the family he once said 'to understand the past one must first leave it'. That is true. But it can also happen that one must first look at the present, or what was recently the present, in order to understand the past. For reasons which will emerge, this is the method imposed on agrarian studies by the present state of the evidence.

The agrarian life of France only emerges into the full light of history from the eighteenth century onwards. Until that time, with the exception of a few specialists who concentrated on technicalities, writers tended to ignore the subject, as did administrators. Few if any of the legal treatises or published customs deal directly with the most important rules governing rural economy, such as the right of grazing on the arable waste. As we shall see, the older documents can be made to yield much valuable information, but one must know how to find it. The first essential is to form an overall picture from which the general lines for research can emerge. It is impossible to form any such overall picture for a period earlier than the eighteenth century. As a rule men only notice their environment when changes are afoot, and sudden changes at that. If agrarian customs appear to remain static over several centuries it is because they in fact altered very little and because whatever small advances were made usually took place without commotion. In the eighteenth century the techniques and principles of land cultivation began to change more rapidly. Furthermore, there was now an active impetus towards change. Agronomists described the old agricultural routines in order to attack them. Administrators analysed the state of the country to gauge the extent of practicable reform. The three great commissions of enquiry initiated between 1766 and 1786 to investigate the problems posed by grazing on the arable and by enclosures presented their results on a scale which had no previous equivalent; and they were but the first link in a long chain which extends into the next century.

In addition to these written accounts we have some almost equally invaluable maps, which lay bare the anatomy of the land. The oldest of these handsome objects (mostly of seigneurial origin) belong to a slightly earlier period, the reign of Louis XIV, and it is again only in the eighteenth century that their numbers start to increase. In order to understand French field patterns in all their rich diversity it is necessary to turn to the survey made under the First Empire and the July Monarchy, at a time when the tide of agricultural revolution was at its height but its achievement still incomplete.[2]

These documents of relatively recent date must be our starting-point for the study of French agrarian history, which I take to include the technicalities of farming as well as the customs by which rural life was to a greater or lesser extent governed. An example will bring home more succinctly than lengthy explanations the reasons for this roundabout approach.

About the year 1885 Frederick Seebohm, a scholar who contributed as much as anyone to the history of rural England, wrote to Fustel de Coulanges (the two had many ideas in common concerning the origins of European civilisation) to ask whether the open-field system with long furlongs, for which there was clear evidence in England, had ever been at all common in France. Fustel replied that he had found no trace of it.[3] I intend no disrespect to a revered memory if I point out that Fustel de Coulanges was not a man on whom the external world made much impact. It is quite probable that he never took any special notice of the characteristic pattern of plough-lands visible all over northern and eastern France which so irresistibly call to mind the open-fields of England. And since Fustel had no particular interest in agriculture, the debates on grazing on the arable which were engaging both Chambers at the very moment he was receiving Seebohm's letter also failed to attract his attention. Fustel based his answer on documents, very ancient documents. Now these were texts he knew very well; how was it then that they failed to reveal for him any trace of the phenomena they in fact quite plainly attest? Maitland in an unworthy moment accused Fustel of having suppressed the evidence on patriotic grounds; but is it necessary

[2] On the eighteenth century inquests, which will be referred to with some frequency, see *Annales d'histoire économique*, 1930, p. 551, and for the maps, *ibid.*, 1929, pp. 60 and 390.

[3] F. Seebohm, 'French peasant proprietorship', *The Economic Journal*, 1891.

to assume that open-fields were of Germanic origin? The true explanation is of a different order. Fustel concentrated solely on his documents, without considering them in the light of the more recent past. Like so many great minds of his age, he was fascinated by the question of origins and always remained faithful to a strictly chronological approach, by which he moved forward step by step from the most remote to the most recent past. If he ever reversed the process he did so unconsciously, for the good reason that at some stage the inverse method will always force itself on the historian, whether he likes it or not. Since the facts of the distant past are also the most obscure, there is really no escape from the discipline of working back from the better to the less well-known. When he was working on the origins of the 'feudal' system, Fustel must surely have had least a provisional mental image of what 'feudal' institutions were like in their heyday; is it unfair to suggest that he would have done better to decide what were the essential features of the finished model before plunging into the mysteries of its inception? The historian, especially the agrarian historian, is perpetually at the mercy of his documents; most of the time he must read history backwards if he hopes to break the sceret cypher of the past.

But trying to break the code from the wrong end has its dangers, which should clearly be understood: to be forewarned is to be forearmed.

The more recent documents raise a number of questions to which the older ones supply at least some of the answers. Properly interrogated, they yield more than one might at first dare to hope; especially valuable are the records relating to legal proceedings, for example judgments and records of litigation, although at present their interpretation is unfortunately seriously hindered by our technical deficiencies. Even so, these documents are still a long way from supplying satisfactory answers to all our questions. The temptation to draw unwarranted conclusions from these reluctant witnesses becomes difficult to resist and a diverting anthology could be made of flights of fancy engendered in this way.

But worse than this can happen. Writing in 1856, Wilhelm Maurer said: 'Even the most hasty survey of the counties of modern England shows that the separate farm is by far the commonest unit of cultivation . . . Since this is so in our own day, we can safely conclude that in the earlier period'—by which he means Anglo-Saxon times—'the population was also settled in isolated homesteads.' What Maurer totally overlooked was nothing less than the revolutionary Enclosure Movement, which interposed a yawning gap between England's rural past and present. The majority of his 'separate farms' had been produced by evictions and grouping together many different plots of land, long after the arrival of Hengist and Horsa. This particular error is all the more culpable since the development in question was relatively recent and easy to recognise and evaluate. But there is real danger in the method itself, for unless one is careful a host of errors may enter in its train, of a kind peculiarly difficult to detect. A method which is quite reasonable in itself becomes vulnerable when linked with some quite arbitrary postulate, in this example the immutability of agrarian custom. The truth of the matter is very different. Admittedly, agrarian habits were much less liable to alteration in the past than they are now; they were protected by the many material difficulties which impeded change, by the less sensitive economy and by the prevailing respect for tradition. It should also be noted that sources which might shed light on such changes as did occur are often meagre and inexplicit. But, as will become plain, there was no question of their being immutable. Any break in the continuity of village life, caused perhaps by some sudden devastation or by resettlement at the end of a war, might cause the villagers to retrace the pattern of their furrows; or again, as in Provence in our own day, a community might abruptly decide to abandon its ancestral way of life; or finally, which was more common, there might be a gradual and unintentional drift away from the old order. Meitzen has a fine romantic passage in which he describes that almost nostalgic feeling familiar to anyone who has spent part of his life immersed in agrarian antiquities. 'In every village our footsteps lead us among prehistoric ruins more ancient than the romanesque rubble of cities or the tottering ramparts of towns.' And this is no exaggeration. It is a fact that in more than one place the pattern of the fields is older by far than even the most venerable stones. But, and this is the point, these survivals have never been 'ruins'; they are better compared to a composite building of archaic structure, never deserted but constantly remodelled by each fresh generation of occupiers. It is not surprising to find that few field systems have come down to us in their original form. Our villages wear an ancient dress, but one that has often been made over. Deliberate refusal to notice and investigate these changes is tantamount to a denial of life itself, since all life is change. Let us then agree, since we have no choice, to follow the trail backwards, one careful step at a time, examining irregularities and variations as they come, avoiding the all too common error of trying to leap at a bound from the eighteenth century to the Neolithic age. If we use our common sense, we shall see that the picture presented by the recent past is not an image we merely need to project over and over again in order to reproduce that of centuries more and more remote; what the recent past offers resembles rather the last reel of a film which we must try to unroll, resigned to the gaps we shall certainly discover, resolved to pay due regard to its sensitivity as a register of change.

*Strasbourg, 10 July 1930*

# Bibliographical Orientation

IT is always difficult to know what policy to adopt over references in a book of this kind, which is essentially a synthesis. To give none at all, which might make for easier reading, would be a breach of the historian's obligation to put forward nothing which cannot be verified. But if all the references were given they would take up most of the page. I have decided to act on the following plan. I omit any reference where the fact or source in question is one which an experienced scholar will be able to find for himself: for example, the fact may be taken from some very familiar document, or from a source mentioned in the body of my text and thanks to the existence of excellent calendars easy to trace, or from some secondary work listed in the bibliography below. In each case the source consulted will be abundantly clear from the nature of the evidence. On the other hand, I have been careful to give precise details where it is obvious that even well-informed readers would be at a loss to know where to look. I am well aware that this plan has its inconvenient side; it cannot help but be somewhat arbitrary in practice and may make me appear ungrateful towards some historians whose work I have drawn on to a much greater extent than will appear. But a choice had to be made.

The bibliography which follows is deliberately limited to the books most essential to my subject. It contains only works dealing with France. I must, however, make brief acknowledgment of the help I have received from studies in the rural history of other countries made by foreign scholars; my own book could never have been written without this basis for comparison and the lines for research they suggested. A bibliography which mentioned them all would have to cover the whole of Europe. Space must, however, be found for mention of some of the great maestros, whose names any historian of rural societies cannot but pronounce with the deepest gratitude:

## Bibliographical Orientation

Georg Hanssen, G. F. Knapp, Meitzen, Gradmann (Germany); Seebohm, Maitland, Vinogradoff, Tawney (Great Britain); and Des Marez (Belgium).[1]

I. *Studies of French rural populations at various epochs.*

M. Augé-Laribé, *L'évolution de la France agricole,* 1912.

M. Augé-Laribé, *L'agriculture pendant la guerre,* s. d. (*Histoire économique de la guerre, série française*).

Fustel de Coulanges, *L'alleu et le domaine rural pendant l'époque mérovingienne,* 1889.

B. Guérard, *Polyptyque de l'abbé Irminon,* t. i. (*Prolégomènes*), 1844.

N. Kareiew, *Les paysans et la question paysanne en France dans le dernier quart du XVIII^e siècle,* 1899.

J. Loutchisky, *L'état des classes agricoles en France à la veille de la Révolution,* 1911.

H. Sée, *Les classes rurales et le régime domanial en France au moyen âge,* 1901.

II. *Important regional studies.*

A. Allix, *L'Oisans, étude géographique,* 1929.

P. Arbos, *La vie pastorale dans les Alpes françaises,* 1922.

C. De Robillard de Beaurepaire, *Notes et documents concernant l'état des campagnes de la Haute Normandie dans les derniers temps du moyen âge,* 1865.

Y. Bezard, *La vie rurale dans le sud de la région parisienne de 1450 à 1560,* 1929.

R. Blanchard, *La Flandre,* 1906.

A. Brutails, *Etude sur la condition des populations rurales du Roussillon au moyen âge,* 1891.

A. de Calonne, *La vie agricole sous l'Ancien Régime dans le Nord de la France,* 1920. (*Mém. de la Soc. des Antiquaires de Picardie,* 4th series, vol. ix.)

L. Delisle, *Etudes sur la condition de la classe agricole et l'état de l'agriculture en Normandie pendant le moyen âge,* 1851.

A. Demangeon, *La plaine picarde,* 1905.

D. Faucher, *Plaines et bassins du Rhône moyen. Etude géographique,* 1927.

L. Febvre, *Philippe II et la Franche Comté, Etude d'histoire politique, religieuse et sociale,* 1911.

[1] I have also derived profit from H. L. Gray's *English Field Systems,* 1915 (not an easy book) and various English studies on enclosure, of which the most convenient and compendious are G. Slater, *The English Peasantry and the Enclosure of the Common Field,* 1907, and H. R. Curtler, *The Enclosure and Redistribution of our Fields,* 1920.

ANDRÉ GIBERT, *La porte de Bourgogne et d'Alsace (Trouée de Belfort)*, 1930.

C. HOFFMANN, *L'Alsace au XVIII<sup>e</sup> siècle*, 2 vol., 1906.

R. LATOUCHE, *La vie en Bas-Quercy du XIV<sup>e</sup> au XVIII<sup>e</sup> siècle*, 1923.

V. LAUDE, *Les classes rurales en Artois à la fin de l'Ancien Régime*, 1914.

G. LEFEBVRE, *Les paysans du Nord pendant la Révolution française*, 1924.

M. MARION, *Etat des classes rurales dans la généralité de Bordeaux*, 1902 (and *Revue des études historiques*, same year; covering the eighteenth century).

R. MUSSET, *Le Bas-Maine*, 1917.

P. RAVEAU, *L'agriculture et les classes paysannes dans le Haut-Poitou au XVI<sup>e</sup> siècle*, 1926, supplemented by two further articles by the same author: *La crise des prix au XVI<sup>e</sup> siècle en Poitou* in *Revue Historique*, clxii, 1929, and *Essai sur la situation économique et l'état social en Poitou au XVI<sup>e</sup> siècle*, in *Revue d'histoire économique*, 1930.

C. DE RIBBE, *La société provençale à la fin du moyen-âge d'après des documents inédits*, 1897.

G. ROUPNEL, *Les populations de la ville et de la campagne dijonnaises au XVII<sup>e</sup> siècle*, 1922.

T. SCLAFERT, *Le Haut-Dauphiné au moyen-âge*, 1925.

H. SÉE, *Etude sur les classes rurales en Bretagne au moyen-âge*, 1896 (and *Annales de Bretagne*, xi and xii).

H. SÉE, *Les classes rurales en Bretagne du XVI<sup>e</sup> siècle à la Révolution*, 1906 (and *Annales de Bretagne*, xxi to xxv).

A. SIEGFRIED, *Tableau politique de la France de l'Ouest sous la Troisième République*, 1913.

J. SION, *Les paysans de la Normandie orientale*, 1909.

THÉRON DE MONTAUGÉ, *L'agriculture et les classes rurales dans le pays toulousain depuis le milieu du XVIII<sup>e</sup> siècle*, 1869.

L. VERRIEST, *Le régime seigneurial dans le comté de Hainaut du XI<sup>e</sup> siècle à la Révolution*, 1916–17.

# CHAPTER ONE

# The Main Stages in the Occupation
# of the Soil

## I. THE BEGINNINGS

AT the beginning of the period we call the Middle Ages, when a state and nation we can recognise as French was slowly starting to emerge, agriculture was already an established feature of the countryside, and had been for a thousand years past. The archaeological evidence is clear; innumerable villages of present-day France are direct descendants of neolithic agrarian settlements, whose fields were harvested with implements of stone long before men had metal sickles to cut their corn.[1] Although our rural prehistory lies outside the scope of this book, its influence will be obvious throughout. If the puzzling variety of our agricultural systems often seems difficult to explain, the reason is that their roots are sunk so far back in the past that the basic structures of their parent societies elude us almost completely.

Under the Romans Gaul was one of the great agricultural regions of the Empire. But even so, settlements and their fields were surrounded by uncultivated land, and in the later days of the Empire waste land increased as holdings were deserted in consequence of general unrest and declining population. In some remote places which were recovered from scrub or forest during the Middle Ages, or which are still uncultivated (or at least uninhabited) to this day, excavation has brought ruins dating from antiquity to light.

Then followed the great invasions of the fourth and fifth

[1] Cf. the valuable synthesis by A. Grenier, 'Aux origines de l'économie rurale', *Annales d'histoire économique*, 1930.

centuries. Although the numerical strength of the barbarians was not great, it must also be remembered that the population of Roman Gaul, particularly at this period, was probably far below its present figure. It was, moreover, very unevenly distributed and the barbarians likewise did not settle with uniform density in every part of the country. Thus although new arrivals may have made little impression on the country as a whole, in some places their impact must have been relatively heavy. There were parts where it was so considerable that the native tongue was eventually superseded, for example in Flanders where settlement in Roman times appears to have been much less dense than it has been since the Middle Ages and where the towns, few in number and somewhat rudimentary, could not as elsewhere lend support to the ascendancy of Latin culture. Again, to take a less extreme example, there is no denying that although the dialects of northern France retained their fundamentally Romance character, they betray many Germanic influences in phonetics and vocabulary, and the same influence is to be seen at work in certain institutions. We know very little of the nature of the barbarian settlements. The one obvious fact, that the conquerors could not afford to disperse, is borne out by archaeological evidence, particularly from the barbarian cemeteries, which confirms that they avoided this mistake. The conquerors settled on the land in small groups, each probably centred on a chieftain. Some of these petty groupings, reinforced to a greater or lesser extent by *coloni* or slaves from the subject population, probably developed into new centres of settlement carved from the ancient Gallo-Roman estates, which the aristocracy were now forced to share with their conquerors.[2] It is also possible that this period saw the cultivation of land previously virgin, or which had been abandoned on account of the invasions. A fair number of our village names date from this time. Some of them show that the barbarian group settled there was an actual clan or *fara*: these are the place-names Fère or La Fère, for which there are exact equivalents in the Lombard parts of Italy.[3] Still more common is to find a village name formed from a personal name—that of

[2] C. Jullian, *Revue des études anciennes*, 1926, p. 145.
[3] For examples see A. Longnon, *Les noms de lieux de la France*, 1920, No. 875 and D. Faucher, *Plaines et bassins du Rhône moyen*, 605, No. 2 (Rochemaure).

a chieftain—in the genitive followed by a common noun such as *villa* or *villare*: for example *Bosonis villa*, which has become Bouzonville. Here we have two typical features, an inverted word order (in Roman times compounds were formed with the genitive in second place) and still more revealing, a distinctly Germanic-sounding name. This is not to say that all eponymous heroes of our villages were Germans. Under the rule of barbarian kings it was fashionable for families of native stock to adopt names in use among their conquerors. Boso need have been no more Frankish or Gothic than the Percies and Williams of present-day America are Anglo-Saxon. But even if their names post-date the invasions, the same need not be true of the settlements themselves, for there can be no doubt that some places of very ancient occupation lost their original names. All the same, it is still true to say that areas for which the map shows a cluster of place-names in this form must certainly have suffered the intrusion of a foreign element. Such was the fate of districts remote from the larger towns and the influence of Roman civilisation, in particular the Beauce, which had been somewhat neglected by prehistoric farmers on account of its aridity but is now one of the richest corn-growing regions of France.

The sources contain references to land clearance throughout the Frankish period. Gregory of Tours says of Duke Chrodin, a leading magnate, 'he set out *villae* (country estates), planted vines, built houses and brought land under cultivation'. Charlemagne directed his bailiffs to make clearings at suitable places in his forests, and to see that once a field had been laid out the woods were kept at bay. Among those very valuable sources for this period, the wills of wealthy landowners, there is scarcely one which does not contain some reference to farm buildings recently erected and land converted to productive use. It must be realised, however, that in most cases these were not fresh acquisitions but reclamations following one of those periods of local depopulation which may easily occur in an unstable society. Thus Charlemagne and Louis the Pious encouraged Spanish refugees to settle in Septimania (Bas-Languedoc), where they established new areas of tillage among the scrub and forest. There was Johannis, who came to Les Corbières 'in the heart of a great wilderness' and established his *coloni* and serfs, first in the neighbourhood of 'la fontaine aux Joncs' and later close to 'the springs' and 'the charcoal-burners' huts'.[4] This territory, reconquered from the Saracens, had been ravaged from end to end in prolonged fighting. Even if some of the land now cleared was actually virgin, these triumphs of man over nature must have been very unequal compensation for the serious and extensive losses already sustained. From the beginning of the ninth century references in seigneurial inventories to vacant holdings (*mansi absi*) increase at an alarming rate; according to a document drawn up before 816, more than a sixth of the '*colonges*' belonging to the church of Lyons were in this state.[5] The struggle against recurrent devastation was unremitting and can be taken as a sign of vitality; but it is difficult to believe that the net result was gain.

For when all is said and done, the contest ended in defeat. After the breakdown of the Carolingian Empire the French countryside has an undeniably depopulated aspect, riddled with pockets of emptiness. In many places cultivation had ceased altogether. The sources for the succeeding period beginning c. 1050, when land clearance started again, tell a unanimous tale of recovering lost ground before fresh advances could be made. A passage taken at random from the chronicle of the monks of Morigny can be matched from countless other sources. 'We acquired' (in 1102) 'the village of Maisons' (in the Beauce) 'which was nothing but a wilderness . . . we took it over in this neglected state in order to clear it.' At a relatively late date (1195) and in a very different region, the Albigeois, the prior of l'Hôpital granting out the village of Lacapelle-Ségalar says 'when this gift was made the village of Lacapelle was deserted; not a soul was living there, it had been deserted for a long time'.[6] The picture which begins to emerge is one of settlements comprising a handful of dwellings and surrounded by a modest tract of cultivated land interspersed among vast areas which never saw the plough. Furthermore, as will shortly be explained, the prevailing methods of cultivation condemned arable lands to lie fallow in at least one year out of two or three,

[4] A full record of how these settlements came into being has fortunately survived, *Dipl. Karol.* I, No. 179; *Histoire du Languedoc*, ii, Nos. 34, 85, 112 and v, No. 113; cf. *Bulletin de la commission archéologique de Narbonne*, 1876-7.

[5] 275 out of 1239: A. Coville, *Recherches sur l'histoire de Lyon*, 1928, pp. 287 ff.

[6] C. Brunel, *Les plus anciennes chartes en langue provençale*, 1926, No. 292.

often for several years at a time. Tenth and eleventh century society rested on occupation of a soil far from fully exploited; it was a society in which the connecting links were extended to the limit, where men lived in small isolated groups. This fact was fundamental to the age and determined many other of its essential features. Yet there was no break in continuity. Here and there a village might disappear—for example the *villa* of Paisson in the Tonnerrois, whose lands were later assarted by the inhabitants of a neighbouring place although the settlement itself was never revived[7]—but the great majority survived, their fields reduced by a greater or lesser extent. In some localities there was a loss of traditional skills; the people of Poitou, for example, whom the Romans considered expert at marling, appear to have lost all knowledge of this art until its revival in the sixteenth century. But ancient prescriptions for the basic processes retained their virtue and were handed down from one generation to another.

## 2. THE AGE OF LARGE-SCALE LAND CLEARANCE

Around the year 1050—in some favoured regions such as Normandy and Flanders perhaps a little earlier, in others somewhat later—a new era dawned, which was to last until the late thirteenth century. This was the period of large-scale land clearances, and to all appearance it saw the most considerable additions to the total area of land under cultivation in this country since prehistoric times.

Man's most formidable obstacle was the forests, and it was in the forests that his efforts bore most obvious fruit.

The trees had for centuries halted the progress of the plough. Neolithic farmers, who probably enjoyed a drier climate than our own, set their villages in expanses of grassland, scrubland, heathland and steppe;[8] the primitive implements at their disposal would have been inadequate for the task of deforestation. In Roman and Frankish times the efforts of woodsmen were

[7] M. Quantin, *Cartulaire générale de l'Yonne*, 1854, i, No. CCXXXIII.

[8] There is some interesting work on Germany by R. Gradmann; for his most recent article see *Verhandlungen und Wissenschaftlichen Abhandlungen des 23 d. Geographentags* (1929), 1930; for France the most obvious starting point is the *Tableau de France* of Vidal de la Blache (p. 54).

apparently more successful. In the early ninth century for example, when Tancred needed land for his completely new village of Le Nocle, he took it from dense forest, *de densitate silvarum.*[9] But even where there were no cultivated clearings, these forests of the early Middle Ages, the ancient forests of France, were by no means unexploited or empty of men.[10] The forest had its own population, often highly suspect in the eyes of more sedentary folk, who roamed about the woods or lived in shacks they built themselves: huntsmen, charcoal-burners, blacksmiths, gatherers of wax and wild honey (described in the texts as *bigres*), dealers in wood-ash, which was important in the manufacture of glass and soap, and bark-strippers, whose wares were used for tanning hides or could be plaited to make cords. At the end of the twelfth century the lady of Valois employed four servants in her woods at Viry: one was an assarter (this was when land clearance was just beginning), one a trapper, a third an archer and the last an 'ash-man'. Hunting in the shady forest was not merely a pleasant sport; it also produced hides for urban and seigneurial tanneries and for the binderies of monastic libraries; it supplied meat for everyone, including fighting-men—in 1269 Alphonse de Poitiers ordered the slaughter of a large number of wild boars from his great forests in the Auvergne, to provide salted carcasses for taking overseas on his projected crusade. In an age when the primeval instinct of foraging was nearer the surface than it is today, the forest had greater riches to offer than we perhaps appreciate. People naturally went there for wood, a far greater necessity of life than in this age of oil, petrol and metal; wood was used for heating and lighting (in torches), for building material (roof slats, castle palisades), for footwear (sabots), for plough handles and various other implements, and as faggots for strengthening roadways. There was also a demand for a wide variety of vegetable products, for mosses or dried

[9] A. de Charmasse, *Cartulaire de l'église d'Autun,* i, No. XLI.

[10] The most important studies of the forests (apart from the works listed in the General Bibliography and various monographs, too numerous to be mentioned here) are: A. Maury, *Les forêts de la Gaule et de l'ancienne France,* 1867; G. Huffel, *Economie forestière,* 3 vols., vols. i and ii, 2nd ed., 1910, 1920, vol. iii, 1st ed., 1919; L. Boutry, 'La forêt d'Ardenne', *Annales de Géographie,* 1920; S. Deck, *Etude sur la forêt d'Eu,* 1929 (cf. *Annales d'histoire économique,* 1930, p. 415); R. de Maulde, *Etude sur la condition forestière de l'Orléanais.*

leaves as bedding, for beechmast on account of the oil, for wild hops and the tart fruit of wild trees—apple, pear, cherry and plum—as also for some of the trees themselves (pear and apple), which were dug up to be used as orchard grafts. But the principal economic contribution of the forest was in a role we no longer demand of it: the presence of fresh leaves, young shoots, grass in the undergrowth, acorns and beechmast made it a first-rate grazing ground. For centuries, in the absence of any standard measurement, the commonest way of indicating the size of a stretch of forest was by reference to the number of pigs it could sustain. Neighbouring villagers sent their cattle into the forest, great lords kept vast herds there and even set up stud-farms for their horses. These hordes of animals lived almost in a state of nature, and the habit died hard; even in the sixteenth century, the squire of Gouberville in Normandy had to take to the woods at certain times of the year to round up his stock, and could fail to find them all at one fell swoop. Once he met only the bull 'who was limping', 'whom no-one had seen for two months past'; on another day his servants managed to catch 'the wild mares . . . whom for two years none had contrived to take'.[11]

As a result of this relatively intensive and quite unregulated exploitation the ranks of the trees became progressively thinner. Bark-stripping alone must have accounted for many a fine oak. By the eleventh and twelfth centuries, despite the obstructions offered by dead tree-trunks and some remaining thickets where penetration was difficult, there were already places where the woodland was sparse. Abbot Suger's foresters were doubtful whether the forest of Iveline could produce the twelve massive timbers he needed for his basilica; Suger himself regarded the

---

[11] The references given here relate only to less familiar evidence: lime-tree bark used 'ad faciendum cordas', Arch. Nat. S 275 No. 13; the lady of Valois and her servants, B. Guérard, *Cartulaire de l'église de Notre-Dame de Paris*, i, No. 191; Alphonse de Poitiers and his boar-hunt, H. F. Rivière, *Histoire des institutions de l'Auvergne*, 1874, i, p. 262, No. 5; wild hops, *Polyptique de l'abbaye de Montierender* c. xiii, ed. C. Lalore, or C. Lalore, *Collection des principaux cartulaires du diocèse de Troyes*, iv, 1878; apple and pear trees, J. Garnier, *Chartes de communes et d'affranchissements en Bourgogne*, 1867, ii, No. CCCLXXIX c. 10; C. de Beaurepaire, *Notes de documents concernant l'état des campagnes de la Haute-Normandie*, p. 409; the forest herds of the lord of Gouberville, A. Toemer, *Journal manuscrit d'un sire de Gouberville*, 2nd ed. 1880, pp. 372 and 388, and cf. H. du Halgouët, *La vicomté de Rohan*, 1921, i, pp. 37 and 143 ff, for the dairy and stud farms of the Breton forests.

happy discovery which crowned his work as little short of a miracle.[12] The hand of man and the tooth of beast had between them created such havoc among standing timber that the way was prepared for clearance on a larger scale. Even so, the great forests of the early Middle Ages were still so isolated from communal life that they remained largely outside the network of parochial organisation which covered every inhabited area.

During the twelfth and thirteenth centuries deliberate efforts were made to bring them in. Patches of tilled land, *ipso facto* liable to tithe, could now be seen at every turn, and their tillers took up permanent residence. Forests on the uplands, hillsides and alluvial lowlands all came under attack from hatchet, billhook and fire. Very few, perhaps none, were totally destroyed, but a large number were reduced to a small remnant of their former extent. They often lost their names as well. There had been a time when, in common with rivers and the principal relief features, each of these sombre smudges on the agrarian landscape had its own place in a geographical vocabulary which descended from a period older than any whose memory has been conserved in the historic languages. By the end of the Middle Ages the ancient entities once known as Bière, Iveline, Laye, Cruye and Loge were reduced to fragments whose names were borrowed from a neighbouring hunting-lodge or township, Fontainebleau, Rambouillet, Saint-Germain, Marly and Orleans. Henceforward the forest was to be first and foremost the hunting-ground of kings and nobles. At much the same time as lowlands were losing their covering of trees, peasants of Dauphiné were mounting their attack on alpine forests which had already been broached from within by the settlements of hermit monks.

It would be a mistake, however, to assume that land-clearance was achieved solely by uprooting trees. There was also much activity in marshlands, particularly along the coasts of Flanders and in Bas-Poitou, and on many uncultivated wastes formerly covered with thickets or wild grasses. The chronicle of Morigny already mentioned tells us that brushwood, brambles, bracken and 'all such obstructive plants rooted in the bowels of the earth' were enemies attacked by peasants armed with

[12] *De consecratione ecclesiae S. Dyonisii*, c. ii.

plough and hoe. In fact assarting[13] often seems to have started in open country of this type, and where this happened attack on the forest took second place.

The men responsible for such gains often established new villages in the heart of the assarted territory. Some were a spontaneous growth, like the hamlet of Froidville on the banks of the Orge, whose piecemeal development house by house over the previous fifty years can be traced from the record of an unusual inquest held in 1224;[14] but the majority came into being following a set plan and were the creation of some enterprising lord. In the absence of other sources, examination of the map alone may be enough to show whether a settlement dates from this period; for example, the houses may be grouped in a regular chequer-board formation as at Villeneuve-le-Comte in Brie, founded in 1203 by Gaucher de Chatillon, and as in the *bastides* or fortified villages of Languedoc; or, as is characteristic of forest villages, the houses and their adjoining plots may be strung out along a specially constructed road, with the fields spread out in herring-bone fashion on either side of this central axis. Examples of this last formation are the hamlet of Bois-Saint-Denis (Plate I) in the Thiérarche and those extraordinary Normandy villages in the great forest of Aliermont, built by the archbishops of Rouen all along the interminable length of two branching roads.[15] But such indications may be lacking; one may find an apparently random huddle of houses and plots whose arrangement differs in no way from that of neighbouring parishes. Anyone who did not already know that Vaucresson, in a valley south of the Seine, owed its existence to

[13] I shall use 'assart' and its derivatives in the medieval sense of clearance, clearing. The term cannot by itself be taken as an indication of whether a clearance was permanent (the type I have in mind here) or temporary (of the type to be dealt with in the next chapter, some of which prepared the way for permanent exploitation). To restrict the term to this second meaning, as J. Blache appears to do in his otherwise very illuminating article (*Revue de géographie alpine*, 1923) seems an unwarranted distortion.

[14] Arch. Nat. S. 206; cf. B. Guérard, *Cartulaire de Notre-Dame de Paris*, ii, 307, No. 1

[15] Cf. the map in J. Sion, *Les paysans de la Normandie Orientale*, fig. 14, and for the arrangement of plots the admirable plan of the county of Aliermont, 1752, made from an original of 1659, Arch. Seine-Inférieure *plans* No. 1. These are the *Waldhufendörfer* of the German historians. Comparison with Chinese land clearance can be made by consulting the map in J. Sion, *L'Asie des Moussons*, i, 1928, p. 123. The arrangement of plots is very similar, although the houses are not set in a straight line.

Suger would certainly not deduce it from the lay-out of the plots. Often the name is the tell-tale factor, although admittedly it is not infallible as a guide, since more than one new settlement simply took over the name given to the place in the days before it was cultivated—Torfou, for example, which owed its name to the beech-grove cleared by its first settlers with the consent of Louis VI. But as a rule a new settlement has a more expressive name. It may take the form of a direct reference to the fact of clearance, Essarts-le-Roi, for example, or to recent occupation of the site, Villeneuve, Neuville,[16] perhaps with some distinguishing suffix to commemorate the rank of the founder—Villeneuve-l'Archévêque—or some feature of the surrounding country, as in the idyllic Neuville-Chant-d'Oisel.[17] Some names have an opportunist ring, stressing the privileges open to inhabitants: Francheville, Sauvetat. Sometimes the founder uses his own name, for example Beaumarchais and Libourne. Or again, as so often happened later with colonies overseas, some illustrious godparent might be appropriated as namesake from the cities of older civilisations; for example Damietta, the Syrian city and battlefield, inspired Damiatte, Florence gave rise to Fleurance and Pavia to Pavie. Just as in the United States there are at least six places called Paris, and Memphis and Corinth stand almost side by side on the banks of Mississippi, so we find Bruges and Ghent cheek by jowl in Béarn during the early thirteenth century, while a lord who had perhaps been on crusade was building Jerusalem, Jericho, Nazareth and Bethphage in the humid forests of La Puisaye, between the Loire and the Yonne.[18]

Some new foundations developed into large towns, cities even. But there were plenty which stayed quite small, especially those in the ancient forests; it was not so much that they lacked opportunities for growth but that the manner of colonisation imposed its own restrictions. Movement among the woods was

[16] Some *villeneuves* were founded well before the eleventh century and are Frankish or even Roman in origin. Villeneuve-Saint-George[5], near Paris, was already quite a large village in Charlemagne's day.

[17] Its official name is now Neuville-*Champ*-d'Oisel; but a charter of St. Louis, which must be almost contemporaneous with the foundation, definitely refers to the place as *Noveville de Cantu Avis* (L. Delisle, *Cartulaire normand*, No. 693.

[18] Vathaire de Guerchy, 'La Puisaye sous les maisons de Toucy et de Bar', in *Bullet. de la Soc. des sciences historiques de l'Yonne*, 1925, p. 164; the four places (the last spelt Betphaget) are dependencies of the commune of St. Verain.

difficult and could be dangerous. Assarters found it safer to split up into little groups, each making its own modest clearing among the trees. The Argonne with its patchwork of minute forest villages still stands out between the densely populated open spaces of Champagne and Lorraine. In the forest to the south of Paris a parish formed from several small settlements had two names, Magny-les-Hameaux and Magny-les-Essarts, and was equally familiar under either; the interchange is characteristic. It seems that over large parts of France during the late Roman and early medieval periods there was a tendency for men to close their ranks; we know that reasons of security led to the desertion of a number of small hamlets or *viculi* at this period.[19] The large-scale clearances, when they came, led to further dispersals.

We must be careful, however, to make some necessary distinctions. The term hamlet definitely implies occupation by a group, however small. An isolated farmstead is something else again, implying a different social order and different customs, based on rejection of the cheek by jowl existence of communal living. Settlements of this kind were probably not unknown in Roman Gaul; the *villae* dispersed among the fields, where their remains have been uncovered by archaeologists, must have brought together a considerable labour force which was perhaps housed in cabins arranged round the principal dwelling, flimsy structures which could well have disappeared without trace.[20] However this may be, with the invasions these *villae* were destroyed or abandoned. The peasants of the early Middle Ages lived side by side in communal groups, an arrangement which obtained even in regions which, as we shall see, remained innocent of large villages. It is not until the era of land reclamation that we find isolated 'granges' springing up here and there in addition to the new villages and hamlets. Many such granges were established by monastic communities, usually offshoots of the new religious orders thrown up by the great spiritual movement which set its seal on the late eleventh century; where the older Benedictines had founded villages, the monks of the new style, in flight from the world, were assarters

[19] E.g. Guérard, *Cartulaire de l'abbaye Saint-Père de Chartres*, i, 93, No. 1.

[20] Not all have disappeared completely, cf. F. Cumont, *Comment la Belgique fut romanisée*, 2nd ed., 1919, p. 42.

on a grand scale. Hermits living in the forests and unattached to any regular community had already made some attempts at tilling the ground round their cells. Although these independent spirits often finished up as members of officially recognised orders, the orders themselves tended to be eremitical in outlook. The Rule of the most famous of them, the Cistercians, can be taken as typical: the order was not to live from rents; 'White Monks' should live by the labours of their hands. Cistercian isolation was zealously protected, at least in the beginning. The abbey itself was always situated in some place remote from human habitation—usually a wooded valley, whose stream, thanks to a convenient weir, could supply the type of food demanded by rules of monastic abstinence; and the subsidiary 'granges' also avoided the neighbourhood of peasant dwellings. They were established in 'desert solitudes', where the religious, assisted by lay brothers and quite soon by paid labour as well, ploughed and worked a few fields of arable. The adjacent land was given over to grazing, for the order was rich in flocks, particularly sheep; on large estates which could not be divided into tenures (because living from rents was prohibited) and where the labour force was inevitably restricted, animal husbandry was a better proposition than agriculture. But it never happened (or so rarely as to make no difference) that a grange or abbey became the nucleus of a *ville neuve*; this would have led monks to mingle with laymen and so violate the basic principle of the order. In the grange, then, we have a type of settlement whose form was determined by a monastic ideal. There were other isolated estates of the same type, founded perhaps in conscious imitation. It seems they were never the spontaneous creation of ordinary country people. The majority owed their existence to wealthy promoters of land-clearance, whose attachment to communal habits was naturally less binding than that of humbler folk; for example, there was the prudent dean of St. Martin's who in 1234 erected the handsome grange in the forest of Vernou in Brie, providing it with stout walls, a wine-press and a tower, all vividly described in the cartulary of Notre-Dame de Paris.[21] Even nowadays it is by no means rare to come across a large farm at some distance from a village, whose medieval origin is revealed by some

[21] Guérard, *Cartulaire de Notre-Dame de Paris*, ii, 235, No. xliv.

significant architectural detail, an abnormal thickness in the walls maybe, or a turret, or the shape of a window.

But to think of land clearance only in terms of the areas surrounding new settlements would be to distort and diminish the total achievement. Much older fields, attached to settlements of much greater antiquity, were also enlarged, by more or less systematic accretion as land won from heathland or thicket was added to fields tilled since time immemorial. The worthy priest of La Croix-en-Brie who wrote the ninth continuation of the *Roman de Renart* c. 1220 knew that every rogue had his 'novel essart'. This slow and patient labour shows up less clearly in the texts than is the case with the *villes neuves*, and the evidence comes chiefly from records of disputes provoked by the tithes levied on *novales*. What seems certain is that a sizeable, perhaps even the major, part of the fresh land brought under cultivation was land which depended on the older villages and was reclaimed by their inhabitants.[22]

Once the detailed studies we now lack become available, we shall no doubt discover that the progress made by the plough at any one period varied considerably in extent from region to region. In some places clearance was linked with migration, as people moved from poorer to richer soil, and from over-exploited fields to regions where virgin lands were still abundant. In the twelfth and thirteenth centuries the wooded region on the left bank of the lower Creuse was settled first by Limousins and later by Bretons; the region known as Entre-deux-Mers (between the Garonne and the Dordogne) was colonised with the help of migrants from Saintonge.[23] But in the present state of our knowledge the only differences we can appreciate are the most obvious ones, above all the time-lag between the progress of the movement over France as a whole as compared with the regions of the South-West, where reclamation started later and continued longer than, for example, in the lands of the Seine and Loire. The explanation is probably to be found in events taking place on the far side of the Pyrenees. The rulers of Spain were obliged to attract aliens to populate the great empty spaces of the Iberian peninsula, which were most

[22] Cf. Pl. VI, *infra*.
[23] E. Clouzot, 'Cartulaire de La Merci-Dieu', in *Arch. historiques du Poitou*, 1905, Nos. viii, cclxxi, cclxxv, Arch. de la Gironde, *Inv. sommaire*, *série* H, Vol. i, p. VII.

extensive on the borders of the former Muslim emirates; not surprisingly a number of Frenchmen found their way south through the Pyrenean passes, drawn by the privileges held out in charters of *poblaciones*. There can be no doubt that most of the immigrants came from the parts of France nearest to Spain, above all Gascony, or that this drain on the labour force entailed a postponement of internal colonisation.

The point may serve as a reminder that the movement was a European phenomenon. It took a number of different forms: the steady stream of colonisers from Germany and the Netherlands towards the Slavonic plains, the cultivation of the wastes of northern Spain, the growth of towns all over Europe, and, in France and her neighbours at least, the clearance of large tracts of country hitherto barren. Gascony apart, colonisation in France (as compared with what we know of it in Germany for example) was distinguished by the absence of any outward movement other than the inconsiderable migration which attended the crusades and the occasional transfer of population en masse, to lands conquered by the Normans for example, or to the cities of Eastern Europe, especially those of Hungary; French colonisation was an almost exclusively internal and unusually intensive operation. The facts of the matter are clear enough, the underlying causes less so.

There is no great difficulty in understanding why the more powerful elements in society favoured colonisation and expansion. The interest of the landlords, generally speaking, was engaged by the extra revenues they could expect from new or enlarged holdings: hence the inducements to colonists in the form of privileges and franchises of all sorts, sometimes promoted by what can only be described as a propaganda campaign—in Languedoc heralds rode round the countryside proclaiming the foundation of *bastides* to the sound of the trumpet.[24] Hence also the kind of megalomaniac intoxication which appears to have possessed some proprietors, for example the abbot of Grandselve, with his vision of a thousand new houses, which tripled almost from one moment to the next.[25]

Ecclesiastical landlords had motives of their own, in addition to those they shared with the seigneurial class as a whole. In

[24] Curie-Seimbres, *Essai sur les villes fondéeˢ dans le Sud-Ouest*, 1880, p. 297.
[25] Bibl. Nat., Doat 79, fol. 336v° and 80, fol. 51 v°.

the period after the Hildebrandine reforms, churchmen were now largely dependent on tithes for their revenues; and since the amount paid in tithe was proportionate to the return from the soil, the more land was under cultivation the better. Ecclesiastical estates were built up from charitable donations; but the benefactors were not always generous enough to grant away land already in production. It was often easier to acquire uncultivated stretches, which the abbey or chapter proceeded to clear and cultivate. Land reclamation normally required the investment of capital; it might also be necessary to make advances to those who cultivated it and certainly to have the ground surveyed; where all or part of an estate was to be reserved for direct exploitation by the lord, suitable provision had to be made. Large communities usually had quite ample resources which could legitimately be used for these purposes. If a community was unwilling or unable to draw on its own reserves, there was no great difficulty in finding what was needed from one of its own members, or from some well-disposed cleric prepared to take charge of the operation in return for a handsome benefice. Although a less familiar figure in Germany, the 'clearance contractor' was by no means unknown in France. Many were ecclesiastics: in the first half of the thirteenth century the brothers Aubri and Gautier Cornu, both destined for high rank among the French clergy, agreed under contract to clear several parcels of land carved from the forest of Brie, and discharged their task by distributing the lots among sub-contractors. It is impossible in the present state of our evidence to apportion credit for the great work of clearing the waste between prelates and religious on the one hand and secular lords on the other. But there can be no doubt that the churchmen, with their more consistent habit of thought and wider range of vision, played a very important part.

Lastly, there was the defence factor, which weighed with monarchs and the heads of feudal principalities, including the great abbots; in the hotly contested territories of the Midi, for example, it was the new fortified villages or *bastides* which protected bases lying along the Anglo-French frontier. There was also the question of public order: the denser the population, the less scope there was for brigands. Several charters expressly state that a grant has been prompted by the urgent need to take an axe to some forest 'hitherto a den of robbers' or to guarantee safe passage for 'pilgrims and travellers' journeying across territory long infested with criminals.[26] In the twelfth century the Capetians established new centres of settlement all along the road from Paris to Orleans, the axis of their monarchy, thus foreshadowing the policy adopted by the Spanish kings in the eighteenth century when faced with the same problem on the notorious road between Madrid and Seville.[27]

The foregoing observations are valuable for the light they shed on the progress of land clearance, but still tell us nothing of the circumstances which made it possible. Now the one essential prerequisite for colonisation is a ready supply of colonists; and land reclamation is impossible unless the existing labour force can be augmented—though in this context it would be more correct to say it was impossible in the absence of technological advance on a scale far beyond the grasp of eleventh and twelfth century societies. So it looks as though only a spontaneous and significant increase in population can account for the immense advances made at this period in the occupation of the soil. Admittedly this merely pushes the problem one stage further back, into a position where at present it must remain insoluble: has anyone yet offered a convincing explanation for demographic fluctuation? We must content ourselves with registering the population increase as a fact. We can, however, go on to remark that few other events in the history of European civilisation, and of French civilisation in particular, have had such weighty consequences. There is no doubt that it promoted greater ease and frequency of exchange between men, since people were now brought closer together than at any earlier time in our history. This interchange took place on various levels, intellectual as well as material, and proved a potent source of rejuvenation in every field of en-

[26] Curie-Seimbres, *ibid.*, pp. 107 and 108; J. Maubourguet, *Le Périgord Méridional*, 1926, p. 146; Suger, *De rebus in administratione sua gestis*, c. vi; G. Desjardins, *Cartulaire de l'abbaye de Conques*, No. 66.

[27] R. Leonhard, *Agrarpolitik und Agrarreform in Spanien*, 1909, p. 287. In the reign of Charles VII the dues exacted by the abbot of St. Germain-des-Prés became so oppressive that the village of Antony, lying on the road between Paris and Orleans, was threatened with depopulation; requesting the abbot to moderate his demands, the king pointed out the dangers to travellers along the road if the place became uninhabited. D. Anger, *Les dépendances de l'abbaye de St. Germain-des-Prés* ii, 1907, p. 275.

deavour. Bédier somewhere remarks that in France this century saw 'the first stained-glass window, the first pointed arch and the first *chanson-de-geste*'. We might add that in Europe as a whole it saw the revival of trade and the beginnings of urban self-government, and in France, on the political plane, the recovery of monarchical authority accompanied by interior consolidation of the great feudal principalities, a further symptom that seigneurial anarchy was on the wane. All this blossoming was made possible by the increase in population; and the ground had been prepared by the mattocks and billhooks of assarters.

### 3. MEDIEVAL LAND CLEARANCE TO THE AGRICULTURAL REVOLUTION

Around the year 1300, earlier in some places, later in others, the attack on virgin lands slowed down and finally ceased, despite the fact that there was plenty of ground still occupied by woodland or waste. Some of this was admittedly either quite unsuitable for cultivation or so unpromising as to offer no adequate return to justify the labour and expense of reclamation. But there was other land which might have been profitable to work, even with the somewhat crude techniques of the time, but yet remained unexploited. One reason may well have been a dearth of man-power; the labour supply was not inexhaustible, and we know of at least some attempted village settlements which failed from underpopulation. But the chief reason seems to have been that reclamation had come close to the reasonable limit. There was no point in continuing the conversion of forest and heath into ploughlands indefinitely. If deforestation continued, where would the animals graze? Where would men look for the natural products they could get from the forest? The preservation of the forest was of particular concern to the leading members of society; as a hunting ground it was the scene of their pleasure, as a source of profit it was valuable as never before. Towns were growing up, to be devourers of beams and billets; the countryside was dotted with new houses where new hearths burned; more and more forges were being set up, often in the very shadow of the trees. Assarting, on the other hand, had entailed the nibbling away of the total area of land planted with trees. All things considered—growing scarcity and increased demand, the two classic elements of a price rise—it is no wonder that timber was now regarded as a valuable commodity or that the lords of the forest were more interested in squeezing the most out of their timber and kindling than in converting woodlands and coppices to arable. It should also be remembered that nature had never been the only enemy in the way of land clearance. Villagers accustomed to benefit from the grazing or the free enjoyment of the forest's wealth had always fought to defend their rights. It was often necessary to sue them or buy them off, especially where they had the support of some lord who shared their interest or by whatever title claimed forest privileges; the archives are full of records relating to litigation of this kind. It would be a mistake to imagine that the disputes were always conducted according to the rules of orderly legal pleading; and just as wrong to assume, whether force was used or not, that the decision always went in favour of tillage. The fate of the *ville neuve* established c. 1200 by a man named Frohier among the coppices on the right bank of the Seine was not unique; attacked by the villagers of Moret and Montereau, who had rights of common in the wood, the place was demolished by order of the chapter of Paris and never rebuilt. At much the same time, but at the other end of the country, the villagers of Six-Fours on the coast of Provence were busy resisting the advance of tillage at the expense of their pastures.[28] In the early days of land clearance however, when so much land lay uncultivated and the arguments in favour of tillage were strong, the plough usually won the day. Later, when a rough balance had been achieved, the great drive to occupy the soil was halted, though not before the agrarian face of France had been decisively altered.

For centuries to come men had a hard struggle to preserve what had been achieved. The second half of the fourteenth and the whole of the fifteenth centuries—to which we shall return—was an era of declining population everywhere in Europe, in France even more than elsewhere. Once the

---

[28] Guérard, *Cartulaire de Notre-Dame de Paris*, ii, 223, No. xviii; Arch. Nat. S. 275 No. 13; Guérard, *Cartulaire de l'abbaye de Saint-Victor de Marseille*, ii, No. 1023 (1197, Feb. 27).

Hundred Years' War was over and the onslaughts of plague less violent, lords and peasants were faced with a common task: but their problem was not to make new villages and enlarge their fields but to rebuild old ones and free existing fields of encroaching brush.

Progress was slow; in places the former level of occupation was by no means achieved[29] before the wars of the seventeenth century in their turn created havoc throughout eastern France, in Burgundy and Lorraine and doubtless in other regions still to be studied. Some villages were left deserted over a long period, in some places the boundaries between plots completely disappeared; once the storm was over, a village often had to be reconstructed piece by piece, as happened in our own day in zones devastated by the Great War.

Despite all these setbacks, so tenacious is man in his contest with the soil that in some areas land reclamation started up again in the sixteenth century, although there was no general movement comparable with that of the Middle Ages. Here and there some progress was made in clearing marshlands, including some which had been common pastures; new villages were established in certain regions, the northern Jura for example, where the medieval assarters had left considerable stretches virgin.[30] The initiative for these ventures rarely came from the peasant community, more jealous than ever of their communal privileges. The credit must go to individual lords and a few semi-bourgeois land-owners, impelled by a radical transformation of society towards taking an interest in the fuller utilisation of the soil. The draining of marshlands, undertaken throughout the kingdom in the reigns of Henry IV and Louis XIII, provides one of the earliest examples of the application of capitalist methods to agriculture; directed by an association of technical experts and business men, the operation was financed by a few large business-houses, mostly Dutch.[31] The movement gained momentum in the eighteenth century, but still followed the same pattern; companies were founded for the express

[29] The great crisis of the fourteenth and fifteenth centuries will be studied in greater detail below, Chapter IV.

[30] Four new villages were founded in the county of Montbéliard between 1562 and 1690; and two earlier villages which had been destroyed were rebuilt, one in 1671, the other in 1704: C.D., *Les villages ruinés du comté de Montbéliard*, 1847.

[31] De Dienne, *Histoire du dessèchement des lacs et marais*, 1891.

purpose of financing—or indeed speculating in—land reclamation, which now also received government patronage. Even so the results fell far short of the medieval achievement: there was some nibbling at the edges of heathlands and sand-dunes, notably in Brittany and Guienne, some large estates grew even bigger, a few new ones came into being; but no new villages were founded, and the total gain was unimpressive. The contribution of the 'agricultural revolution' of the eighteenth and nineteenth centuries lay elsewhere. It was no longer a question of bringing waste land under the plough—quite the reverse, since technical improvements which allowed fuller use of good soil also permitted the abandonment of poorer land which had formerly been cultivated. Instead, as we shall see, since there was no need to leave land fallow, the ploughlands themselves were no longer exposed to the regular resurgence of the encroaching waste.

# CHAPTER TWO

# Agrarian Life[1]

## I. GENERAL CHARACTERISTICS OF ANCIENT AGRICULTURE

DOWN to the eve of the nineteenth century the rural life of France is dominated by a single, ancient and probably indigenous word, *blé*,[2] which owes nothing to Latin, and may well be of Gallic origin, like numerous other words in our agricultural vocabulary which are such eloquent testimony to the antiquity of our agrarian life—*charrue*, *chemin*, *somart* or *sombre* (in the sense of fallow land), *lande* and *arpent*. During the Middle Ages, and for a long time after, *blé* was not restricted to wheat, as seems to have become the modern literary usage; in the language of the countryside *blé* covered all cereals from which bread could be made, whether it was the fine wheat bread which delighted the rich or the heavy black bread of the peasants, which might contain wheat, rye—which when diseased caused the spread of erysipelas—*maslin* (a mixture of wheat and rye), spelt, oats or even barley.[3] By far the greater part of cultivated land was devoted to *blé*, corn in its closest English equivalent.* Corn held pride of place in every village

[1] For this chapter as a whole cf. M. Bloch, 'La lutte pour l'individualisme agraire au XVIII siècle', *Annales d'histoire économique*, 1930, where references to the great inquests of the eighteenth century will also be found.

[2] J. Jud in *Romania*, 1923, p. 405; cf. other useful papers by the same author, *ibid*, 1920, 1921, 1926 and (in collaboration with P. Aebischer) in *Archivum Romanum*, 1921.

[3] At times even beans and peas were included; see Guérard, *Cartulaire de Notre-Dame de Paris*, ii, 314, No. xiii. For English bread see W. Ashley, *The Bread of Our Forefathers*, 1928. In 1277 the canons of the small chapter of Champeaux in Brie complained that the place was disagreeable because white bread was not always available: Bibl. Nat. lat. 10942, fol. 40.

* Translator's addition.

and on every estate. It was cultivated even on ground apparently unpromising, rugged alpine slopes and those waterlogged lands of western and central France, soaked with incessant rain, which to us might seem more appropriate as pasture. In 1787 the commissaries of the Provincial Assembly of the Orléanais could still remark: 'agriculture, in the great majority of the provinces of France, may be considered a huge factory for the production of corn'. For a very long time conditions of life militated against any more specialised use of the soil. Bread was an essential food for everyone, for the poor their staple diet. Flour was vital but could not readily be obtained by purchase; although probably never completely non-existent, trading was for centuries a rare and difficult operation. The safest course was to look to one's own fields; and so the lord had his demesne lands sown for him, the peasants worked their own. There was of course nothing to prevent a lord or well-provided peasant from diverting his surplus grain to regions where the harvest had failed.

Later on, especially from the beginning of the sixteenth century, the organisation of society was admittedly once again more favourable to the circulation of goods. But economic climate is not the only factor; if a country is to adopt a trading economy a buying and selling mentality must also be generated among the population at large. The first to adapt themselves were the landed proprietors who were great merchants, men accustomed to take the wider view in handling affairs and backed by capital or credit. The small producer, and probably also the small-town bourgeois, of the type still to be found at the time of the Revolution who made his own bread from the corn of his *métayage*, long remained faithful to the mystique of a closed economy based on corn.

The predominance of cereals gave the countryside a far more uniform appearance than it has today. There were no single-crop regions to compare with the vast vineyard which is modern Bas-Languedoc or with the pastur lands of the Auge valley. The most that can be claimed is that from some quite early date—certainly from the beginning of the thirteenth century— there were a few communities devoted wholly to the cultivation of the vine. Wine had a unique value as a commodity, since it was easy to transport and certain of a market in regions condemned by nature to abstinence or the consumption of inferior local wines. But even this departure from the traditional subsistence economy was possible only for communities within reach of a great highway, preferably a waterway. It was not by chance that the port of Collioure was the only township of Roussillon c. 1290 where corn had been supplanted by the vine; and Salimbene, writing a little earlier, had been quick to see why the villagers of the winegrowing valley dominated by Auxerre had 'neither to sow nor to reap': the river at their feet 'flows toward Paris' where wine sells 'famously'. Yet specialisation in viticulture was slow to spread. In seventeenth century Burgundy there were still only eleven places where it engaged the whole population. Wine, like corn, continued to be produced on the spot, even in regions of poor soil and poorer climate, where a season good enough to yield a vintage produced at best a miserable rot-gut. Wine production was continued in Flanders and Normandy until the sixteenth century, in the valley of the Somme even later. This conservatism was only natural, given the uncertainty of communications and the extent of the demand, which arose partly from the pleasurable qualities of wine but also owed much to its liturgical importance. Without wine there could be no Mass, nor, until the chalice was reserved to the priest in the thirteenth century, any Communion for the faithful. A Mediterranean religion, Christianity brought with it to the North the grapes and vine-branches indispensable to its mysteries.

Although cereals were in most places the dominant crop, they never had the fields entirely to themselves. A variety of auxiliary crops was grown. Cereals might be alternated with forage crops, particularly vetch, and sometimes with peas and beans. Other types of produce were kept to their own ground, quite distinct from the arable: vegetables in the garden, fruit-trees in the orchard, hemp in special fields, usually enclosed, and vines in vineyards—although in Provence the vine-plants were often raised with the corn. The siting of these areas was determined by natural conditions, which gave some variety to the local scene. It was among these special crops that time brought its most obvious changes. Advances in the cloth industry during the thirteenth century stimulated the production of woad (the medieval equivalent of indigo) in many

23

places, for example the country around Paris. As the influence of America made itself felt, the maize plant gained ground in regions with a warm, moist climate, and the broad bean retreated before the haricot. The last new arrival was buckwheat, which came from Asia Minor in the sixteenth century, probably by way of Spain, and was at first of interest only to dry goods merchants; as time went on, however, it gradually replaced rye and maslin on the poorer soils of Bresse, the Massif Central and Brittany, where it was especially popular. The great revolution marked by the advent of artificial fodder and root crops would come only at the end of the eighteenth century, entailing a complete break with the agrarian traditions of the past.

In France, as elsewhere in Europe, medieval agriculture was based not on crop-raising alone but on a combination of arable and animal husbandry. This is one of the most important differences distinguishing our western, technological, civilisations from those of the Far East. Domestic animals were necessary to medieval man in a number of ways; they provided some of his meat (the rest came from the forests and the poultry-yards), his dairy foods, leather, wool and motor power. Animals were equally essential in the cultivation of corn, for drawing the plough and, more important still, manuring the fields. Feeding these animals was one of the most pressing problems facing any village. Where there was natural pasturage beside rivers and streams, in the moist lands of valley bottoms, animals could be sure of at least some fodder for the winter and a grazing place after the hay was cut. But even at their best the meadows were never completely adequate, and some places had none at all. Their scarcity value is clearly brought out by the price they commanded, almost invariably higher than that paid for arable, and by the eagerness with which they were snapped up by well-to-do landowners, the nobility and the wealthy bourgeoisie. The occasional forage crops grown on the arable fields as an alternative to corn were also insufficient to meet the demand. In fact there were only two methods, usually employed turn and turn about, to ensure the sustenance of livestock. The first was to set aside forest or waste land as permanent grazing, where the herds could feed on the free-growing plants of heath and steppe in all their abundant

24

variety. The other was to turn the animals on to the arable itself, to feed on the stubble and wild grasses during the more or less lengthy period which intervened between harvest and seed-time. Both methods were attended by serious difficulties, admittedly legal rather than practical in nature, arising from communal bye-laws and the organisation of collective services on the fields. But even without these difficulties of a social order, the equilibrium between stock-rearing and cereal cultivation was bound to be unstable and insecure. Manure was by no means plentiful, in fact quite scarce and therefore valuable: so much so indeed that some lords demanded 'pots of excrement' as part of their dues, to the great indignation of some over-sensitive scholars who have mistaken what was merely prudent husbandry for a gross and calculated insult.[4] It was in fact this scarcity of manure that was mainly responsible not only for the rule sometimes found that sturdier but inferior crops such as rye should be sown instead of wheat, but also for the generally low yields.

The low yields were also due to other causes. Methods of cultivation were often inefficient, and remained so for centuries. One of the great achievements of medieval agriculture, and of the twelfth century in particular, was to plough land sown with grain three or even four times, instead of twice, an improvement probably made possible by the increase in the labour force which, as we have seen, must have been responsible for the large clearances. The perennial difficulty of feeding livestock, however, meant that plough teams were kept below strength and worse still were often unsuited to the task. Donkeys were quite often used as plough animals, in some places down into the eighteenth and nineteenth centuries; although economical in their diet (like the Algerian cuddy of our own day), they were deficient in motor power. Agricultural equipment also left much to be desired. It would be absurd to try to give figures for an average yield, pretending that they could apply to every century before the eighteenth and to every type of husbandry. But the records agree in showing that a yield

[4] *Archives historiques de la Corrèze*, ii, 1905, p. 370, No. lxv; and cf. the comments of the editor, G. Clément-Simon. The more usual practice was for the lord to insist on the peasants' flocks occupying his fields for stated periods so that he might reap the benefit of their dung.

between three and six times greater than the amount of seed sown was a reasonable result. When one considers all the patient observation, practical intuition and willing co-operation, unsupported by any proper scientific knowledge, which from the dawn of our rural history must have gone into the cultivation of the soil, one is filled with feelings of admiration akin to those which inspired Vidal de la Blache, after a visit to the Museum of Ethnography, to one of his finest flights of prose. But our sense of gratitude to those remote forefathers of ours who discovered corn, invented ploughing and joined arable, woodland and pasture in a fruitful union, should not blind us to the imperfections of their labours, to the poverty of their fields and to the narrowness of the margin which separated them from famine, their ever-present companion.

## 2. SYSTEMS OF CROP ROTATION

Although corn was everywhere the staple crop, the rules governing cultivation varied considerably according to the region. These differences can best be appreciated by concentrating on the arable fields and excluding the areas of minor activities.

It had long been recognised that unless fields were intensively manured they needed intermittent periods of rest; in other words, to avoid exhausting the soil it was not only necessary to vary the crop but also to interrupt cultivation altogether for a time. Although now quite outmoded, in its context the idea was reasonable; the scarcity of dung and the narrow choice of crops available for rotation (narrow because of the necessary predominance of cereals) meant a mere change of crop was insufficient to refresh the soil and keep the weeds at bay. This general rule, learned from experience, was applied in a variety of ways. It was obviously necessary to introduce some kind of order, more or less rigidly observed, into the sequence and treatment of the active and passive periods. Many permutations are possible and several were in fact used—the various systems of crop rotation.

Until well into the eighteenth century, it was still the custom in some places where the soil was very impoverished—the

Ardennes, the Vosges, the granite and schist zones of the west—
to crop a patch of ground for a few years and then pass on to
another, under a system of 'temporary cultivation'. A patch of
waste would be cleared, often by burning,[5] ploughed, sown and
perhaps fenced off, as a protection against grazing cattle.
Cultivation continued for several years, eight at most; when
the declining yield indicated that the soil was exhausted, the
patch was abandoned once again to its natural vegetation of
weeds and brush. But although now left undisturbed, the
ground was by no means unproductive; having been a field it
now became a pasture; and even the bushy undergrowth, which
could provide litter and faggots and sometimes compost from
its bracken and furze, had its uses. At the end of a period
which was at least equivalent to the time previously spent under
cultivation and often longer, the patch would be judged again
fit for cultivation, the plough brought back and the cycle begun
afresh. It was quite possible to conduct these operations more
or less systematically by making a distinction between lands
earmarked for temporary periods of cultivation on a fixed cycle
and those of the permanent waste; local custom probably in
fact imposed some such rule, though it may not always have
been rigorously applied. To the agronomists of the eighteenth
century the system seemed not merely barbarous but positively
anarchic; they remark that in these villages 'no set courses are
observed'. The circumstances which caused other places to set
a strict limitation on individual initiative were here absent.
The plots under temporary cultivation were scattered, which
meant there was little danger of friction among those who
worked them. Moreover, the grazing was always so much more
extensive than the arable that the problems of maintaining a
proper balance between arable and animal husbandry, elsewhere such a major preoccupation, scarcely arose.

By the eighteenth century there were few places where this
loosely-organised programme was still followed in full; at one
time, however, it must have been quite common and was
probably one of the earliest—perhaps indeed the earliest—of all

[5] Since both implements and manure were hard to come by, burning was a
favourite method of clearing the ground and had the advantage of leaving ashes
rich in potash; vegetation was sometimes burned right down to the stubble.
A. Eysette, *Histoire administrative de la Beaucaire*, ii, 1888, p. 291; R. Brun, *La ville de
Salon*, 1924, p. 309, c. 63.

the regimes devised by man for working the soil without danger
of exhaustion and combining corn with grazing. When the
villages where the system was still practised in the eighteenth
century finally went over to crop rotation (either of their own
accord or under external pressure), they were forced to undertake the redistribution of their properties.[6] Such villages appear
to have passed at a single bound through an evolution which
elsewhere had been far more gradual and was already ancient
history.

Even so, the change to a more orderly system was often only
partial. Although few places still kept all their land under
temporary cultivation, until quite recently there were villages
and hamlets where a fair proportion of the arable was treated
in this way, the rest being given over to a more systematic
rotation. This was the rule in Béarn, for example, where nearly
every community had both its *plaine* (permanent arable) and its
*coteaux* (hillsides covered with bracken, dwarf furze and grass,
where the peasants came each year to clear enough space for a
few ephemeral fields). The same practice prevailed in inland
Brittany, in Maine, in the Ardennes, in the Hautes Vosges
(where the short-lived clearances were chiefly at the expense of
forest), on the plateaus of German Lorraine, in the Jura, in the
Alps and Pyrenees, in Provence and on the uplands of the
Massif Central. In all these regions there were many settlements where the regularly sown *terres chaudes* lay alongside
wide tracts of *terres froides* (in the north-east usually known by
the Germanic name *trieux*), for the most part uncultivated but
with temporary furrows traced here and there. In the plains to
the north of the Loire, however, the custom had almost died
out. Here fewer spaces had been left untouched by medieval
assarters; such virgin lands as remained were either totally
unsuitable for ploughing or indispensable as grazing and a
source of wood and peat. But this had not always been the case.
Permanent cultivation may frequently have been preceded by
temporary cropping. As an example one may cite the rules
concerning deforestation laid down by Louis VI for villagers in

[6] Mariembourg and subdelegation of Givet: Arch. du Nord, Hainault, C 695
bis. Cf. also the very curious ordinances issued by the princes of Nassau-Sarre-
brück (and thus affecting regions very close to our frontiers), J. M. Sittel, *Sammlung
der Provincial und Partikular Gesetze* . . . i, 1843, pp. 324 and 394.

the forest of Corbreuse, which although a dependency of the Chapter of Paris was under a form of royal protection, very lucrative to the king because of the accompanying privileges known as *gruerie*: 'the villagers shall take only two harvests; then they shall move to another part of the wood and again take two successive harvests, sowing on assarted ground'.[7] The highlander of Indo-China and Indonesia also moves his *ray* and his *ladang* from place to place in the jungle or scrub, and sometimes creates a permanent rice-field in the process.

When compared with these makeshift methods, continuous crop rotation certainly presents a striking contrast. But it would be a mistake to imagine that medieval farmrs regularly alternated several different types of crop, as is done in the modern systems which have nearly everywhere replaced the old system of fallowing. In villages where continuous crop rotation was an ancient practice, a portion of the arable would be occupied by successive cereal crops, without any thought of intermission; the only alternation practised, and this tended to be irregular, was between winter and spring sowing, a truly astonishing application of the principle of 'resting' the land! It may be asked how land which under this treatment should have been exhausted and a prey to weeds could still yield a harvest. The explanation is that only a small part of the arable, for which all the manure was reserved, received such intensive cultivation. The surrounding land was grazing, from which temporary assarts were cut as required. Moreover, there is clear evidence that even with concentrated manuring the yield remained unimpressive. This regime was widespread in the British Isles, above all in Scotland, but in France was exceptional. Traces of it appear here and there, in the neighbourhood of Chauny, in Picardy, in a few Hainault villages, in Brittany, Angoumois and Lorraine.[8] It may perhaps once have been

[7] Guérard, *Cartulaire de Notre-Dame de Paris*, i, 258, No. xvi.

[8] Arch. Nat., H. 1502, Nos. 229, 230, 233 (Chauny) and H. 1503, No. 32 (Angoumois), Arch. du Nord C Hainaut 176 (Bruille-Saint-Amand and Chateau l'Abbaye): the dossier includes a plan of Bruille, showing very irregular plots—this village was devastated during the wars of Louis XIV and later rebuilt, its inhabitants were very poor; H. Sée, *Les classes rurales en Bretagne du XVI siècle à la Revolution*, pp. 381 ff.; Borie, *Statistique du département d'Ille et Vilaine*, Year IX, p. 31; C. Etienne, *Cahiers du bailliage de Vic*, 1907, pp. 55 and 107. The *pays de* Chauny is the only region where continuous and temporary cultivation almost certainly took place

more common; one can well believe that villages emerging from a system of temporary cultivation sometimes passed through this phase.

Both the main systems of crop rotation, by which almost all the arable land was cultivated in orderly sequence instead of by fits and starts, were based on the fallowing principle; where they differed was in the length of their cultivation cycle.

The shorter of the two was biennial: a field would be ploughed and sown one year—usually in autumn, sometimes in spring as well—and spend the next lying fallow. This meant that in any given year approximately half the tillage of each holding (and therefore half the total extent of arable) was under cultivation, while the rest remained unsown; in the following year the roles would be reversed, and so the cycle continued, by simple alternation.

Triennial rotation allowed for a more subtle relation between the crops and the nutritive properties of the soil. It was based in principle on a distinction between two categories of harvest. The lands of each holding—and thus of the total arable—were divided into three more or less equal-sized parts.[9] The names for these divisions vary with the region and include *soles, saisons, cours, cotaisons, royes* or *coutoures* and, in Burgundy, *fins, épis* or *fins de pie*. Rural terminology is idiosyncratic in the extreme; although conditions over a wide area might be fundamentally the same, the settlements which were the centres of gossip and argument were so small and self-centred that the words men used to describe their affairs varied from region to region, even from village to village. Let us place ourselves at the point in the cycle when the harvest is just over;

side by side; and here it may perhaps represent an ill-fated effort at improvement. At all events, no system of crop rotation practised in 1770 entailed artificial meadows, so there is no chance that the Chauny fields could have resulted from changes introduced by the agricultural revolution. On the yield from land under continuous cultivation and unmanured see *The Economic Journal*, 1922, p. 27; although the yield is low, it is by no means non-existent.

[9] Here are some figures taken at random. At Saint-Seine-l'Eglise, Burgundy, 1736–7, the three *soles* were made up of 227, 243 and 246 journaux respectively; at Romagna-sous-Mont-Faucon, Clermontois, in 1778 the figures were 758, 649 and 654 '*jours*'; at Magny-sur-Tille in Burgundy in 1728 one *laboureur* (J. B. Gevrey) possessed from 4 to 5 journaux in each *sole*: Arch. Côte d'Or E 1163 and 332; Chantilly, reg. E 33.

what happens next? One *sole* will be sown in autumn with the winter corn (*blés d'hiver, hivernois, bons-blés*), wheat, spelt or rye. The second is reserved for spring corn' (*blé de printemps, gros blés, marsage, trémois, grains de carême*), and will be sown in the first fine days of spring, with barley, oats, some kind of forage crop, vetch for example, or legumes, probably peas or beans. The third *sole* will be fallow throughout the year, to be sown with winter corn in the following autumn, when the others will progress from winter to spring corn and from spring corn to fallow. And so the triennial succession will proceed from year to year.

The exact geographical distribution of these two rotations has not so far been established. It would probably not be difficult to reconstruct the pattern as it was in the late eighteenth century, before the more flexible rotation introduced by the agricultural revolution put an end to fallowing; but for this we should need detailed studies which are at present lacking. What is certain is that the two systems occupied distinct blocks of territory, and had done so since the Middle Ages. Biennial rotation was the rule in the Midi, that is to say in the lands watered by the Garonne, in Languedoc, along the southern reaches of the Rhône and the southern watershed of the Massif Central. North of Poitou we enter the domain of triennial rotation.

This picture is of course oversimplified; closer inspection reveals that there were always exceptions and that changes took place with the passage of time. The exceptions become more frequent the further back one goes. It is true that on certain types of land material considerations and necessities always acted as a check on individual deviations from the rule. Consider the case of the Artois peasant of the early fourteenth century who took possession of a parcel in the *sole* sown with winter corn too late for the autumn ploughing and had to be content with sowing oats in March. In the following year he was again made to sow his parcel in the spring, to keep his land in line with that of his neighbours.[10] But in a season when labour or seed was short the situation was very different; then the only solution was to depart from the rule and leave more land fallow. On the other hand, in a year when there were

[10] *Biblothèque de l'Ecole des Chartes*, liii, 389, No. 5.

more mouths to feed everyone might agree to increase the area sown, at the expense of a little grazing. The primitive habits of temporary cultivation were never far below the surface and might even influence the regular order of rotation; we shall see that in Maine, for example, cycles in which the fallow period never exceeded one year were followed by a resting period which lasted for several. This must still be described as a mixed regime, although it has all but achieved stability. Elsewhere the old prescription of lengthy resting periods was applied only in exceptional situations. The foundation charter (1225) issued for the village of Bonlieu in the Beauce by the nuns of Yerres stipulates that the ploughlands shall be cultivated 'following the usual *soles*', but then goes on to make provision for the peasant who might wish to leave his parcel uncultivated for several years 'because of poverty or in order to improve his land'.[11]

Finally, it should be remembered that there were long periods when times were so troubled that the regular rhythm of agrarian life, as of much else, was profoundly disturbed. Edicts issued by the seventeenth-century Dukes of Lorraine complain that peasants resettled in their former villages after a period of war are not observing 'the customary courses'.[12] We should be careful to exaggerate neither the rigidity of the restrictions suffered by our rural forefathers nor the perfection of continuity from one generation to the next. Respect for the virtues of regularity and consistency is the hallmark of periods closer to our own and of societies of greater tranquillity and stability. However disturbing to the officials of Lorraine, the confusion of the seventeenth century had the positive merit of facilitating the changeover from one system of crop rotation to another.

It is time we took a closer look at the distribution of the two main systems of rotation, biennial and triennial. If the distribution were plotted on a map, it would be seen that while

[11] Arch. Nat. LL. 1599B p. 143.

[12] Ordinance of Jan. 20, 1641, in a *Mémoire* of the Parlement of Nancy, Arch. Nat., H 1486, No. 158; judgment of the *Cour Souveraine* 18 April 1670, printed in François de Neufchateau, *Recueil authentique*, ii, 1784, p. 164; cf. the undated petition from the farmer of the demesne at Epinal, Arch. Meurthe-et-Moselle, B 845, No. 175; and for the county of Montbéliard, the ordinances of 19 September 1662 and 27 August 1705, Arch. Nat., K 2195 (6).

some regions were wholly given over to one type, others presented a less homogeneous appearance. Triennial rotation was virtually unknown in the Midi. On the other hand, biennial rotation continued to be practised alongside the three-course system over extensive regions lying quite far to the north, and lingered on over a large part of the Alsatian plain (from the Strasbourg gap as far north as Wissembourg) right down to the time of the agricultural revolution. The same is true of several villages in the highlands of Franche Comté and on the northern coasts of Brittany.[13] These pockets were at one time much commoner; quite extensive areas of biennial rotation have been uncovered in medieval Normandy and also in Anjou and Maine for much the same period.[14] In Maine the biennial cycle survived in some places right down to the beginning of the nineteenth century, in an unusual combination of temporary cultivation with a tripartite division of the soil. This singular system worked as follows. There were three courses. In each course the land spent six years alternating between bearing a cereal crop of wheat or rye and lying fallow; then followed three years under grazing.[15] These curious arrangements must have survived from an earlier age, and we can guess what the intermediate stages must have been. The Carolingian estate surveys make a distinction between spring and autumn sowing, which suggests that three courses were being observed on seigneurial demesnes north of the Loire; but, as emerges very clearly from what we know of the services demanded from the tenants who worked the demesne, winter corn always took up more space than that sown in spring. There are two possible explanations: either part of the demesne still followed a biennial

---

[13] R. Krzymowski, *Die landwirtschaftlichen Wirtschaftsysteme Elsass-Lothringens*, 1914; cf. P. Hammer, 'Zweifeldwirtschaft im Unterelsass', in *Elsass-Lothringisches Jahrbuch* 1927 (the ethnographical conclusions of this last article are quite unproved); R. Pyot, *Statistique générale du Jura*, 1838, p. 394; A. Aulanier and F. Habasque, *Usages . . . du departement des Côtes du Nord*, 2nd ed. 1851, pp. 137-9.
[14] Reconstruction of the cartulary of Saint-Serge d'Angers, by Marchegay, Arch. de Maine-et-Loire, fol. 106, 280, 285; G. Durville, *Catalogue du Musée Dobrée*, 1903, p. 138, No. 127 (a reference to two courses).
[15] Marc, in *Bulletin de la Soc. d'agriculture . . . de la Sarthe*, 1st series, vol. vii (1846-7). Despite the assertions of R. Musset, *Le Bas-Maine*. p. 288 ff., this cannot be an example of triennial rotation since there is no alternation of spring and autumn sowing. It seems however that triennial rotation, mixed to some extent with temporary cultivation, was also being practised side by side with the system outlined above.

regime, or else, which is more likely, certain parcels were obliged to lie fallow for two years, so that the single year of fallow allowed to the others was always preceded by spring sowing. Whichever explanation is correct, a threefold cycle is already clearly present in embryonic form. There can be no doubt that triennial rotation was of great antiquity in the north, going back certainly to the Frankish period and probably much further still. Over the centuries however there was some mingling with the biennial system, which produced certain modifications; the same phenomenon has been observed just across the Channel, in the British Isles.

But let there be no mistake. The fundamental contrast between the two main zones occupied by each system of crop rotation is in no way lessened by these qualifications. Triennial rotation was born in the North and has left its mark there. The Midi obdurately resisted its intrusion, as though it were a foreign element. As the population of the North increased there was a definite move away from the biennial system, which left half the total arable uncultivated in any given year, in favour of the triennial system in which only a third was omitted. The needs of a growing population must also have made themselves felt in the Midi; but there the biennial habit seems to have been so deep-rooted that the idea of increasing production by changing over to the three-field system apparently never occurred to anyone before the time of the agricultural revolution. This contrast in attitude is a genuine enigma of agrarian history. It cannot be explained by reference to geographical factors in their narrowest sense; the areas concerned are too vast, their physical characteristics too diverse. Moreover, the boundaries of both zones extend far beyond the frontiers of France. The biennial cycle was practised by the Greek and Italian farmers of antiquity, sung by Pindar as well as Virgil. The triennial cycle was widespread in most of England and over all the great plains of northern Europe. The confrontation of the two systems in France represents the collision on our soil of two major forms of agrarian civilisation, which may conveniently be called the northern and southern types; how these civilisations came to take their distinctive form is still a mystery, although it is likely that historical, ethnic and no doubt also geographical, factors all played their part. For example,

34

although physical conditions cannot by themselves have
determined the ultimate distribution of the two systems, they
may well help to explain why triennial rotation had its origin
in a region remote from the Mediterranean. Roman agronomists recognised the advantages of crop rotation, and indeed
practised it, to the extent that exceptionally fertile soils were
allowed no fallow periods at all. But the crops they rotated
with cereals were either legumes or flax; they attempted no
regular alternation between different kinds of cereals. The
Romans were also familiar with the idea of spring sowing, but
regarded it merely as a useful expedient in seasons when the
autumn-sown crop had failed.[16] The Romans, after all, had no
reasonable expectation of a drought-free summer, which may
well have been why they never adopted a system of cultivation
based on alternation between spring and autumn sowing. All
this is guess-work. One thing is certain, and will emerge still
more clearly in later pages: the coexistence in France of
agrarian institutions belonging to both main systems of
agriculture, the southern and the northern, is at once one of the
most striking features of our rural life and, for the light it sheds
on the deeper roots of our whole civilisation, among the most
valuable lessons to be learned from the economic history of our
countryside.

### 3. AGRARIAN REGIMES: OPEN AND ELONGATED FIELDS

An agrarian regime is not characterised solely by its crop
rotation. Each regime is an intricate complex of techniques
and social relations. It is time we tried to identify the regimes
found in France.

Certain types of land must be omitted from this survey,
although we shall later need to clarify some points about their
origins. We cannot, for example, include land wholly under
temporary or 'haphazard' cultivation, to borrow an expression
used by an agronomist from Franche Comté; for this was land
where the husbandman drove his plough in the direction he
alone decided,[17] and although the shadowy outlines of a more
regulated system might appear, it was unlikely to become

[16] Columella, ii, 6.     [17] R. Pyot, *Statistique générale du Jura*, 1838, p. 418.

permanent. We shall also have to refrain from dwelling on the peculiarities of settlements with an unusual physical environment. The agrarian economy of the high mountains has always been markedly different from that of the lower slopes and plains, because of the inevitable predominance of pastoral farming. It should be pointed out, however, that in the past this contrast was much less obvious than it is today. Our rural civilisations originated in the plains and on the hill-sides; the high altitudes took over their institutions instead of creating any specifically adapted to their own needs. Despite the danger of over-simplification, it has seemed best for my present purpose to single out the basic features of each agrarian system; the nuances would require a volume to themselves.

The obvious place to start is with the most easily recognisable and coherent regime, that of open fields with long furlongs.

Picture a compact rural settlement. It will be fairly large, since this was a regime designed primarily for villages rather than hamlets, although it was by no means incompatible with a more dispersed form of settlement, especially where the clearance was of relatively recent date. The houses will be surrounded by gardens and orchards, all enclosed. Originally garden or *jardin* (a Germanic word) simply meant close, *clos*; the two terms are in fact synonymous and were constantly interchanged. The land inside the enclosure was sacrosanct, secured against intrusion from the communal herd. There will also be some enclosed areas on the open fields where hemp or vines are growing. (Vines were only enclosed in the north; in the south the vines were more sturdy and once the vintage was over could be safely exposed to the depredations of grazing livestock.) The ground bordering the stream, if there is one, will be meadow; then come the ploughlands, interspersed with or surrounded by grazing.

The most striking feature of the ploughlands is the uninterrupted vista they present. This is not to say there will be no fences of any kind. There is an obvious initial distinction to be made, between barriers that were permanent and those which were temporary. During a large part of the Middle Ages it was customary on the approach of the growing season to erect temporary wattle fences, not indeed round each field, but around groups of fields; sometimes ditches were dug instead.

Rustic calendars mention this chore among the tasks of spring. In the twelfth century one of the villages dependent on the abbey of St. Vaast's of Arras still had a hereditary official whose task it was to 'reinstate the ditches before harvest-time', presumably on the seigneurial demesne.[18] Once the harvest was over these temporary obstacles were removed. The custom started to die out in the twelfth and thirteenth centuries. It had originated in an age of less systematic cultivation, when the waste, roamed by grazing herds, encroached on the arable from all sides. Once the arable became more compact and distinct from the grazing land, as the result of the large clearances, this labour of Penelope lost its point. In many open-field regions it was now the practice to maintain permanent barriers at certain points along the borders of the arable. In Clermontois villagers were obliged to erect fences separating their fields from the highway; although at first temporary structures, in time these barriers developed into stout thorny hedges.[19] In Hainault and Lorraine border fences along roads or commons became the normal rule. In Béarn fences were needed to protect the permanent cultivation of the *plaines* from animals wandering on the *coteaux*, where the temporary fields were also enclosed; one finds a similar arrangement in Scotland, where walls separate the infield from the outfield, which was devoted to grazing and intermittent cultivation. Elsewhere, as in the Haguenau region of Alsace, barriers were sometimes used to divide up the arable into a few large compartments.

But once these defences—often totally lacking—have been crossed, there is no further obstacle to impede the gaze or obstruct footsteps. There may be some kind of demarcation between groups of parcels (never between individual parcels), but it will rarely be anything more substantial than a few stones sunk in the soil or perhaps an uncultivated furrow; it may even take the form of a purely imaginary line. Here was temptation indeed for 'devourers of furrows', to use a graphic rural idiom. A plough driven year after year only a little beyond its lawful course could add several furrows to a parcel, which might well represent a considerable accretion, especially where the new

[18] *Cartulaire de l'abbaye de Saint-Vaast*, ed. Van Drival, 1875, p. 252.
[19] *Description de la terre et seigneurie de Varennes* (1763): Chantilly, reg. E 31, fol. 162 v°.

furrows were as long as the old, as was usually the case. It is on record that one parcel was enlarged to more than a third of its original size in the course of sixty years. These 'thefts', 'as surreptitious and difficult to prove as any we are likely to encounter', were denounced by medieval preachers and magistrates of the *Ancien Régime* with equal fervour; they were a social evil peculiar to 'champion' country (they may be still), where field succeeds field with nothing to show where one property ends and another begins, so that unless some rising ground intervenes 'the husbandman sees at a glance all that is happening on the parcels he possesses in a single *quartier*, or even over the whole field', to quote an eighteenth century writer.[20] In its visual aspect such countryside has altered little, and one recognises the 'uncluttered' landscapes so dear to Maurice Barrès.

But although unmarked by any physical barrier, boundaries certainly existed. The lines they traced produced a curious pattern in parallel compartments.[21] The major divisions, varying in number from ten to a score and more, were known by many different names, which as usual change from region to region, even from village to village: *quartiers, climats, cantons, contrées, bènes, triages, delles,* to name only a few. *Delle*, which must be Scandinavian in origin (it also occurs in eastern England, long under Danish occupation) belongs to the lowlands around Caen. *Quartier* (the English equivalent is furlong) will be the term used here. Each had its proper name, in census

---

[20] Arch. de la Somme, C 136 (subdelegation of Doullens). The expression 'devourers of furrows', *mangeurs de raies*, occurs in any number of texts. The example of an enlarged parcel comes from F. H. V. Noizet, *Du cadastre*, 2nd ed. 1863, p. 193; the remark about thefts comes from a memorandum of 1768, Bibl. Nat. Joly de Fleury, 438, fol. 19; for a sample of a medieval sermon see Jacques de Vitry, *Sermo ad agricolas*, Bibl. Nat., 17509, fol. 123.

[21] See the map of Hubert-Folie and Bras (Pl. III), which may be compared with the maps of Spoy, Thomirey and Monnerville (Plates VI, XIII, XIV and XV) and the earlier map of the small estate of Bois-Saint-Denis (Pl. I). The fact that some of these places were Germanic settlements, as is betrayed by their names (Monnerville) or agrarian vocabulary (*delle*, at Hubert-Folie and Bras), is beside the point. The choice of illustrative plates was dictated by technical considerations alone; had the maps of Jancigny or Magny-sur-Tille in Burgundy (Arch. Côte d'Or, E 1126 and 334), to take two examples, been suitable for reproduction, the reader would have seen that the arrangements in these places of impeccably Roman origin were identical to those that appear so clearly in the maps of Hubert-Folie and Bras.

language a *lieu dit*: for example, the *quartier de la Grosse Borne*, the *climat du Creux des Fourches*, the *delle des Trahisons*. On occasion a *quartier* might be bounded by a visible limit, a hump in the ground, a stream, a man-made embankment or hedge. But often the only feature distinguishing one from another was the orientation of the furrows, for all the furrows of a *quartier* had to run in the same direction. The crime of cross-ploughing was among the charges levelled by officials in Lorraine against peasants who ignored the old customs when they came to reoccupy their lands after the wars.

The village lands were in fact laid out like a chequer-board, subdivided into a tissue of innumerable minute parcels which produced a very odd effect, since they were nearly all of the same markedly assymetrical shape. The length of the parcels corresponded to that of the furrow. But their width, perpendicular to the axis traced by the plough, was exiguous, in many cases less than a twentieth of the length. Strips made up of several consecutive furrows might be as much as a hundred metres long. It is possible that this particular effect has been accentuated by partitions among heirs at a relatively recent date; the more usual way of dealing with strips which had become impossibly long and thin was to allow the next partition to be made crosswise at the widest point, in contravention of the rule that both ends of a strip should touch the boundary of a *quartier*. It is also likely that the number of elongated strips increased when the rather larger parcels which had previously formed part of the lord's demesne were redistributed among the peasants between the eleventh and twelfth centuries. In its fundamental characteristics the pattern was certainly very ancient. The relatively frequent amalgamation of plots in more recent times has tended to obliterate rather than accentuate the identity of the separate parcels, as we shall see. Even medieval records usually indicate the position of a particular strip merely by reference to the *quartier* where it was situated and the names of the strip-holders on either side, so that each was known merely by its place in the bundle.

It is obvious that whatever its length, the total area occupied by each narrow segment must have been small. Even the most modest individual holding would have to consist of several such parcels, scattered over the *quartiers*. Dispersal and fragmentation had long been the rule governing village lands laid out on this pattern.

Two further customs, touching agrarian life at its roots, were also essential to the regime: compulsory crop rotation[22] and communal grazing on the stubble.

The cultivator was obliged to crop his land in accordance with the traditional courses; each parcel observed the rotation of its *quartier*, in the sequence of autumn sowing, spring sowing (where triennial rotation was in force) and fallow. The *quartiers* were often grouped into definite *soles* or courses, and these, like the *quartiers*, had their own names, recognised in law: at Nantillois in Clermontois there were the three *royes* of Harupré, Hames and Cottenière; at Magny-sur-Tille in Burgundy the *fins* of Chapelle-de l'Abayotte, Rouilleux and Chapelle-des-Champs. In some places the lands grouped in a *sole* were all contiguous, so that in the growing season two or three contrasting zones of cultivation might be visible, in one part the winter or spring corn, distinguished by their difference in height and colour, in another the fallow *sombres* or *versaines*, their brown earth dotted with the green of wild grasses. This was particularly characteristic of many Lorraine villages in more recent times, perhaps because the ploughlands reinstated after the devastations of the great wars of the seventeenth century were then arranged in more regular fashion. Elsewhere, even where the *sole* was sufficiently a unit to possess its distinctive name, it was made up of several different groups of *quartiers*, often as a result of the vicissitudes attendant on the conquest of the soil. Sometimes however, as in the Beauce, scattering was so extreme that the *sole* as such disappeared from view and the *quartier* became the unit for purposes of crop rotation. But whether the unit was the *sole* or the *quartier*, strict uniformity was the rule; sowing, harvesting, and the main works of cultivation all had to be done at the dates fixed by the community or its custom.

Although founded on tradition, this regime was not wholly inflexible. It was possible to change a *quartier* from one *sole* or

[22] This expression, analogous to the *Flurzwang* of the German historians, is taken from a Poitevin agronomist of the early nineteenth century, who admired the system so keenly that he was inspired to a eulogy of its merits: De Verneilh, *Observations des commissions consultatives* iii, 1811, pp. 63 ff.

course to another by communal decision: at Jancigny in Burgundy the course of the *climat Derrière l'Eglise* was altered shortly after 1667, so that the autumn sowing followed that of *Champs-Roux* instead of *Fin-du-Port*. There were even some deviations from the sacrosanct principle of compulsory rotation. For example, in the eighteenth century there were three places in the Meuse and Aire valleys (Dun, Varennes and Clermont) where certain lands, most of them close to the houses and therefore easy to manure, were 'sown at will'; they were 'out of course'. These lands admittedly represented a minute fraction of the total arable, leaving all the rest 'subject to the rules of cultivation by the regular *roye*'. Moreover there is no other trace of 'free' fields throughout the whole of Clermontois, a region for which we have exceptionally full information, and the three places just mentioned were all small townships, whose bourgeois inhabitants doubtless had a greater inclination to act individually than was common. So far as the villages are concerned, the remark applied to one of them in a document dated 1769 seems a safe generalisation: 'all the land' was divided 'among three courses . . . unalterable by the cultivators'.[23]

Let us imagine the harvest is done. The corn-fields are cut; they are 'empty' or 'waste' land (*vide* or *vaine*, it makes no difference.) If biennial rotation is in force, they will remain in this state for more than a year. If the rotation is triennial, the fields which bore the winter corn will not be sown again until spring; those which had the spring corn now enter on their fallow year. Must the void remain barren? Most certainly it must not. There is nourishment for livestock in the stubble and in the spontaneous growth which appears so rapidly on unsown land and will continue after the stubble has gone. An eighteenth century memorandum on the peasants of Franche Comté remarks 'for two-thirds of the year the inhabitants of the countryside make almost no provision for their herds apart from grazing on the waste'.[24] But this did not allow each man to graze his beasts on his own stubble, just as he pleased.

[23] Jancigny: comparison of the survey of 1667 and the table, which is a little later in date, Arch. Côte d'Or, E 1119. Dun, Varennes, Clermont. Montblainville, Chantilly, E reg. 39 (1783), key; E reg. 31 (1762), fol. 161; E reg. 28 (1774), key; cf. Plates IV and V.

[24] Arch. Nat. E 2661, No. 243. Cf. E. Martin, *Cahiers de doléances du bailliage de Mirecourt*, p. 164: 'the countryside is only kept alive by common pasture.'

Pasture on the waste was essentially a communal matter. All the animals of the village were formed into a common herd, which roamed over the harvested arable lands in a sequence fixed by the local authorities or by tradition (always the faithful protector of communal interests), browsing as they went; and the owner of each plot had to welcome the whole herd as his own.

The roaming herd needed so much space that barriers between communities as well as between properties went down before it. In most of the regions where common grazing on the stubble was the rule the villages allowed commonage or inter-commoning; under this arrangement each community was entitled to graze its livestock on some or all (it varied with the region) of the fields of the adjacent village; sometimes as many as three villages were involved. There could be no more convincing proof that the arable waste was treated very differently from land with growing crops.

The meadows, which like the arable were unenclosed, were also subject to the overriding demands of grazing, especially after the first hay had been cut. Only the 'first coat', as the old texts have it, belonged to the owner of the meadow. The aftermath fell to the community, who might allow the herd to graze on the hay as it stood (doubtless the traditional practice) or else have it cut, either for distribution among the villagers or even for sale. The owners of meadows and fields, known in eighteenth century legal language as *'detenteurs du fonds'* enjoyed 'only a restricted right of possession, subordinate to the rights of the community'.[25]

A system in which the freedom of the producer was so severely limited must obviously have contained some element of compulsion. Enclosure of strips was not merely contrary to custom; it was formally prohibited.[26] Compulsory rotation

[25] P. Guyot, *Répertoire*, 1784–5, art. *Regain* (by Henry).

[26] In certain customary codes the only enclosure expressly forbidden is of land held in *champart*, that is under the obligation of making payment to the lord in kind in an amount proportionate to the yield. But we should not take this to mean that enclosure of other lands was allowed. The customs are based on the assumption that no-one would enclose arable unless he meant to convert it to some other type of cultivation, i.e. to make a garden or a vineyard or a hemp-field, and it was this that was forbidden in the case of plots which owed part of the harvest to the lord, except, of course, where he had had given his permission; cf. the very explicit passage in the *Coutumes du baillage d'Amiens* c. 115 (*Coutume reformée*, c. 197).

was not practised merely as a habit or from convenience; it was a strict rule. Acceptance of the common herd and its grazing privileges was an inescapable duty. But since the sources of law were so diverse and relatively unco-ordinated, the legal origins of these obligations varied with the different regions: though perhaps a better way of putting it would be to say that they rested on tradition, but a tradition expressed in divers forms. When provincial customs came to be set down in writing, a task begun on the orders of the monarchy in the late fifteenth century and continued during the sixteenth, many codes were found to include the obligation of common grazing on the stubble and prohibitions against the enclosure of arable. In others, however, these provisions were absent, due perhaps to inadvertence, or to the difficulty of finding a common formula for regions with a variety of agrarian systems, or even, as in Berry, to the contempt of lawyers trained in Roman Law for customs so far removed from the conception of ownership enshrined in the Civil Law. But the law courts were on the watch. From the reign of St. Louis the Parlement consistently opposed enclosure of ploughlands in Brie, and in the eighteenth century forced several villages in Champagne to maintain compulsory rotation in all its rigour.[27] In 1787 the intendant of Tours declared 'the customs of Anjou and Touraine make no mention of common grazing on the stubble . . . but immemorial usage has been so generally regarded as the law on this point that any proprietor in these provinces would have no chance of protecting his lands against it before the courts'. Finally, even if written law was lacking and the time came when magistrates showed growing repugnance at enforcing a tradition attacked by agronomists and highly irksome to owners of great estates, collective pressure was often sufficiently powerful to secure respect for the old agrarian customs, whether by persuasion or violence. As the intendant of Bordeaux wrote in 1772, these customs 'had no force in law apart from the will of the inhabitants'; but they were none the less binding for that. Woe to the

---

[27] *Olim*, i, 516, No. vi, Arch. Nat., AD IV 1 (Nogent-sur-Seine, 1721; Essoyes, 1779). The seventeenth century judgments printed in Delamare, *Traité de la Police*, ii, pp. 1137 ff. confine themselves to withholding the right of grazing on the arable from villagers who fail to observe the rules about crop rotation. For the significance of these decisions see *infra*, p. 218. Cf. an ordinance of the county of Montbéliard, 30 August 1759, Arch. Nat., K 2195 (6) and also *supra*, pp. 40 and 41.

proprietor who erected a barrier round his field! 'A hedge would serve no purpose' said an Alsatian landowner who was being urged (*c.* 1687) to make agricultural improvements which were incompatible with communal grazing 'since it would certainly be torn down'. In eighteenth century Auvergne it was said that if an individual dared to transform his field into an enclosed orchard, as by written custom he was fully entitled to do, his neighbours would destroy the fence 'and criminal proceedings ensue, the result of which would be the dispersal and disruption of whole communities without bringing about their submission'.[28] Many eighteenth century texts make approving references to 'the strict laws forbidding men to enclose their patrimony' and the 'law of three course husbandry'.[29] In fact, prohibition of enclosure, communal grazing on the stubble and compulsory crop rotation were all so strongly felt to be 'laws' (whether they were written or unwritten, whether they were imposed by official sanction or the imperious will of the group was quite immaterial) that when the great agricultural transformations of the late eighteenth century made their suppression unavoidable it took an entirely new code to replace them.

The fact that these rules survived even when they had lost all legal sanction was perhaps mainly due to the smoothness of their interaction in practice. It is difficult to imagine a more coherent system, and even in the nineteenth century its 'harmony' could still arouse the grudging admiration of the most sophisticated critics.[30] The lay-out of the fields and the practice of communal grazing on the stubble were powerful and allied incentives to the adoption of compulsory rotation. Such improbably narrow strips, which were often so situated that they could only be reached by crossing those on either side, would have been impossible to work except under an agreed cycle of cultivation. Again, it is doubtful if the village livestock would have found enough fallow to guarantee their sustenance without a system of compulsion. Deference to the needs of

[28] J. M. Ortlieb, *Plan . . . pour l'amélioration . . . des biens de la terre*, 1789, p. 32, n.*, Arch. Nat., H 1486, No. 206; for an actual example, see Puy de Dôme, C 1840 (*subdélégue de Thiers*).

[29] *Procès-verbal . . . de l'Assemblée provinciale de l'Ile de France . . . 1787*, p. 367; Arch. de Meurthe-et-Moselle, C 320.

[30] See the fine passage in Mathieu de Dombasle's *Annales agricoles de Roville*, i, 1824, p. 2.

communal grazing ruled out the possibility of erecting permanent fences on the arable which would obstruct the movements of the herd. Enclosure was also made difficult by the layout of the fields; to fence off each of those elongated parallelograms would have been tedious and absurd, quite apart from the inconvenience of the resulting shadow and of getting from one strip to another. Finally, given the difficulty of preventing grazing animals from straying outside the narrow pasture offered by the single strip, a system of communal grazing may well have seemed the most sensible arrangement.

Only a society of great compactness, composed of men who thought instinctively in terms of the community, could have created such a regime. The land itself was the fruit of collective labour. The various *quartiers* must have been built up little by little as fresh uncultivated land was taken in. Moreover, there is uncontestable evidence to show that the methods adopted for the creation of some of our earliest, perhaps prehistoric, fields were still used as new gains were made over the centuries. It is possible to point to more than one village, whose name betrays it as at latest a Gallo-Roman foundation, in which the outlying bundles of strips can be shown as medieval additions, recognisable as such either by their names (*Rotures*, for example, from *ruptura*, clearance) or by their assessment for tithe as *novales*. Still more common is to find *villes neuves*, established during the twelfth and thirteenth centuries in predominantly open-field regions, in which the pattern of *quartiers* and strips characteristic of the older settlements is repeated. The lands of the ruined village of Bessey in Burgundy which were recovered from brush by the inhabitants of neighbouring townships during the fifteenth and sixteenth centuries present all the features set out above. And as late as the nineteenth century, when villagers in Auxois came to share out their commons they shaped the resulting plots into very long strip fields, arranged side by side.[31] Now, no matter whether a *quartier* was of recent or ancient origin, it is hardly likely that so precise an arrangement of the narrow parcels could have been achieved without a master plan, reached by common agreement. We need not at present concern ourselves with the possible existence of a leader. A group is no

[31] Assarts and *villes neuves*: pls. I and VI and *infra*, p. 53, n. 46; Bessey, *infra*, p. 115, n. 10; Auxois, *Bullet. de la soc. des sciences histor. de Semur*, xxxvi, p. 44, n. 1.

45

less a group for having a superior. The arrangement also implies agreement over crop rotation, which must surely have been foreseen and equally surely accepted, since it corresponded so closely to the general idea of what was natural and right.[32]

So far as communal grazing on the stubble is concerned, we cannot in honesty say that it was made inevitable by the shape of the fields, awkward though this was. The inconvenience of keeping animals to individual strips could have been avoided by tying them up, as was (and is still) the practice under certain other agrarian regimes. The truth is that communal grazing arose first and foremost from an attitude of mind, from the notion that once land became unproductive it was no longer capable of individual exploitation. It is interesting to see what the older legal authorities have to say on this point. Among many admirable expositions there is none better than that of Eusèbe Laurière, writing in the reign of Louis XIV: 'Under the general law of France'—he means in the parts of France covered by open-fields, the only regions he knew well—'the plots are under care and protection only while the crops are showing; once they have been taken in, the ground becomes as it were

[32] One wonders if there may not have been at first periodic redistributions of land rather than a disposition made once and for all on the basis of a common plan drawn up at the time of the initial clearance. There is definite evidence that periodical partition, coupled with temporary cultivation, was practised at Schaumburg in the late eighteenth and early nineteenth centuries (Arch. Nat., H 1486, No. 158, p. 5; Colchen, *Mémoire statistique du département de la Moselle*, Year XI, p. 119); but this was simply a version of the well-known Moselle institution of *Gehöferschaften*, which cannot be discussed here in any detail; although they were probably of fairly recent origin, the *Gehöferschaften* can be taken as evidence of an ancient and deep-rooted community feeling, cf. F. Rörig, *Die Entstehung der Landeshoheit des Trierer Erzbischofs*, 1906, pp. 70 ff. In other places and also at a relatively recent date we find cases of 'alternate ownership', which in Lorraine affected some of the meadows (Arch. Nat., F[10] 284: *Soc. des Amis de la Constitution de Verdun*—cf. the very widespread English custom of lot-meadows) and in some unenclosed pockets of Mayenne applied to the arable (Arch. Parlementaires CVI, p. 688): but these examples are much too isolated and the course of development too obscure to allow of any general conclusions. As for communal ploughing, which Seebohm (surely quite mistakenly) held to be responsible for the origins of the open-field system in England, I can only say I have discovered no trace of it in France; peasants certainly helped one another, '*laboureurs*' lent or hired their equipment to *manouvriers*; but this was from a sense of moral duty or in order to make the best use of a capital asset; neither lending nor hiring led to working as a group. F. Steinbach ('Gewanndorf und Einzeldorf' in *Historische Aufsätze Aloys Schulte gewidmet*, 1927) has recently put forward the theory that the fragmentation of holdings and the collective obligations were later developments, but I can see no proof for this whatsoever.

subject to the law of nations and the common property of all, rich and poor alike'.[33]

There were still further manifestations of the strength of the collective idea. The Biblical custom of gleaning, which might be thought a good example, was actually so common in one form or another that it cannot be linked with any particular agrarian regime, although it was certainly a dominant feature of open-field regions, where in practice if not in law it was likely to be available over the whole arable and to the whole population, not merely to the women and infirm. The right to 'stubble' on the other hand, is full of significance for our present discussion. When the harvest was over and before the livestock were given the run of the fields, the villagers were entitled to gather straw from the stubble, which they used as thatch for their houses, litter for their stables, and sometimes fuel for their fires; everyone was free to range over the entire field, without regard to parcel boundaries. This right was so highly regarded that no grower was allowed to minimise its value by cutting his corn too close to the ground. Scythes were not allowed, except on meadows; the cornfields had to be reaped with sickles, which cut much higher; even in the eighteenth century Parlements were still concerned to enforce this rule. Thus in the many places where this obligation existed—always open-field country—even the harvest was not the sole property of the land's master: the ear was his, but the straw belonged to the community.[34]

It must be admitted that the system was not quite so egalitarian as Laurière makes out. Both rich and poor certainly observed their communal obligations, but they were not on an equal footing. The usual rule was that each inhabitant, however small his holding, had the right to contribute so many animals to the common herd; beyond this minimum, the number of beasts allowed to each individual depended on the extent of his lands. Rural society was composed of clearly

---

[33] *Commentaire sur les Instituts de Loysel*, II, II, 15. This particular remark does not appear in the first edition, 1710, and is first found in the second edition, 1783, from which it passed into the Dupin edition, 1846. It is likely—though not certain—that as with other additions to the edition of 1783 the passage is based on notes left by Laurière.

[34] The owners of the field might sometimes be allowed a preferential share in the stubble and the lord also took his share: Arch. Nat., F¹⁰ 284 (Gricourt).

defined classes. Rich and poor alike were bound by the custom of the whole group, which helped to preserve some kind of balance between these social classes and the different ways of exploiting the soil. This 'rudimentary communism'—to borrow an expression used by Jaurès in the brilliant and prophetic early pages of his *Histoire de la Révolution*—was at once the hall-mark of the type of agrarian civilisation which found its expression in open-fields with long furlongs and the very reason for its existence.

Although very widespread in France, there was nothing uniquely French about this regime. Its precise frontiers would be impossible to trace without the help of much more detailed studies. Roughly speaking, it reigned supreme in the whole of France north of the Loire, except in the tablelands of Caux and the enclosed areas of the west, and was equally dominant in both Burgundies. This French zone, however, was itself only a part of a much greater area which covered much of England, almost the whole of Germany and even took in large tracts of the Russian and Polish plains. The question of origins, to which we shall have to return, must be looked at in a European context. What was peculiar to the regime in its French setting was its co-existence with two other regimes, to which we must now turn.

4. AGRARIAN REGIMES: OPEN AND IRREGULAR FIELDS

Imagine an expanse of arable, without any visible enclosures. So far the picture is similar to that presented by the fields just discussed. But now imagine that the plots instead of being long narrow strips neatly grouped in their *quartiers*, all pointing in the same direction, are of many different shapes, none much longer than they are broad, and scattered over the ground as though by chance, so that the territory as a whole has the look of a meaningless puzzle. This was (and is still, for those who have eyes to see it) what our southern ancestors saw when they looked at their countryside. It is typical of most of the Midi watered by the Rhône, Languedoc, the Garonne region, Poitou, Berry, and, further north, the Pays de Caux (Plates VII-IX). We happen to have information about the size of Provençal fields from the eleventh century onwards, which shows that their breadth varied from between 48 to 77 per cent of their length.[35] This regime, like that of the open-fields with long furlongs, was European rather than specifically French; unhappily the agrarian structure of other countries where it appears has been much less closely studied than that of Germany or England. For want of a better name, we must call it the regime of irregular open-fields.

This was not a regime based of set purpose on individual initiative. In its earliest forms compulsory common grazing on the stubble (*compascuité* in the legal language of the Midi) was an essential feature, and from this it followed that enclosure was forbidden and that some measure of uniformity in crop rotation was probably prescribed.[36] But, as we shall have occasion to show, these obligations disappeared much more quickly here than in the long-furlong regions, and were apparently never so rigidly enforced. Even communal grazing, the rule most generally observed and longest lived in the Midi, often appears without the complementary duty of forming a common herd. The fabric of social obligations lacked the solid framework elsewhere conferred by the lay-out of the fields. The possessor of a long strip sandwiched between two similar strips could scarcely entertain thoughts of branching out on his own; any such initiative would founder on almost insuperable practical difficulties. But with a broader and more isolated plot the temptation was much stronger. Moreover, as the pattern itself suggests, there can never have been any set plan for the lay-out of these fields. In long-furlong country one sometimes comes across places where although the general plan of the fields may conform to the normal pattern, the parcel boundaries of a small portion follow an irregular course; or again, one may

[35] Guérard, *Cartulaire de Saint-Victor*, No. 269; in the Uzégeois fields seem to have been somewhat longer, No. 198.

[36] Ancient rights of grazing on the arable, in regions of irregular open-fields: for Provence see *infra*, p. 198; for Languedoc and Gascony there are numerous examples, see E. Bligny-Bondurand, *Les coutumes de Saint Gilles*, 1915, pp. 180 and 229, B. Alart, *Privilèges et titres relatifs aux franchises . . . du Roussillon*, 1874, i, 270, *Arch. histor. de la Gascogne*, v, p. 60, c. 34; for Caux, Berry and Poitou, any number of examples down to the eighteenth century and later note the very interesting judgment relating Poitou printed in J. Lelet, *Observations sur la coutume*, 1683, i, p. 400. Compulsory fallow: see Villeneuve, *Statistique du département des B. du Rhône*, iv, 1829, p. 178. Within the jurisdiction of the Parlement of Toulouse, by the late eighteenth century enclosure was almost everywhere regarded as legal; this does not mean to say there were no difficulties about it in practice.

find broad, almost square, patches, all in one piece, situated either at the edge of the cultivated zone or in a clearing of the waste. These odd corners represent later assarts, undertaken without reference to any over-all plan. In regions of long-furlong fields these individual exploitations were the exception; in regions of irregular fields they must have been the rule. But the prime reason for the contrast between the two types appears to lie in an opposition between two techniques.[37]

Two kinds of plough divided between them the task of tilling our ancient fields.[38] Many features were common to both and evolved in the same way, so that in both cases the single primitive digging-stick came to be replaced by the double action of share and coulter, with the cutting parts reinforced by a mould-board. Nevertheless they differed profoundly in one fundamental feature: the *araire* was wheel-less and had to be dragged across the fields, while the *charrue* was mounted on wheels.[39]

[37] Naturally there may be places where redistribution of the land at a later date —perhaps in consequence of the tardy introduction of the wheeled plough, whose role in the matter will shortly be explained—has given rise to groups of parallel strips even in irregular-shaped fields. One finds the same thing in regions where enclosure was the rule. But it is not difficult to see that this was exceptional.

[38] The bibliography on this subject is voluminous but uneven in quality. Surviving pictorial representations of ancient ploughs are relatively few and difficult to use. The following are worth noting: K. H. Rau, *Geschichte des Pfluges*, 1845 (still useful); H. Behlen, *Der Pflug and das Pflügen*, 1904; R. Braungart, *Die Ackerbaugeräthe*, 1881, and *Die Urheimhat der Landwirtschaft*, 1912 (cf. *Landwirt-schaftliche Jahrbücher*, xxvi, 1897), all to be treated with great caution; certain archaeological studies, e.g. J. C. Ginzrot, *Die Wagen und Fuhrwerke der Griechen und Römer*, 1817, Sophus Müller in *Mémoires de la Soc. royale des Antiquaires du Nord*, 1902; the work of some Slavonic scholars, e.g. J. Peisker, *Zeitschrift für Sozial- und Wirtschaftsgeschichte* and sundry writings in French and Czech by L. Niederlé; and above all contributions from philologists, e.g. R. Meringer, *Indogermanische Forschungen* xvi, xvii, xviii, A. Guebhardt, *Deutsche Literaturzeitung*, 1909, col. 1445. The map labelled *Charrue* in the *Atlas Linguistique* edited by Gilliéron and Edmont is practically useless since it fails to distinguish the different types of plough and thus assumes that the various names used all describe the same object, not realising that the variety of nomenclature corresponds to a variety of quite distinct objects. However the map provoked an illuminating article from W. Foerster, *Zeitschrift für romanische Philologie*, 1905 (with appendices).

[39] Some authorities regard the coulter as an essential feature of the wheeled plough, which is certainly a mistake. What is true is that the cutting pieces were often much less useful to the *aratrum*, since where the soil was more compact it had less thrust than the wheeled plough; where they were merely a nuisance, the cutting parts might be removed, and so are less commonly found on the *aratrum*. Very occasionally a Provençal plough might carry a single wheel, placed in quite a different position from the wheels of the *charrue* and intended simply to serve as a guide in tracing the furrow.

The names given to these implements are highly instructive. The wheel-less model was the ancient tool used by farmers whose ancestors spoke tongues from which our own are descended; in France, and throughout most of Europe, this plough has retained its Indo-European name, which to us has come down by way of Latin: *araire* in Provence (*aratrum*), *éreau* in Berry and Poitou, *érère* in Walloon country, *erling* in High German dialects, *oralo* in Russian and its Slavonic congeners.[40] But there is no word of Indo-European root for the rival model, which arrived too late and occupied too limited a field for this to be possible. Even its French name owes nothing to Latin, since this plough was either unknown or spurned in ancient Italy, except in the Cisalpine parts. In France the word was *charrue*, indisputably Gallic. Nor can there be any doubt as to its original affiliations: a near relation of *char* or *charette*, *charrue* was originally used to describe a particular form of carriage. It was only natural that a vehicle whose salient feature was its wheels should lend its name to this new assemblage in which the plough-share was linked to a wheel.[41] Virgil was guided by the same logic when he called the plough he describes not an *aratrum* but a *currus* or chariot; brought up in a region more than half Celtic, he could not imagine an unwheeled plough.[42] The Germanic languages of the West used an entirely different word, in modern German *Pflug*, to describe the wheeled model, and their term passed into the Slavonic languages. If we are to believe Pliny, this mysterious word was invented by the Rhaetians living to the south of the upper Danube, which would make it of very ancient origin, derived from a language long since vanished and perhaps a stranger to the Indo-European family.[43] Pliny seems to suggest—his text is un-

[40] Naturally there were some deviations from this general rule. Foerster claims that in northern Italy for example *pio* (derived from the Germanic word which has produced *Pflug*) came to be used of the *aratrum*, while I learn from M. Jaberg that *ara* was used of a wheeled plough. It appears that in Norway *ard* is nowadays used only of the archaic types without a mouldboard, or with a mouldboard with two inclines; *plog* is used for the more sophisticated implements, also wheel-less.

[41] In Rouergue, which is in *aratrum* country, *carrugo* is still used as the name for a small cart; see Mistral, *Tresor*, under the heading *carrugo*.

[42] See Servius' comments on *Georg.* i, 174.

[43] *Hist. Nat.* xviii, 18, as restored by G. Baist, *Archiv für lateinische Lexikographie*, 1886, p. 285: 'Non pridem inventum in Gallia duas addere tali rotulas, quod genus vocant *ploum* Raeti.' (The manuscripts have 'in Raetia Galliae' and 'vocant plaumorati.')

fortunately obscure and must have been restored—that the
wheeled plough itself was invented in 'Gaul'. But how far can
we trust this opinion? Pliny had seen the wheeled plough in
use among the Gauls, but what more did he know? Only one
thing seems certain; wherever and whenever it originated—
perhaps before either Celts or Germans had become settled in
their historic territories—the wheeled plough must undoubtedly
be regarded as a creation of the agrarian technology which
ruled the northern plains, where the wheel in all its aspects was
put to ingenious and comprehensive use, as the Romans were
quick to notice. In any case, how can we doubt that the
wheeled plough was a child of the lowlands? It was first
invented to draw clean straight lines across wide tracts of loam
gouged from the primeval steppe. On rugged ground the
wheeled plough is useless, even today; it could never have been
born in such an environment.

If anyone had bothered to gather the necessary information
while there was still time—the task would not be impossible
even now, though haste is vital—we might be able to form a
fairly accurate picture of the distribution of the two ploughs on
the eve of the great agrarian revolution of modern times.[44] In
the present state of research the pattern is difficult to reconstruct
even for an epoch so close to our own. *A fortiori*, the details and
deviations become more and more confused the further back
one goes. And there are other complications: the older instrument, the unwheeled plough, was sometimes retained for
lighter soils even in regions where the wheeled plough had long
since been accepted as standard. Despite these difficulties,
however, what we can see is enough to show that the area now
occupied by the wheeled plough (and by the same token we can
deduce that its limits were fixed at a very early date) corresponds very closely to the region of long-furlong open fields; the
unwheeled plough on the other hand belongs to the country of
irregular open-fields. The champion lands of Berry and
Poitou provide us with a really crucial test. One might think,
from their geographical constitution, that their field patterns

[44] I have myself made some very rewarding enquiries of *Directeurs Départementaux
de l'Agriculture*, and am glad to set on record my gratitude. To arrive at a correct
interpretation of the facts as they are now it is important to remember that in
some places the wheel-less plough recommended by the agronomist Mathieu de
Dombasle was adopted during the first half of the nineteenth century.

would be similar to those of the Beauce or Picardy; I must
confess that this was my own expectation before I came to
know them. But this is *éreau* territory.[45] So, instead of long
strips grouped in *quartiers*, we find a somewhat haphazard network of plots, roughly square in shape.

The Pays de Caux poses a more delicate problem. The
peculiarities of its agrarian map can probably be explained by
the way the region was settled. In the Scandinavian peninsula
the wheeled plough long remained unknown, as it still is in
many parts; the traditional plough was the *aratrum*. When
Rollo's companions settled *en masse* in the Caux region, as we
know they did, they doubtless redrew the plots after the custom
of their homeland, using the implements with which they were
familiar. Admittedly, this is all conjecture and can only be
substantiated by a minute examination of the terrain. The
history of the Scandinavian occupation, which has hitherto
been based almost exclusively on place-names, needs to be
studied by reference to field patterns as well. To be fruitful any
such investigation should ideally be undertaken jointly by
scholars of different disciplines and perhaps also of different
nationalities. One of its incidental rewards might be the solution of another conundrum which has long puzzled scholars,
the distribution on our soil of the various ethnic groups among
the Scandinavian invaders. It should at least be possible to
distinguish the Danish settlements from the rest, on the strength
of their field patterns: unlike the Swedes and Norwegians, the
Danes were familiar from an early date both with the wheeled
plough and with strip fields arranged in groups. For the
moment, however, if we want confirmation of the influence of
Scandinavian (i.e. Swedish and Norwegian) settlement on the
field patterns of Caux we shall do best to look at the fields around
*villes neuves*, which were taken into cultivation in the great age
of assarts. We shall find that the pattern of fields with long
strips grouped in *quartiers* is again predominant, in striking
contrast with the older settlements.[46] The agrarian habits of

---

[45] For the Poitevin plough see the very interesting document Arch. Nat.,
H 1510³, No. 16.

[46] In addition to the plans of Aliermont referred to above, see also the admirable
map of Neuville-Champ-d'Oisel made in the eighteenth century, Arch. Seine Inf.,
plan No. 172.

the early days after the conquest have been forgotten, the wheeled plough has come into its own again and is everywhere in use, as in Upper Normandy today.

There is nothing inherently odd about finding the two main types of plough associated with two different types of fields. The wheeled plough is an admirable tool; given a well-balanced team it attacks the earth much more thoroughly than the *aratrum*. But because of the wheels it requires more space in which to turn, and allowing for the necessary tacking to and fro once the furrow had been traced presented quite a problem, as much legal as technical in character. Sometimes the difficulty was met by leaving a strip of land unploughed at each edge of the *quartier*, at right angles to the axis of the furrow, which was ploughed when the rest of the field was finished; in Picardy these headlands were known as *fourrières*, in the lowlands of Caen as *butiers*. Alternatively, there might be an obligation on the strip-holders on the edge of adjacent *quartiers* to allow the plough to turn on their strips, the duty known as *tournaille*: one can imagine what a hornet's nest of lawsuits this must have raised! But whatever the means, the aim was to reduce the number of turns, which accounts for the excessive elongation of the strips. The more easily manoeuvred *aratrum* invited a squarer formation, which allowed for variations in the direction of the furrows where necessary and even for criss-cross ploughing.[47] Wherever this lighter plough is found in Europe— in Scandinavia, in the ancient Slav villages of eastern Germany, which go back to the time of the *oralo*—the field patterns will be based on squarish plots.

But are these purely material factors a sufficient explanation ? It is certainly very tempting to trace the whole chain of causation back to a single technological innovation. The wheeled plough produced long-furlong fields; long-furlong fields provided a powerful and constant incentive to collective practices;

---

[47] Meitzen probably exaggerated the importance of cross-ploughing; however it cannot be doubted that the *aratrum* gave rise to numerous lightly traced furrows running in all directions. This feature is in fact noted in the document relating to Poitou referred to above, n. 45. By way of counter-demonstration, cf. the modifications introduced into the shape of certain vineyard parcels when the wheeled plough was introduced in place of the mattock: R. Millot, *La réforme du cadastre*, 1906, p. 49. It seems that in China the wheeled plough also led to the formation of long fields, cf. *supra*, p. 9, n. 15.

and hey presto, a set of wheels fixed to a plough-share becomes the basis of an entire social structure. But we must be careful; such reasoning would fail to take account of the thousand and one subtleties of human behaviour. It is true that plots had to be long if they were to accommodate the wheeled plough; but did they also have to be narrow? There was nothing in practice to prevent the occupants from dividing the land into a smaller number of larger plots, of sizeable length and breadth, so that each holding was composed of a few well-shaped plots instead of a host of very narrow strips. But far from being sought after, such concentrations appear to have been generally avoided. If the plots were dispersed, then everyone shared the same risks and enjoyed the same opportunities; everyone had his share of the different types of soil; everyone had some hope of avoiding the full impact of the natural or human disasters—hailstorms, plant diseases, devastation—which might descend upon a place without destroying it completely. This line of thought, so much a part of peasant mentality that it can still stand in the way of a rational redistribution of land, was almost as influential in determining the shape of irregular fields as it was in long-furlong regions. But where the *aratrum* was in use it was possible to keep plots to a modest size simply by curtailing their length, while maintaining a reasonable width. This solution was not practicable in wheeled plough regions, where the only way to avoid making parcels either too small or too large was to make them long and thin; this in turn meant aligning them in regular sized bundles, since otherwise—ridiculous idea!—they would run criss-cross. But this arrangement also assumes a prior understanding among the occupants and their acquiescence in certain communal restrictions. This discipline seems such an essential feature of the system that we might feel justified in reversing our previous argument: we might say that without communal habits of cultivation the wheeled plough could never have been adopted. There are obviously inherent difficulties in attempting to make such exact appraisals of cause and effect for a development whose course can only be plotted by guess-work. So let us content ourselves with a less ambitious observa-tion: for as far back in time as we can go, the wheeled plough (parent of the long-furlong field) and a collective habit of culti-vation are the twin characteristics of one very distinct type of agrarian civilisation; where these criteria are lacking, the civilisation will be of a totally different type.

### 5. AGRARIAN REGIMES: ENCLOSED FIELDS

In striking contrast to the two 'open' systems, found always in association with collective obligations more or less rigorously observed, we have the regime of enclosures. (Plates X–XII).

English agronomists of the eighteenth century tended to look on enclosure as a mark of agricultural advance: in the more fertile parts of England enclosure was accompanied by the abandonment of outdated crop rotations and of communal grazing on the arable. But when Arthur Young crossed the Channel in 1789 he was in for a surprise. He discovered whole provinces of France where the arable was divided up into enclosed fields and yet continued to be cultivated by the hide-bound methods used in neighbouring regions..., 'the marvellous folly is, that in nine-tenths of all the enclosures of France, the system of management is precisely the same as in the open fields, that is to say, fallows as regularly prevail...'[48]

Throughout these disgracefully anomalous areas the plough-lands were enclosed by fences, which as a rule surrounded each parcel: these were permanent enclosures made of durable material, clearly meant to last. They usually took the form of quick-set hedges, sometimes, as in the west, mounted on high banks of earth known as *fossés*—in these parts the *fossé* (ditch) of standard French is called *douve*. When viewed from a distance, this wealth of foliage—hedges often include bushes and trees—creates the illusion of a 'moving forest' sprinkled with isolated clearings, to borrow an eighteenth century description.[49] Hence the old name *bocage*, spontaneously applied in popular speech to enclosed regions in direct antithesis to the *champagnes* and *plaines* so evocative of open vistas. Writing c. 1170, the Norman poet Wace describes a gathering of peasants as coming

cil del bocage e cil del plain,
some from enclosed, some from open country.

[48] Arthur Young, *Travels in France*, ed. C. Maxwell, 1929, p. 291.
[49] Arch. Nat., H 1486, No. 191, p. 19.

Enclosures were not always made from growing things. Climate, soil, or mere custom might dictate some different method: on the windtorn coasts of Brittany, and in Quercy, men built low dry-stone walls which turned the countryside into one huge chequer-board.

As in the regions of open-fields, these material manifestations were the outward expression of underlying social realities.

We cannot claim that the regime of enclosures was wholly individualist in tendency. Villages where it was in force normally possessed extensive common pastures over which the villagers enjoyed collective rights, often jealously defended, as in Brittany for example. Again, except in northern Brittany and Cotentin, the meadows, unlike the ploughlands, were unenclosed and the livestock of the whole population would be turned out to graze there after the first hay was cut. What we can say, however, is that collective practices stopped short at the arable; and this is all the more remarkable when we remember that in unenclosed country, especially where the fields were long, it was the ploughlands that were subject to strictest regulation.[50] Secure within its hedge or wall, no enclosed field was exposed to the common herd; fallow land was of course used for grazing as it was elsewhere, but each man could reserve his fields for his own livestock, and follow his own system of rotation.

These independent habits were so much part and parcel of the regime that they could even survive the disappearance of the enclosures which were its outward sign. An example of what might be described as the triumph of the enclosure mentality can be found in seaward parts of south-western Brittany, where hedges were out of the question and even walls often dispensed with; yet collective obligations were apparently completely unknown. In 1768 the subdelegate of Pont-Croix, whose evidence is corroborated by slightly later sources, observed: 'each landholder tethers his beasts to a stake on his own plots, so that they shall not stray and graze on those of others'.[51] This respect for the principle of keeping oneself to oneself was liable to prevail

[50] Nothing is more revealing than an old maxim of country law, almost universally applied in open-field country: where a hedge separated two parcels of differing character, it was presumed to belong to the parcel most apt for enclosure, i.e. to garden or vineyard rather than meadow, to meadow rather than ploughland. This rule was much less common in enclosed regions.

[51] Arch. Ille-et-Vilaine, C 1632.

even when several holdings came to occupy a single enclosure. It seems that originally each field was in the hands of a single owner, and had its own quickset or stone fence, just as it had its own name—as is still largely the custom in these parts. In general the fields were fairly large and somewhat irregular in shape, though without any great disproportion between length and breadth. The *aratrum* was in use in many enclosed regions, probably because much of the ground was very uneven; even where, as in Maine, the wheeled plough was used, there was no difficulty about making fields reasonably wide, since for reasons which will shortly become clear, dispersal of properties was not the rule so the total area might be quite extensive. But in course of time these fair-sized plots might become divided up among several holders, the result of alienations or inheritance. Sometimes fragmentation resulted in fresh enclosures. On maps from Normandy which enable us to compare the same piece of land at two different dates, the boundary between two plots originally contained by the same enclosure solidifies from a purely notional line into an actual hedge.[52] It seems that the peasant preferred to work ground sheltered by a hedge. But he was often reluctant to undertake the expense and difficulty of providing his own protection, especially when his plot was small. When this was so, a single enclosure was made to embrace a small group of parcels, often quite long and narrow, whose pattern on a map where the hedges are left unmarked might persuade a casual observer that he was seeing long-furlong open-fields; in Brittany this formation was described by the significant French expression *champagne*. The holders of the various plots were pretty well bound to come to some kind of agreement over crop rotation, which might include a measure of communal grazing. Such agreements are on record, and had the effect of reproducing the customs of open-field villages in isolated pockets of the countryside.[53] But the surrounding

[52] Cf. Pl. X. In the Breton district of Broerech no enclosures could be set up without the consent of the landlord; this was because the normal tenancy was the type known as *domaine congéable*, under which the ground belonged to the lessor and the buildings to the lessee; since new enclosures counted as buildings, if the tenant who put them up were to be evicted the landlord would have to defray their cost; cf. E. Chénon, *L'ancien droit dans le Morbihan*, 1894, p. 80.

[53] Numerous examples from eighteenth and nineteenth centuries. A somewhat enigmatic judgment of the Breton Parlement probably relates to these *champagnes*: Poullain du Parc, *Journal des Audiences*, iii, 1763, p. 186.

climate of individualism was too strong for them. I remember showing a plan of one of these *champagne* fields to a man employed in the Manche survey office, who was very well versed in the rural customs of his region; when I remarked that some form of communal grazing must have been adopted, he replied with a pitying air: 'But of course not; everyone would keep their beasts tied up'. How true it is that all rural customs take their origin from an attitude of mind! In 1750, when there was a proposal to introduce into Brittany a modified form of the common herd, under which the arable would still be protected, the representatives of the Breton Estates rejected as unpracticable a measure accepted as part of the natural order by the peasants of Picardy, Champagne and Lorraine. 'It seems impossible,' they said, 'to hope that reason and the community spirit could triumph among the inhabitants of the same village to such an extent that they would be prepared to bring their sheep into one flock under one shepherd.'[54]

How did such a regime come into being? How was it even possible? Before attempting to answer these questions we must look at the enclosures in their geographical and social setting. There is nothing specifically French about enclosure, just as there is nothing specifically French about the other regimes described in this chapter. If he had looked carefully, Arthur Young would have found places in England where enclosure was accompanied by those same outmoded techniques he derides. There is even a striking parallelism in the terminology: in Middle English there was a distinction between open 'champion' land, and 'woodland', which was interrupted by hedgerows. Here, however, we are concerned only with French enclosures.

In the present state of our knowledge, a distribution map would show the following as areas of enclosure: the whole of Brittany, apart from the region of Pontchâteau near the Loire, which was open-field and subject to collective obligations; Cotentin, together with the hilly country bordering the lowlands of Caen to the east and south; Maine; Perche; the *bocages* of Poitou and Vendée; most of the Massif Central, with the exception of the loamy low-lying areas scattered like so many indeterminate oases; Bugey and the Pays de Gex; and finally the Basque lands of the extreme south west. This summary

[54] Arch. d'Ille-et-Vilaine, C 3243.

picture will doubtless have to be modified in the light of further research. But we can at least see from it that the regime is found where the soil is poor and the terrain for the most part hilly.

Further, the regime is found in lightly populated areas. Enclosed fields almost invariably centre on a hamlet rather than a village proper. Nowadays one sometimes sees enclosed fields attached to a single dwelling, but this is likely to be a relatively recent development, evidence perhaps of an individual effort at land clearance or self-aggrandizement, all the lands of the hamlet having been acquired by a single proprietor. In its earlier form, a settlement although small will always be a cluster, not an isolated farmstead.

So small a group of men could not keep all their land under permanent cultivation. The ploughlands, which were intersected by hedges or walls, would be surrounded by great stretches of waste; the Breton *landes* are a good example. The waste was used as pasture and for intermittent cultivation, on a fairly large scale. These small communities thus had no pressing need to resort to communal grazing on the arable, since the waste provided the free-range area which was lacking in regions where clearance had been more complete. It also becomes clear why the permanent plots, which formed only a small fraction of the total area, could be large, compact, and few in number, while those under temporary cultivation were scattered.

All the same, we must start with the temporary plots if we are to explain how the enclosed portions came into being. The course of development is admittedly difficult to follow, but a general idea can be formed from a study of the Breton evidence. We know a fair amount about the regime of *terres froides* as it existed in eighteenth century Brittany, by which land alternated between waste and intermittent cultivation. One part, perhaps the smaller, was set aside for commons; the remainder was given over to individual exploitation but remained subject to collective obligations, a condition which was never applied to *terres chaudes*. Each cultivator had both permanent fields, which were enclosed, and a number of plots scattered about the waste. Every now and again, at fairly lengthy intervals, he would sow his outlying lands with rye and take a single harvest. He was then entitled to cultivate broom (used for bedding and the muck-heap) on this land for a somewhat longer period, during which he was allowed to fence it off, strictly on the understanding that the closure was temporary. The intendant of Rennes has left a full account in a very interesting report written in 1769. 'By an inveterate custom which has almost passed into law, brooms are allowed to remain in the ground for only three years . . . and after this fatal term the enclosures set up to protect the crops of these *terres froides* must be destroyed.' In other words, when its period of exemption expires, the ground must once again be thrown open to the herd. It seems that at first most, if not all, of the plots established by these small groups of husbandmen fell into the category of *terre froide*, which meant that the rules about communal grazing had to be observed except where land was actually under cultivation. Although often somewhat obscure, the provisions of the *Très Ancienne Coutume*, the earliest Breton custumal written down at the beginning of the fourteenth century, clearly reflect the uncertainties of a transitional period. Enclosure is allowed, yet at the same time the practice of *guerb*—common grazing on the arable, known by this name because the owners are obliged to surrender (*guerpir*) their fields—is apparently still widespread. The custom is justified as beneficial to the community and therefore entitled to certain legal validity. It also appears that cultivation might still be intermittent.[55] In the same way, although common pasture on the arable is quite unknown in Marche today, in the thirteenth century it appears to have been the rule.[56] Little by little, however, clearances made by individuals at various spots became clearly defined and permanent as a random scattering like the temporary assarts on the edge of heathlands; but since

[55] Ed. Planiol, 256, 273, 274, 279, 280, 283. If their fields were large enough the nobles could protect without enclosure or by a merely token fence; in either case they retained their right of *guerb* over other fields. Non-nobles were allowed to enclose, but their fences had to be strong; if, having omitted to build fences they still wanted to protect their land, they were entitled to do so, but only to the extent of expelling wandering cattle—they could claim no damages or compensation, since communal pasturage was 'for the good of the community' and should be encouraged. Non-nobles who enclosed or protected their properties no longer had the right to graze their livestock on other people's arable. Note finally the remark in § 280 that no-one can know until mid-April whether a piece of land will be ploughed or left fallow, sure indication of a very irregular system of rotation.

[56] See the grants of rights of pasture over all land 'both open and woodland' 'except on sown land and meadows', in the cartulary of Bonlieu, Bibl. Nat., lat. 9196, fol. 33, 83, 74, 104, 130.

this was ground taken in from waste lying close to houses, where animals were accustomed to have free range, the fields had to be enclosed to protect the growing crops.[57] The regime of enclosure was in fact only possible because these communities still had so much uncultivated land at their disposal, so that collective rights over the small fraction which was permanent arable could safely be abandoned.

Historians have long been impressed by the contrasts between the various agrarian regimes just described, although some have appreciated the differences more clearly than others. In the days when it was fashionable to see race as the key to every historical problem, there was an understandable inclination to make the *Volksgeist* responsible. This was the aim of Meitzen's ambitious project, a praiseworthy pioneer effort now completely demolished. Quite apart from his various misconceptions, he made the mistake of confining his attention to the historic peoples, the Celts, Romans, Germans and Slavs. But one would need to go much further back in time than this, to the anonymous prehistoric groups of men who first created our fields. 'Race' and 'people' are words best left unmentioned in this context; in any case, there is nothing more elusive than the concept of ethnic unity. It is more fruitful to speak of types of civilisation. Even so we must recognise that the facts of agrarian life are no tidier than those of language: just as there are always certain forms and usages which straddle dialect boundaries, so there are no geographical areas whose limits are exactly coterminous with one particular set of agrarian forms and techniques. True, the wheeled plough and triennial rotation were probably both children of the northern plains; but their spheres of influence by no means coincided. The wheeled plough is normally linked with long open-fields, yet is also found in regions of enclosure. Taking into account both the existence of border zones, always a fruitful source of hybrid forms, and sundry instances of overlapping, it is still possible to distinguish three main types of agrarian civilisation in France, each standing in close relation to its physical and human environment. There is the type found in regions of poor soil and sparse settlement, a regime in which cultivation long remained

<hr>

[57] This was why hedges were often obligatory: Poullain du Parc, *Journal des Audiences et Arrets du Parlement de Bretagne*, v, 1178, p. 240.

intermittent and was largely to continue so down into the nineteenth century; this was the regime of enclosures. Then we have two types proper to more closely settled areas, both based in principle on collective exploitation of the arable as the sole means, given the length of the plots, of maintaining the vital balance between crops and grazing, and both necessarily innocent of enclosures. One of these types, the 'northern', invented the wheeled plough and is markedly communal in its agricultural practices; externally, it takes the form of long-furlong fields arranged in parallel strips. Triennial rotation probably had its origin in the same environment; but although it spread southwards, in other directions it made less headway than the wheeled plough and the strip field system, as is shown for example, by the evidence from the lowlands of Alsace. The prescription for the other type of open-field, which for the sake of convenience may be called 'southern' although the label cannot be accepted without some reserves, is compounded of loyalty to the *aratrum* and to biennial rotation (in the Midi proper, at least), taken with a much weaker dose of the communal spirit, especially in matters concerning the distribution and cultivation of the soil. It is not impermissible to think that these pointed contrasts of organisation and outlook among our older rural societies could not fail to have had far-reaching effects on the evolution of the country as a whole.[58]

[58] Throughout this discussion I have treated field forms as though they were a purely economic phenomonen. One may ask whether religion, always a very potent factor in primitive societies, may not also have played a part. Religious rites, which later degenerated into magic, were long regarded essential to secure a good harvest. There is also the fact that all boundaries, and this would of course include field boundaries, were held to have a sacred significance, cf. S. Czarnowski, *Actes du Congrès international d'histoire des religions . . . en octobre 1923*, vol. i. Diverse agrarian patterns could have been the product of differing religious concepts. But here we are entering on very uncertain ground, which crumbles away as soon as we try to examine the issue instead of merely stating it as a hypothesis. There is also the possibility that the Roman *centuriatio* left some traces in this country, on the analogy of the survivals discovered in Italy, Africa and perhaps also the Rhineland. The point has been raised (cf. *Revue des Etudes Anciennes*, 1920, p. 209), but no answer yet been found. And what, after all, do we know of the internal organisation of the *centuriatio*? What shape were the plots, what agrarian methods employed? Once again it is not enough simply to look at a map; agrarian customs have to be studied as well. And here we come back to the problem raised at the beginning of this note: the Roman field may perhaps have been a religious formalisation, *templum*, of the almost square field demanded by the *aratrum*. It will be seen that the note of interrogation is still strongly dominant.

# CHAPTER THREE

## The *Seigneurie* Down to the Crisis of the Fourteenth and Fifteenth Centuries

EVERY study of the *seigneurie* must have its point of departure in the early Middle Ages. This is not to deny that the institution is not in fact much older; we shall try to explore its deepest roots in the appropriate place. But it is only in the eighth and ninth centuries, when documents (charters, laws, and above all the invaluable seigneurial inventories known as *polyptiques*) become relatively plentiful, that a comprehensive picture begins to emerge with a clarity unattainable for centuries more remote.

Frankish Gaul appears as a land divided into a very large number of *seigneuries*, which are usually described as *villae*, although this expression is already acquiring the meaning of inhabited place. In territorial terms a *seigneurie* or *villa* means an estate so organised that a large part of the profits from the soil accrue directly or indirectly to a single master; in human terms it is a group of people subjected to a single superior.

The land of a *seigneurie* is divided into two parts, each quite distinct but linked to the other by very close ties of interdependence. On the one hand we have what amounts to a large home farm, cultivated under the immediate direction of the lord or his agents; in the Latin of the period this portion is usually described as *mansus indominicatus*, which in French became

64

*domaine* (and in English is usually rendered demesne*). On the other, we have a number of small or middle-sized holdings whose tenants owed the lord various customary dues and, still more important, helped in the cultivation of his demesne. Historians describe these holdings as 'tenures', a word borrowed from the legal vocabulary of the later Middle Ages. From the economic point of view, this combination of large and small scale farming within a single unit is the essential characteristic of the *seigneurie*.

Let us look first at the demesne. We find it consists of houses, farm-buildings, gardens, heathland or forest, but above all of fields, meadows and vineyards: in all essentials, an agricultural estate. Was it a compact estate? Naturally we have no maps. But where the texts happen to admit a ray or two of light, we can see that the lord's arable was usually divided up into several fields or *coutures*, dotted about more or less indiscriminately among the tenants' holdings. Although the parcels of demesne land admittedly varied considerably in size according to circumstances (they average 89 hectares at Verrières in the region of Paris, $5\frac{1}{2}$ at Neuillay in Berry and less than 1 at Anthenay near Rheims), as a rule they were much larger than the plots composing the tenements of the peasantry, and this was so even in the regions of long-furlong fields. Since he had more lands the lord to some extent escaped the fragmentation imposed by law (in an effort to give everyone an equal chance) on small and medium holders who had gradually extended their furrows. In the normal way the demesne was in fact very large. Leaving the dwellings, woodlands and waste to one side, can we say how much of the cultivated land belonged to the demesne and how much was left for the tenures? This is a question of the first importance: the answer will have a decisive bearing on the whole nature of the *seigneurie*. It is also a highly embarrassing question, since we have so few figures, and those we have are difficult to interpret. Moreover, in all probability there were marked differences not only from place to place but also between *seigneuries* of different categories. The only records which give us even a rough idea relate to wealthier properties, and even here we can only estimate orders of magnitude. However, we shall probably not be far wrong if

* Translator's addition.

we assume that on the estates of the king, the higher aristocracy and important ecclesiastical landlords, the demesne occupied between a quarter and a half of the total arable, an area likely to run into several hundred acres.[1]

We are thus dealing with large estates, some of them very extensive indeed. A considerable labour force would be needed to work them at a profit. In principle a lord had three categories of labour to draw on, and in practice used them all, though in greatly varying proportions: he might pay labourers to work for him, he might own slaves, and he might exact services from his tenants.

Paid labour could be remunerated in one of two ways, either by payment of a fixed wage in money or in kind, or by maintaining the worker at the employer's expense in his own household, which would include provision of board and lodging and sometimes clothing as well; in this second case, any monetary payment would be by way of bonus. The first system, which is our standard modern industrial practice, makes for flexibility, allowing for temporary employment and a constant turnover among employees; it also presupposes an economy based largely on money and exchange. The second system, still in use today for some agricultural workers, presupposes less mobility and a more restricted circulation of goods.

Whatever may have been said to the contrary, both forms of remuneration were certainly known in the early Middle Ages and were practised on seigneurial demesnes. The men employed by the monks of Corbie as gardeners, to dig in the autumn, attend to the spring planting and weed the beds in summer, were undoubtedly paid labourers, who worked in return for a fixed number of loaves or barrels of barley-beer, a stipulated amount of vegetables, even a few pence. So were the peasants mentioned in a capitulary of Charles the Bald, refugees from devastated areas who had hired themselves out for the grape harvest.[2] These are both cases of seasonal employment, where

---

[1] Cf. L. Halphen, *Etudes critiques sur l'histoire de Charlemagne* 1921, pp. 260–1. For Anthenay see B. Guérard, *Polyptyque de l'abbaye de Saint-Rémi de Reims*, 1853; unfortunately the measurements are given in *mappae*, a unit which appears to have varied according to the locality; but none of its known values would produce an average of more than 1 hectare.

[2] *Statuts* ed. Levillain, in *Le Moyen Age*, 1900, p. 361, cf. p. 359; *Capitularia*, ii, No. 273, c. 31.

the demand was for an increased effort over a relatively short period. But the very existence of these temporary workers is an indication of greater mobility among the rural population than is sometimes imagined and also of a margin of surplus labour, attributable no doubt to the low level of cultivation at this period. On the large demesnes, however, paid labourers who were that and nothing more can never have been more than a temporary and exceptional expedient.

Workers described as *provendiers* (because they lived at their master's expense and received their *praebendam—provende* in medieval French—from him) are mentioned in the sources at all periods of the Middle Ages, and especially in those relating to Frankish Gaul. Within this category, however, only those who were free can properly be described as paid labourers; for although slaves were also maintained by their masters, their position was entirely different. Since slavery still existed at the Frankish period, it is not always easy to be sure of the exact legal status of the fairly numerous *provendiers* encountered in the records—records whose chief concern was with practical matters such as the size of the food ration and not at all with the analysis of social conditions. It is not impossible, however, that the often unruly collection of slaves, free craftsmen, men-at-arms and vassals who drew their rations from the lord's cellarer sometimes included farm-workers of both sexes who were there of their own free will. But their numbers would in any case be inadequate for the needs of a really large estate.

Turning now to the slaves, we must again make a distinction, since slaves might be employed as agricultural labour in one of two ways: they might be set to routine daily tasks on the demesne, working under the direct orders of their master or his deputy; or they might be made responsible for the cultivation of a specific area, dividing the profits with their master in a pre-determined ratio. Under this second plan the slave was virtually a tenant, so that any additional labour he contributed to the demesne should really be classed as a *corvée*. We are left with slaves who were *provendiers*.

In the Roman world there were large estates cultivated exclusively by slave-gangs, in much the same way as the colonial plantations in America. However, with the decline of the Empire, this system (which had probably never been universal) was gradually abandoned, for reasons at once psychological and practical. Gang-labour depended on the existence of a plentiful supply of slave labour, which for that reason was also cheap. But Roman agronomists had already noticed that under these conditions slaves worked badly, that too many hands were needed to do even a little work. Moreover, the illness or death of a slave meant a loss of capital and the need for a replacement. It was useless to look to births within the estate to keep up the supply; the young of human cattle are notoriously difficult to rear. So a replacement usually had to be bought, and if the price was high the overall loss might be considerable. The slave markets were kept supplied by warfare, especially by forays into barbarian territory. In its declining centuries, when the Empire was forced on to the defensive, the raw material of the slave trade became scarce and dear. But the tenant slave was another matter. On his own holding, where he was working partly for his own benefit, he was ready to be industrious. He lived in a settled family circle, free from the constant threat of dispersal, which meant that the replacement of the labour force took care of itself. And there is this to bear in mind. A large plantation is a capitalist undertaking; capital and labour must be balanced against profits, income and expenditure nicely calculated, the labour force constantly supervised; all these operations became increasingly difficult in the changing conditions of Western economy and in a society soon to become semi-barbarised. Under the Carolingians the majority of slaves were *casati*, that is to say they were provided with a dwelling (*casa*) and fields to go with it. At least, this is true of such slaves as remained: many had been enfranchised, precisely on condition that they remained on their holdings.

However, the sources of supply were by no means exhausted during this period—there were now wars against the infidel—and traffic in slaves continued, on a fairly large scale. Thus there were still slaves living *non casati*, part of their master's household and always at his bidding. Their labours were no doubt considerable, but their numbers must always have been too few for them to tackle the field work of the demesne unaided or even make any perceptible impact on it. Everything points to the same conclusion. The demesne, if it was to be profitably exploited, relied upon *corvées*, that is to say upon the tenures, whose nature we must now examine.

We need to picture a number of small holdings: just how many will vary according to circumstances. Some will be close to the demesne land, field marching with field, the tenants' dwellings cheek by jowl with the great 'hall'—which may already be a castle—where the lord and his household lived. But sometimes the setting will be less compact: a *mansus indominicatus* could be linked with a number of scattered plots, perhaps as much as a day's journey apart, which had been acquired from chance gifts, divisions of property, sales, or upon contracts establishing ties of dependence between man and man. Again it, is by no means unusual to find that a village or parish contains a patchwork of demesne and tenant lands belonging to different *seigneuries*. We must avoid making our picture too tidy; these older societies could accommodate a large measure of confusion and overlapping in their property arrangements, both on the ground and in the way they were defined in law.

In the eyes of the seigneurial administration most of the tenures, though not all, formed fixed and indivisible units, known usually as *mansi*.[3] The men who occupied and worked them originally belonged to very diverse social categories. Put at its simplest, some were slaves and more, many more, were *coloni*, theoretically free but bound by the legislation of the later Empire to the soil. In Carolingian times, when these laws no longer applied, the *colonus* was nevertheless still under close seigneurial control. There was a tendency to confuse *coloni* with freedmen, that is to say slaves who had been given their liberty against quite stringent conditions. These are only a few of the possible categories; there were many more to add to the juridical confusion. Nor was this all; the land had a status of its own, which did not always match that of its occupant. To mention only one broad classification, *mansi* could be *ingenuiles* or *serviles*, free or servile; in theory each category of holding was assumed to have its own set of obligations. But it might easily happen that a free *mansus*, intended for a *colonus*, came to be

---

[3] I shall have to return in Chapter V to the definition of the *mansus* and the classification of its various categories; here I give only the facts strictly necessary to an understanding of the *seigneurie*.

occupied by a slave, and vice versa; such discrepancies are characteristic of a hierarchical society undergoing transformation. As time went on, these elaborate classifications became devoid of any practical significance. What mattered was that all the tenants now found themselves dependent on their lord; in a phrase which gained currency about this time and whose full meaning was to be made very plain before the Middle Ages had run their course, they were all 'his men'.

The majority of tenures were not granted for a fixed term. It is true that here and there one comes across holdings leased for a certain number of years or for a life or several lives, generally three: these were the *manses censiles* or *mainfermes*. But although quite common in Italy, in Gaul such tenancies were rare, and most were of indeterminate duration. There was no written contract to set a fixed period or to specify the obligations attaching to the tenure, in fact no explicit contract of any kind. Relations between the lord and his men were regulated by the custom of the *seigneurie*, and by that alone.

Here we touch upon a concept which lay at the heart of all medieval thinking about law, and was nowhere more powerful than in its influence on the structure of rural society. Traditionalists to the core, medieval men could be said with slight (very slight) exaggeration to have ordered their lives on the assumption that the only title to permanence was that conferred by long usage. Life was ruled by tradition, by group custom. At first sight such a system might seem inimical to all progress. But this was by no means so. Custom might sometimes find written embodiment in charters, legal decisions, seigneurial inventories drawn up with the help of inquest proceedings; but in the main custom continued to be purely oral. In short, human memory was the sole arbiter. If a certain institution was known to have existed 'time out of mind', then it was assumed to be good and sufficient. Now 'the memory of man' is a singularly pliant and imperfect instrument; it is quite miraculous how thoroughly it can forget and distort. The effect of the appeal to custom was not so much to inhibit all development as to legitimise, by gradually transforming precedents into rights, a host of abuses arising from intentional violation or mere neglect; custom, in fact, was a double-edged weapon which served both lords and peasants in turn. Inter-

preted in this way, tradition had the advantages and dis-
advantages of being relatively supple, and was at least preferable
to the lord's acting as sole arbiter. Under the Carolingians,
when public justice still had some meaning, the custom of the
*seigneurie* might be invoked by a lord against his men, and just
as easily by men against their lord; and it is clear that from this
time onward the rule of custom was extending its sway to
include slaves as well as *coloni*.[4]

One of the most important effects of this extension was that
all tenures, whatever their legal status or that of their holders,
tended to become hereditary, on a more or less uniform basis.
There was no reason for the lords to resist this move, which
indeed they assisted by allowing the creation of precedents. It
is clear that in the normal way a lord would have no interest in
preventing the children of a deceased *colonus* or slave from taking
over their father's holding. It would for example be pointless
to add such land to the demesne, which depended on tenant
labour for its cultivation and could not expand indefinitely
without destroying its main source of man-power. Besides, the
possession of land without men meant lordship without honour.
Looking for another tenant might entail a long vacancy, since
the countryside was under-populated and there was plenty of
waste land available. The real innovation of the Frankish
period was not that 'free' tenures became heritable, for this had
apparently long been an accepted part of rural custom, but
that this traditional rule was extended to all tenants, even if
they were of servile status.

Nothing could be more misleading than to dwell exclusively
on the economic aspects of the relationship between a lord and
his men, however important they may seem. For the lord was
not merely the director of an undertaking; he was also a leader.
He had power of command over his tenants, levied his armed
forces from them as occasion demanded, and in return gave
them his protection, his *mondebour*. The formidably complex
problems posed by seigneurial justice cannot be touched on
here. It is sufficient to recall that from the Frankish period
onward the seigneurial court was the recognised place for
hearing most of the pleas affecting the lord's dependants; at
least, this was the theory and there is no reason to suppose it

[4] *Capitularia*, ii, No. 297, c. 14.

was not so in fact. Many a Frankish and French baron, if asked what his land brought in for him would have answered like the Highlander who said '500 men'.[5]

In economic terms, the tenant owed his lord two types of obligation, the payment of rents and the performance of services.

The complex of rents was so intricate that it is not always easy to grasp the primary significance of each separate strand. Some payments represented a kind of ground rent, at once a recognition of the lord's proprietary right over the soil and a recompense for the tenant's enjoyment of it. Other rents, which were assessed like a poll-tax, were a mark of personal servitude, and only affected certain categories of tenants; others again were payable in respect of auxiliary benefits made available to small-holders, pasturage for example. Finally, there were the archaic charges formerly levied by the state which the lords had managed to usurp for their own profit. Sometimes, though this was rare, a proportion of the harvest was taken as payment. The majority of rents were fixed, sometimes in money, more often in kind. All in all they must have been a considerable burden—but the services were more oppressive still. The tenant of the Carolingian period owed more by way of service than he did in rent. In this essential role he resembled the Norwegian *husmend* of our own time, who are given a few acres of land on condition that they serve on the home farm of the estate.

Viewed as a whole, the services were just as variegated as the rents; but leaving aside minor activities such as cartage, two major categories can be distinguished, agricultural labour and craft work.

Agricultural labour can be subdivided again, into task works and day works. The head of each small-holding was made responsible for the cultivation of a certain stretch of land taken from the demesne; usually he was also given the necessary seed. All the profits went to the lord. This was task work. In addition the tenant owed the lord a certain number of day works, whose nature might be precisely laid down, so many days' ploughing, so many days' wood-cutting etc. The timing was left to the lord or his agents to arrange, as best suited the interests of the demesne.

Everyone was obliged to perform day works; but how many?

[5] S. F. Grant, *Everyday Life in an Old Highland Farm*, 1924, p. 98.

This was the crucial question. The burden might vary from one *seigneurie* to another, even from man to man, according to personal status or type of holding. Sometimes custom failed to impose any officially accepted limit, leaving the lord sole arbiter: the tenant 'performs his days when it is necessary' or 'when he is ordered to do so'. This lack of definition could even apply to free tenures; with servile tenures it was frequent and must have been a relic of slavery—by definition, a slave is always at his master's bidding. Otherwise the number of day works was fixed by tradition and was usually high, three days a week being the norm. Even this was often exceeded at certain seasons, or even all the year round. How then did the peasants find time to cultivate their own plots ? We must remember that the number of day works owed was reckoned by holdings, not heads, the *mansus* being the standard unit. Now each holding supported at least one family, sometimes more. For several days in the week one man from the household would go to work for the lord, taking one or two extra workers with him at very busy times of the year. The rest of the family worked the fields of the small-holding. This arrangement provided the manager of the demesne with a quite substantial labour force without leaving the peasant holdings denuded.[6]

But this was not all. Some peasants, though perhaps not all, owed the lord a fixed number of manufactured articles each year: objects made of wood, cloth, made-up garments or even metal ware. The duty of working in metal was attached to certain *mansi* and the skills were handed down from father to son. Sometimes the tenant had to supply the raw material as well as the labour, and with wooden articles this was probably the normal procedure. In the case of cloth the materials were often supplied by the lord: the peasant and his wife gave only their time, trouble and skill. The work was done either at home or in an estate workshop that was known, irrespective of the sex of the workers, as the *gynaeceum*, a name already current in the late Empire. The workshop was a means of preventing waste and theft, and the obligation to work there, itself a stigma

---

[6] Although compulsory, work done as a *corvée* was not necessarily unrewarded; the lord was sometimes obliged to provide refreshments. See the *Polyptyque* of Saint-Maur des Fossés, c. 10, printed by B. Guérard in *Polyptyque de l'abbé Irminon*, ii, 1844. There are many later examples.

of servitude, was confined to 'hutted' (*casati*) slaves. The tenurial system was thus so thoroughly geared to supplying labour that it could serve industry as well as agriculture. In this sense the *seigneurie* might be defined as one vast enterprise, at once farm and factory but principally farm, where remuneration was in land instead of wages.

Was the *seigneurie* of the eighth and ninth centuries an institution of recent origin, thrown up by social and political change? Or was it an already ancient form of association, deeply rooted in rural tradition? The answer is more difficult than one might wish. Do we always, I wonder, make adequate allowance for our profound ignorance of Gallo-Roman society, especially during the first three centuries A.D.? The combined weight of the evidence, such as it is, seems on the whole to indicate that the medieval *seigneurie* represents a direct continuation of a much earlier custom, going back certainly as far as the Celtic period if not earlier.

The picture of Gaul we get from Caesar is of a tribal society largely dominated by chieftains, who were also the wealthiest men of their communities. There can be no doubt that the greater part of this wealth came from the land. But how was it produced? It is hard to visualise these chieftains as directors of large estates cultivated by gangs of slave labour. We are given to understand that their power rested primarily on their 'clients', men who although free by birth were nevertheless their subjects. Such retainers would clearly be too numerous to live in their master's household; and since they are unlikely to have been concentrated in towns, which were few in number and modest in size, most of them must have been settled on the country. Everything points to the conclusion that the Gallo-Roman aristocracy was a caste of village chieftains, drawing the greater part of their income from dues owed by their peasant subjects. It is again Caesar who mentions in passing that the fortified trading post of Uxellodunum, which was almost a town, lay within the *clientela* of Lucterius, chief of the Cadurci. If this was true of Uxellodunum, why should we doubt that other, more exclusively rural communities, were not also 'clients'? It thus seems possible, though this is only conjecture, that the regime had its origin in an ancient tribal system: the experience of non-Romanised Celtic societies, for example Wales in the later Middle Ages, seems to suggest that the transition from tribal or clan leadership to seigneurial lordship was a relatively simple matter.

Analagous systems for organising the exploitation of the land were to be found up and down the Empire, so the essential characteristics of tribal institutions were probably kept alive beneath the Roman façade. Naturally there had to be some adaptation to changed economic and legal conditions. Initially the abundance of slave labour no doubt stimulated the creation of some huge demesnes, but it is by no means certain that many such existed during the Celtic period. The example of Wales is again pertinent, since it proves that a territorial clientele need not be based on the existence of a demesne, still less on a demesne of vast dimensions; a chief could derive the whole or larger part of his revenues from dues owed by his peasants. Slavery, on the other hand, was an invitation to cultivation on the large scale. But as the supply of servile labour started to shrink, the proprietor who was unwilling to abandon his demesne completely exacted more and more oppressive services from his tenants, either in place of or in addition to the existing dues.[7] The landed aristocracy was a potent force in the Empire and could bring pressure to bear on dependants. Yet in Gaul, as no doubt elsewhere in the Empire, each rural *seigneurie*, even in late Roman times, in practice followed its own law, which was its custom: *consuetudo praedii*.[8]

There is also impressive linguistic evidence in favour of the antiquity of the seigneurial regime in France. We can see it most clearly in the place-names. A very large number of French village names are formed from the combination of a personal name with a suffix of belonging. As already noticed, some of the personal names are Germanic. But there are others, much more numerous and with different suffixes, which are older still, Celtic or Roman. The Roman names are admittedly

[7] Before the Empire started to decline few *corvées* were apparently demanded from *coloni* living on *villae*; but, as usual, we have no information directly concerning Gaul—if only we could discover something like the *saltus* found in Africa! Cf. H. Gummerus, *Die Fronden der Kolonen* in *Oefversigt af Finska Vetenskapssocietetens Förhandlingar*, 1907–8.

[8] Fustel de Coulanges, *Recherches*, 1885, p. 125. Cf. the inscription at Henchir-Mettich, *C.I.L.*, viii, No. 25902, *ex consuetudine Manciane*.

devoid of any ethnic significance; they reflect the general fashion of adopting the onomastic of the conqueror. For example, the Gallic *Brennos* became *Brennacum*, which in French has become Berny or Bernac; *Florus*, which is Latin, became *Floriacum*, giving rise to Fleury, Florac etc. The phenomenon is not peculiar to France: there are plenty of Italian villages whose names preserve the memory of their eponyms. But—so far as can be seen in the present state of comparative studies— the habit was nowhere more widespread or more tenacious than in Gaul. And who, if not chieftains or lords, could have given their names to so many settlements? But we can venture further. In the Germanic languages, the common nouns denoting the focal point of a rural settlement contain a reference to the enclosing fence surrounding it (town, township), or else, though this is less certain, express the idea of a meeting-place (*dorf*); but the Gallo-Romans adopted for this purpose a word used in classical Latin to describe a large estate (usually including both demesne and tenant land), in short a *seigneurie*. This word was *villa*, in French *ville* and much later *village*, a diminutive which emerged when it became necessary to distinguish small rural settlements from the larger urban agglomerations which would henceforth have the monopoly of *ville*. There could scarcely be a more convincing demonstration that most villages must originally have had a lord. I think we must admit that despite all manner of vicissitudes and inevitable transfer of ownership, the lords of the medieval *seigneuries* were in direct line of descent, by way of the masters of the Gallo-Roman *villae*, from the village chieftains of ancient Gaul.

If we ask whether the whole of Gaul was given over to the seigneurial system during the Frankish period the answer should very probably be no. To all appearance there were still small-holders unencumbered by any dues or services—save what they owed the king and his representatives—and in many cases bound only to the performance of the collective duties basic to agrarian life. Such men either lived together in separate villages or were scattered among the tenants of the *villae*, forming part of their community and occupying the same land. Petty proprietors of this sort had always existed in the Roman world, though they were perhaps less numerous in Gaul, with its long tradition of rural 'clienteles', than for example in Italy.

After the barbarian invasions their numbers were no doubt augmented by a proportion of the German immigrants who settled permanently on Gallic soil. This is not to imply that all or even most of the barbarians lived merely on the margins of the seigneurial system; we have Tacitus' word for it that even in their original habitat the Germans were accustomed to render obedience and 'gifts', i.e. customary dues, to their village chiefs, who were thus well on the way to becoming lords. It is quite impossible for us to arrive at even an approximate estimate of the proportion of allodial holdings to the rest (in the early Middle Ages *alleu* was already being applied, as later, to land unencumbered by any superior title). But what we can clearly recognise is that these petty proprietors were under the continual threat of losing their independence, and that this was due to conditions chronic from at least the later days of the Empire. The constant unrest, the habitual resort to force, the insecurity which impelled everyone to seek a protector more powerful than himself, the abuse of power fostered by the absence of government and all too soon sanctioned by custom, all combined to draw an ever-increasing throng of peasants, whether they liked it or not, into the bonds of seigneurial subjection. The *seigneurie* is indeed older than the Frankish period; but it was during the Frankish period that it acquired its indelible character.

## 2. FROM GREAT PROPRIETOR TO RENTIER LANDLORD

Now let us place ourselves around the year 1200, in the reign of Philip Augustus. What has become of the *seigneurie*?

At first sight we can see clearly that it is far from having ceased to dominate the rural scene. In certain respects it seems more firmly and more widely entrenched than ever. Admittedly, peasants with allodial holdings can still be found here and there, in Hainault for example; but they are very few, and although exempt from paying rent for their land, are by no means outside the orbit of seigneurial control. And if their land is free, they themselves are often bound to a lord by ties of personal subjection which, as will be seen, could be very constricting. Moreover, the courts to which they have recourse are usually those of a neighbouring lord.

For the lords now had a monopoly of justice. It is true that the public jurisdictions of the preceding era lingered on, in more than vestigial form. The fundamental distinction observed in Carolingian times between major and minor causes (major canses were those reserved for the count, a royal official, while minor causes were left to lesser officers or the lords) still held good and was still recognisable, albeit somewhat transformed, in the division of justice into *haute* (carrying the right to judge offences carrying the death penalty or in which the duel was the form of trial) and *basse*. There were many regions where the three great judicial assemblies—*placita generalia*—were still held each year, following the rule laid down by Charlemagne in his legislation. In northern France at least, the ancient Carolingian judicial functionaries known as the *échevins* still held their sessions. But the crown had made sweeping concessions in the form of grants of immunity, offices had been allowed to become hereditary, so that the descendants of subordinates had become irremovable principals, and a host of abuses and usurpations had crept in, all of which meant that the state had lost control of its own institutions. It was the lords, in virtue of a right which could be inherited, bought or sold, who appointed the *échevins* or summoned the *placita*.[9] Higher jurisdiction, also heritable and alienable, was the prerogative of a large number of lords who exercised it on their lands (and sometimes on those of less privileged neighbours) without reference to their sovereign. On each *seigneurie*, low justice and a territorial jurisdiction over his estate (the hearing of petty offences and causes relating to the tenures) belonged to the lord, or, which was much the same, to the court which he set up, summoned and presided over (whether in person or through his deputy), and whose decisions he would carry out. In England the ancient popular assemblies known to Germanic law survived, as county and hundred courts; in Germany itself, where in theory at least the sovereign retained the right of appointing the chief justices down to the thirteenth century, courts composed of free men were by no means unknown; but

[9] During the twelfth and thirteenth centuries the inhabitants of a number of towns and even certain villages won the right to nominate the *échevins* themselves, or at least to share in their appointment. This however was part of a general movement towards group autonomy, and was something new.

in France justice was seigneurial justice. At the period we are now speaking of, the French kings, using strategies which do not concern us here but which were far less bold than those deployed in England, had only just embarked on their efforts to regain control of justice.

This almost unrestricted exercise of rights of jurisdiction armed lords with a weapon of economic exploitation whose potentialities seem limitless. It reinforced their power to command, the faculty described in the language of the day as the lord's *ban*, an old Germanic word meaning precisely command, order. As the inhabitants of a village in Roussillon acknowledged in 1246, writing to the Templars who were lords of the place, 'You can compel us to obey these rules' (about using the lord's bakehouse) 'just as a lord can and should compel his subjects'. And consider this incident, which took place in Picardy about 1319. The lord's bailiff had ordered a peasant to go and cut wood; this was not a *corvée*, the job would have been paid for at 'labourer's' rates. The man refused, and was thereupon fined by the seigneurial court for his 'disobedience'.[10] Among all the many possible uses of this authority, in practice one of the most significant and important was in the creation of seigneurial monopolies.

In Carolingian times the demesne frequently included a water-mill among its amenities (windmills had yet to be introduced into the West). There can be no doubt that many of the households occupying *mansi* were in the habit of bringing their corn there to be ground, with considerable profit to the lord. But there is no evidence that they were forced to do so. Many probably still had hand-driven mills in their own homes. From the tenth century a very large number of lords took advantage of their coercive powers to compel all the men living on their land (and sometimes even on neighbouring lands if their jurisdiction or effective authority extended so far) to make use of the seigneurial mill—naturally at a price. The establishment of this monopoly coincided with a technological advance, the final substitution of hydraulic power for human or animal effort as the driving force. The complicated machinery of the water-mill would obviously only be worth

---

[10] B. Alart, *Privilèges et titres . . . du Roussillon*, i, p. 185; A. J. Marnier, *Ancien Coutumier inédit de Picardie*, 1840, p. 70, No. lxxix.

installing if it was to be used by a large group of people, and the river or stream which drove it was often regarded as part of the lord's demesne property. But it was the element of compulsion rather than the technical advance that was really decisive: without compulsion, who knows how long the peasants might not have clung to their domestic mills? It is safe to say that neither the evolution of machinery nor the lord's possession of rights over running water was the overriding factor in this tightening of seigneurial control: for although constraint to use the lord's mill (*ban* in the sources—the word is significant) seems to have been the most widespread of all seigneurial monopolies, it was far from being unique. In its other manifestations seigneurial monopolism owed nothing to technical improvements or to the possession of rights over water.

Constraint to use the lord's bakehouse was almost as common as enforced use of the lord's mill. In wine or cider country the lord's press almost invariably had the monopoly, in beer or ale country the lord's brewhouse. Small-holders who were anxious to increase their flocks were often forced to use the lord's bull or the lord's boar. In the south, where the grain instead of being beaten with a flail was usually trodden out under horses' hooves, many lords insisted that beasts from the demesne stables should be used, in return for a fat fee. And finally, the monopoly could be of a more exorbitant nature still—during certain weeks of the year the lord could reserve to himself the right to sell particular forms of produce, usually wine (*banvin*).

Admittedly, nothing of this was unique to France. England had its suit of mill, its seigneurial monopolies selling beer, even compulsions imposed on tenants to buy beer. Germany had much the same monopolies as France. But it was in France that the system reached its apogee; nowhere else did it embrace so many estates or so many of the different economic activities carried on in a single place. There can be no doubt that this was due to the greater authority of the French *seigneur*, derived from his almost total usurpation of jurisdiction. When the jurists of the thirteenth century set about providing a theoretical framework for this social order, it was a sound intuition that led them to connect constraints and monopolies with the organisation of justice; over this they are unanimous, although the forms in which they clothe their thoughts vary with the author and the cases under discussion. The right to judge was indeed the surest foundation for the right to command.[11]

The older dues also remained in force, quite distinct from these monopolies, and retained their essential characteristics; in detail, however, they showed infinite variety, which arose from the vagaries of local custom and the operation of precedent, disuse or abuse. In addition, two further charges were being introduced, tithe and tallage.[12]

Tithe was actually quite a venerable institution. What was new was its appropriation by the lords. Pepin and Charlemagne had decreed that every Christian should pay a tenth of his revenues, more specifically a tenth of his harvest, to the Church, and had thus given force of law to an ancient Mosaic precept long enjoined as a moral obligation on the faithful, although hitherto unsanctioned by the State. So tithe was to be paid to the Church; but to which of the Church's representatives? The answers given in Carolingian legislation are immaterial here. All that concerns us is the outcome: from an early date the lords were in practice masters of the churches established on their lands; appointing the priests who served them, they also annexed the greater part of the parochial revenues, in particular all or most of the tithes. Then, in the late eleventh century, came that great movement for securing the independence of the spirituality, commonly known as the Gregorian reform. Its leaders made the restitution of tithes to the clergy part of their programme. Little by little many tithes were indeed recovered, by pious donations or redemptions. But, the beneficiaries generally speaking were not the parish priests nor even always the bishops. Grants of tithe went by preference to chapters and monasteries, the custodians of relics who could also offer the prayers of their religious on behalf of

---

[11] In virtue of these same powers of constraint, a lord could compel villagers to patronise certain craftsmen—a barber or farrier, for example—to whom he had granted a monopoly, in return for various advantages to himself. Cf. P. Boissonade, *Essai sur l'organisation du travail en Poitou*, 1899, i, 367, n. 2 and ii, 268 ff.

[12] On tithes see the legal studies of P. Viard, 1909, 1912, and 1914, in *Zeitschrift der Savigny-Stiftung*, K.A., 1911 and 1913; *Revue Historique*, clvi, 1927. On tallage, see F. Lot, *L'impôt foncier . . . sous le Bas-Empire*, 1928, and the studies by Carl Stephenson there referred to, p. 131. Readers will have no difficulty in discovering the points on which I differ from these authorities; cf. also *Mém. de la Soc. de l'histoire de Paris*, 1911.

the donor. If it was a matter of purchase, these rich communities were again in the best position for finding the necessary funds. So the net result was not so much to deprive the tithe of its seigneurial character as to make it primarily (though not of course exclusively) a typical source of income for a certain category of lord. Instead of being distributed among a whole host of petty lords or country priests, these sacks of grain now accumulated in the barns of a few great tithe-owners, who disposed of them in the market. Without this development, whose curve was determined by what were initially religious considerations, how could the towns growing up so rapidly in the twelfth and thirteenth centures have been fed?

In tallage we have an eloquent example of the strict subjection of tenants as a group to their lord. There was another and highly significant name commonly used for this charge: it was an 'aid'. The general feeling was that in times of grave necessity a lord was entitled to assistance from his men. This assistance took varying forms, according to the nature of the case: it could be military support, credit in cash or kind, provision of lodging (*gîte*) for the master, his retinue and his guests, or, where the need was pressing, a sum of money. Suppose then that a lord, whose immediate resources can never be very great, since this is a period when money is scarce and slow to circulate, is faced with the need for some sudden and exceptional outlay: a ransom, a feast for the knighting of a son or the marriage of a daughter, a subsidy demanded by a superior, the King or the Pope for example, a fire at his castle, a building to erect, or the price of some property to round off his estates. He turns to his dependants and 'requests'(tallage sometimes goes by more polite names such as 'request', *queste*) or more precisely exacts (hence *exactio*, yet another synonym) a subvention from their purses. This procedure he applies to all his dependants, whatever their rank. If he has other lords as his vassals, he will not neglect to call on them for help. But the main burden of contribution naturally falls on the tenants. Originally, then, tallage was levied at irregular intervals and was variable in amount, which is what historians mean when they describe it as an arbitrary imposition. Possessing these inconvenient features, which were exacerbated by the impossibility of predicting the date and amount of the charge, too irregular in its returns to become absorbed into the routine of customary payments, tallage long remained a dubiously legitimate impost, a generator of rural revolts and an object of censure, even in religious communities, among men concerned for the good name of the law, which of course meant tradition. Later, as the lords' need for ready money increased, keeping pace with the general economic trend, their demands also became more frequent. The vassals, too powerful to be mulcted indefinitely, as a rule saw to it that their liability to tallage was restricted to certain cases, which varied with the customs of each group of vassals or from region to region. The peasants were less capable of resisting the lords' demands, so that tallage was on the way to becoming an almost universal and annual imposition, levied within each *seigneurie*. The amount was still variable. In the course of the thirteenth century, however, it seems that rural communities, who were everywhere pre-occupied with attempts to regularise their dues, were trying to 'compound' their tallage so as to make it a fixed charge, though certain cases might still be admitted as exceptional. Around the year 1200 this movement had only just begun. But whether compounded or not, tallage provided the lords of Capetian France—and of many other parts of Europe—with quite considerable revenues denied to their Frankish predecessors.

The jumbled complexity of legal status so characteristic of the tenant populations of seigneurial estates during the early Middle Ages was primarily due to the survival of the traditional categories, more or less antiquated, which were inherited from the many diverse legal systems, Roman and Germanic, whose discordant elements intermingled in Carolingian society. The confusion of the succeeding centuries, which in France as in Germany (though not in Italy nor in a sense in England) led to the disappearance of all legal teaching and learning and put an end to any conscious application of specifically Roman or barbarian codes in the courts, produced a great simplification.[13] The same is to some extent true of language, for example the

---

[13] Although Roman law may still have been taught in some Provençal schools, its influence was slight. Canon Law was always taught, but had little bearing on the structure of society.

history of English between the Norman Conquest and the fourteenth century: once a language loses its literary status and is
no longer ruled by grammarians and stylists, the modes of
classification tend to become fewer and more obvious. If we
ignore certain survivals, such as will always subsist throughout
the course of an evolution, we can say that in the France of the
twelfth and thirteenth centuries every tenant, or to use the
terminology of the period, every villein (French *vilain*, Latin
*villanus*, from inhabitant of a *villa*, the old name for *seigneurie*)
was in a condition either of freedom or of servitude.[14]

The free villein was bound to his lord only because he held a
tenure from him and lived on his land. In a way he represents
the norm among tenants, the tenant pure and simple. And so
he is called *vilain* without further qualification, or *hôte* or
*manant*, terms which imply the simple fact of habitation as the
source of his obligations. Let us not be led astray by the fair
name of 'liberty' appearing in this connection. It stands here
in opposition to a very precisely formulated concept of servitude,
as will soon become plain; it has no absolute value whatsoever.
The villein belonged to the *seigneurie*. He was therefore bound
to render to the head of the estate not only the various rents
which were in one way or another a recompense for his enjoyment of the land, but also all those obligations of aid (including
tallage) and obedience (including submission to seigneurial
jurisdiction and its contingencies) which were the ordinary
marks of subjection. In return he had the right to be protected.
Thus in 1160 the Hospitallers engaged 'to guard and defend'
the *hôtes* on their new settlement at Bonneville near Coulmiers
'in peace as in war, as their own'; as *hôtes*, these men would
certainly be free of any servile bond. It was a double-edged
form of engagement that united a group of free villeins with
their lord. When a (free) *bourgeois* of Saint-Denis was killed by
a knife thrust, the murderer paid a composition to the abbot.
If the religious of Notre-Dame of Argenteuil or the canons of
Paris failed to pay a rent for which they were liable under
contract, the creditor seized the persons or properties of their

[14] Here I am drawing on the results of my own research on serfdom; a list of my
articles is given in *Revue Historique*, clvii, 1928, p. 1. For slavery cf. *Annales d'histoire
economique*, 1929, p. 91, and *Revue de Synthèse Historique* xli, 1926, p. 96 and xliii, 1927,
p. 89; in addition to the references given there, see R. Livi, *La schiavitu domestica nei
tempi di mezzo e nei moderni*, Padua, 1928.

tenants.[15] But however powerful the claim on him, once a villein left his tenure the attachment was immediately broken.

The serf also normally lived on a tenure. In this respect he was subject to the same customs as the body of free villeins, of whatever condition. But he also had to obey certain rules arising from his personal status. Already a villein, he was a villein plus. But although he had inherited the ancient Roman name of *servus*, he was certainly not a slave. In Capetian France there were no longer any slaves, or practically none. But neither was he free, as can easily be appreciated. The fact is that the concept of liberty, or if you will, the absence of liberty, was gradually changing in content. The curve of its vicissitudes is identical with that of servility as an institution; what social hierarchy is ever anything but a system of group images, by their very nature subject to change? In eleventh and twelfth century eyes a man was free so long as he escaped all taint of hereditary servitude. The type of villein who changed his lord when he changed his holding was free. The vassal owing military service was free, no matter that in practice he nearly always fought under the same baronial banner as his father had, or that when the baron died he swore fealty to the next in line, on pain of losing his fief; in law the reciprocal obligations of lord and vassal were born of a ceremonial contract, homage, which bound only the two parties concluding it, each of his own free will, hands laid within hands. The serf, on the other hand, was a serf—and already belonged to a predetermined master—from his mother's womb. He did not choose his lord: for him, therefore, there was no 'liberty'.

The other terms used to designate serfs are significant: he is the lord's 'own man' or, which is almost the same, his 'liege man' or even his *homme de corps*. Such expressions all imply a strictly personal bondage. It is possible that the South-West— a region whose institutions, often widely different from those of other provinces, are still little known—was quite early familiar with a type of serfdom incurred simply by residence on certain lands: men in this situation were known as serfs *'de caselage'*. This anomaly seems to confirm what is suggested by other

[15] Arch. Nat., S 5010[1] fol. 43 v°; Bibl. Nat., ms. lat. 5415, p. 319 (1233, 15 May); L. Merlet and A. Moutié, *Cartulaire de l'abbaye de Notre-Dame des Vaux-de-Cernay*, 1857, No. 474 (1249, June); B. Guérard, *Cartulaire de Notre-Dame de Paris*, ii, 291.

indications: that the system of personal relationships, of which serfdom, together with vassalage, was only one facet, must undoubtedly have been less widespread in most of the regions covered by the *langue d'oc* than it was in central and northern France. Everywhere else, despite understandable efforts on the part of lords here and there to make an avowal of serfdom a necessary condition for the occupation of certain lands, the bond of servitude remained essentially 'corporal'. From birth, by the very fact of birth, serfdom was bred into 'the flesh and bone', as the jurist Gui Coquille later put it.

The serf's hereditary attachment was to a man, not to a tenure. The medieval serf must not be confused with the *colonus* of the Later Empire; he might be descended from him by blood, but his status was quite different. The *colonus* was in theory a free man (which according to the categories of his age meant he was above slavery) who had been chained by law to his holding, which his son was obliged to inherit; he was not, it was said, the slave of a person, which would have made him merely a *servus*, but of a thing, the land. This subtle fiction was quite unknown to the robust realism of medieval law, and in any case could only have been enforced by a strong government. In a society where no sovereign power held sway above the dust of the seigneurial courts, the idea of this 'eternal' union of men with the soil would have been quite devoid of content, with no reason to commend its preservation to a legal mentality largely unencumbered, as we have seen, by survivals from the earlier age. Once a man had gone, who was there to seize him by the collar? More pertinent still, who could force his new master, who had perhaps already accepted him, to send him back?[16] Definitions of serfdom arrived at by courts or jurists have survived in some quantity: none before the fourteenth century include 'attachment to the soil' among its characteristics in any shape or form. There is no disputing that the lords, with their vital interest in protecting themselves against depopulation, might not on occasion retain their tenants by force. Two neighbouring lords often reached a mutual agreement not

---

[16] Cf. the difficulties encountered later in Poland in enforcing the rule of attachment to the soil: J. Rutkowski, *Histoire economique de la Pologne avant les partages,* 1927, p. 104 and *Le régime agraire en Pologne au XVIII^e siècle* (off-prints from the *Revue d'histoire economique,* 1926 and 1927), p. 13.

to grant asylum to absconders. But these arrangements, which took their force from the over-all power of the seigneurial *ban*, applied as much to the so-called 'free' villeins as to those whose status is described as servile. To cite only two examples among many: it was 'the serfs or other men, whatsoever they may be' of Saint Benôit-sur-Loire, 'the serfs or *hôtes* of Notre-Dame de Paris' whom the monks of St Jean-en-Vallée and the nuns of Montmartre agreed not to receive at Mantarville or Bourg-la-Reine. And when Sir Pierre de Dongeon made residence a strict condition for holding land of Saint-Martin-en-Bière, he never for a moment dreamed of making a distinction in respect of the legal status of the subjects affected by his order.[17] The departure of a serf was so little a crime against his condition that it was sometimes expressly catered for: 'I give to Saint Martin', says Sir Galeran in 1077, 'all my serfs, both male and female, of Nottonville . . . on the understanding that whoever of their posterity, whether man or woman, removes himself to another place, near or far, village, castle, fortified town or city, shall still remain tied to the monks of Saint Martin by the same knot of servitude'.[18] The only difference, as clearly emerges from this and many other texts, is that the departure of a serf did not, as in the case of a free villein, automatically free him from his chains. Suppose he settles on another holding. Then he will henceforth owe the lord of that holding all the common obligations of villeinage. But at the same time he will continue to be liable to his old master, to whom his 'body' still belongs, for the obligations proper to his servile status. Since he is compelled to give aid to both, he will pay a double tallage. Or at least that was the law. In practice one can well imagine that many of these 'foreigners' ended by losing themselves among the throng of itinerants. But the principle leaves no room for doubt. There was only one way such a powerful bond could be broken, by a solemn act of enfranchisement.

It is time to set out the commonest charges and incapacities which defined the constricting bonds of dependence in which the serf passed his days.

[17] R. Merlet, *Cartulaire de Saint-Jean en Vallée*, 1906, No. xxix (1121); B. Guérard, *Cartulaire de Notre-Dame de Paris*, i, 388 (1152); Arch. Nat., S 2110, No. 23 (1226 n. st. February.)

[18] E. Mabille, *Cartulaire de Marmoutier pour le Dunois*, 1874, No. xxxix (1077).

A lord, even where he could not exercise higher jurisdiction over his other tenants, was sole judge of his serfs in matters 'of life and limb', no matter where that serf might be living. This enhanced the lord's power to command and brought him appreciable profits: the right to judge was lucrative.

A serf was not allowed to marry outside the group of serfs dependent on his lord. This provision was necessary to ensure that the lord kept control of the children. Sometimes, however, a young man or woman sought and obtained permission to marry elsewhere, to 'marry out' (*formarier*). This was naturally obtained only at a price. Here was another source of profit.

A serf, male or female, had to make the lord an annual payment called chevage. This was not an important source of profit, since its main purpose was to provide permanent proof of serfdom and the amount was only small.

In certain situations, or to a limited degree, a lord might inherit from his serf. Two different systems were in operation. One, particularly associated with the extreme north, is almost completely analogous to the custom commonly observed in England and Germany: whenever a serf died, the lord was entitled to a small part of his estate, the best chattel, the best head of cattle, or perhaps a very small sum of money. The other system, generally known as the right of *mainmorte*, was peculiar to France and the more frequently followed there. Where a serf left children—or, according to a later modification of the rule, where he left children living with him at the time of his death—the lord got nothing. If the heirs were only collateral, the lord took everything. Under both systems, apart from some cases recognised as exceptions, the heritability of tenures is clearly as much an established part of the customs affecting serfs as it is for the villeins: and the general tenor of the charters is to treat serfs as *heredes*, men with a patrimony. But whatever method of assessment was used, the profits were either slender or very irregular. Land was still too plentiful and labour too scarce to make a few bits and pieces tempting prey for lords who, as we shall see, were themselves in process of dismantling their demesnes.

Our view of serfdom would be incomplete if we thought of it only as an unusually strong hereditary bond uniting the weaker to the more powerful. By a dualism which is one of its most

patent characteristics, serfdom made a man at once the subject
of his chief and a member of an inferior and despised social class,
near the bottom of the scale. He was not allowed to give
evidence against free men (serfs belonging to the king or to
certain ecclesiastical landlords were exceptions, by reason of
their masters' rank). Under Canon Law serfs were excluded
from Holy Orders unless they first obtained their freedom, on
the grounds that they were too dependent, though in fact this
was simply a transference of a rule originally made for slaves.
The servile condition was an indisputably damaging stigma;
but, at this period at least, it was also and above all a personal
tie linking one human being with another.

Serfs were to be found in nearly every part of France, either
under this name or under others which might carry slightly
different connotations and were peculiar to more remote areas,
for example Brittany and Roussillon.[19] Where studies of
medieval status are concerned, it is a good general rule never
to linger over particular terms, since they vary enormously
from region to region and even from one village to the next.
How could it have been otherwise in a fragmented society,
lacking a common code, lacking any system of legal education
and with no central government, in short lacking all the authorities capable of evolving a standard terminology ? Nor should we
become hypnotised by details, which are also susceptible to
infinite variations, since all the habits of everyday life were ruled
by strictly local custom, which inevitably confirmed and enlarged every difference however slight. If instead we concentrate on the fundamental principles, it is at once obvious
that the basic ideas, which reflect the general trends of common
opinion, are at once very simple and almost everywhere
identical. The terms used to designate a serf, and the practical
implications of his status, may vary from province to province
and from one *seigneurie* to another. But overriding this diversity
in the eleventh and twelfth centuries was a common, perhaps
European, concept of serfdom, which was certainly recognised

[19] The Breton '*mottiers*' and '*quevaisiers*' had a status which, as H. Sée has shown,
must surely be regarded as a variant of serfdom. The *homines de remensa* found in
Roussillon are quite indubitably serfs; if they are not called *servi* this must be
because the word was reserved for slaves, of which there were still a fair number in
Roussillon right down to the end of the Middle Ages; cf. *infra*, p. 95.

and accepted throughout France. It is this concept whose constituents I have sought to analyse.

One province, Normandy, was a region apart. Serfdom seems never to have developed there on any scale; the latest document to mention men who must certainly have been in this category cannot be much later than 1020. As with the irregular open-fields of the Caux region, the explanation is probably to be found in the manner of settlement. In the English Danelaw, the part of the country where Scandinavian occupation left its most decisive imprint, the rural population also retained a greater measure of freedom than is noticeable elsewhere in England. This parallel must at the least give food for thought.

To come back to France, in addition to being so widely disseminated serfs were almost everywhere far more numerous than ordinary villeins; they were in fact in the majority among the rural populations living under the seigneurial regime.

This one class gradually absorbed into itself, 'by a slow and silent revolution',[20] the descendants of men of varying legal condition: 'hutted' slaves, *coloni* enfranchised under Roman or Germanic law, perhaps some allodial small-holders. Some, no doubt the majority, had changed their status gradually without recourse to any definite contract, by one of those imperceptible elisions natural to a society governed by precedent and the ebb and flow of tradition. Others consciously surrendered their liberty; there are plenty of examples in the cartularies. Many peasants formerly free entered the bonds of servitude in this way, ostensibly of their own free will, actually more often driven to it by fear of being isolated, by the spur of hunger or under duress. In fact this was a new kind of servitude. For although men were not fully aware of the change, the old names which were still on everyone's lips had slowly acquired connotations far removed from their original meaning. When ties of dependence started to proliferate after the barbarian invasions, no new names were created to suit the new categories. The complex vocabulary which developed spontaneously drew heavily on the language of slavery. And this happened even in the case of non-hereditary and superior relationships: 'vassal', a Celtic word

---

[20] I have borrowed this expression from Guérard, who despite his somewhat pedantic manner of exposition penetrated further than most in his understanding of the evolution of medieval society: *Polyptyque d'Irminon*, i, 2, p. 498.

taken over into Romance, means slave; the obligations of a vassal are his 'service', a word used in classical Latin only of servile obligations (a free man performed his *officium*). With rather more reason, these transfers of meaning were more frequent in the humbler realm of strictly hereditary relationships. In Carolingian times the language of the law was careful to keep *servus* strictly for slaves; but in current speech it was already being freely extended to all the subjects of a *seigneurie*. As the final term of this evolution we have serfdom, an ancient label applied to one of the lynch-pins of a now transformed social system dominated by ties of personal attachment whose details were regulated by group custom.

What, on balance, did the lords gain from this institution? It certainly brought them very great power, and far from negligible profits. But as a source of labour it was less rewarding. The serf was a tenant, whose principal effort was necessarily devoted to his own land and whose obligations, like those of other peasants, were generally fixed by custom. Outright slavery would first and foremost have provided the masters with abundant labour; serfdom offered the lords only a very limited supply.

Two outstanding characteristics, reaching to the heart of the system, distinguished the French *seigneuries* of the late twelfth century both from their Gallo-Roman predecessors and from the majority of their contemporaries in England and Germany: the erosion of the *mansus*, the indivisible fiscal unit, and the dwindling of the *corvées* or services. Leaving aside the former for the time being, let us concentrate on the latter.

There were no longer any 'manufacturing' services. Lords certainly kept up the custom of granting tenures—generally known as 'fiefs', in common with all tenures based essentially on services—as a means of remunerating the small number of craftsmen retained for the household. But the mass of tenants no longer had to produce wooden tools or scantlings, cloths or garments; the obligation to make scythes and spears was restricted to the few 'fiefs' reserved for blacksmiths; the estate workshops had put up their shutters. At some time in the first half of the twelfth century the *'maires'* of Notre-Dame-de-Chartres—that is, the seigneurial officials responsible for the cathedral lands—were still making the peasants spin and weave wool; but this they did illegally, for their own advantage, and there is no sign that when the canons prohibited the practice they demanded a similar tribute on their own account.[21] From now on, lords fortunate enough to have a town within their jurisdiction exacted what they needed from urban trades-men; others relied on their domestic artisans, who were rewarded by land or other means. But, and above all, goods could now be purchased in the market.

How was it that lords no longer called on their tenants to provide their castles and monasteries with so many objects which, although crudely fashioned, were at any rate serviceable and cost nothing in labour to produce? Is it enough to say that a 'closed economy' had been replaced by an 'economy of exchange', and leave it at that? The formula is no doubt a close approximation to what was happening within the *seigneurie* itself. But it would also imply that the seigneurial economy had been drawn into the wake of a great tide of exchanges running through every region, a tide which by casting a greater number of goods on the market had speeded up their circulation and ended by making bulk purchase a better proposition than production within a closed unit. This hypothesis would only be tenable if we could see the normal sequence of cause and effect in operation, that is to say, if the revival of trade is followed at a decent interval by the disappearance of the manufacturing services. We should also expect to find these services surviving here and there over a longish period, since the return to a more active circulation of trade made itself felt in some parts of France later than in others. Now, as far as can be judged from the all too scanty evidence, the disappearance of manufacturing services was everywhere complete by the beginning of the twelfth century; but this disappearance is much too early and too general to be accounted for by the development of commerce, still very much in embryo. It is more likely to be yet another aspect of a deep-seated and far-reaching change which was taking place within the whole seigneurial organism at this time, which in turn no doubt had its effect on the general rhythm of the economy. Probably there did indeed come a time when the unaccustomed abundance of goods on the market en-

[21] E. de Lépinois and L. Merlet, *Cartulaire de Notre-Dame de Chartres*, i, No. lviii (1116—24 Jan. 1149).

couraged lords to step up their purchases. But the initial and unprecedented expansion of the market may itself need to be explained as a response to fresh seigneurial needs. It looks, then, as though the *seigneurie* should be closely scrutinised by anyone seeking to analyse the exchange mechanism in depth, an undertaking so far barely attempted. The nature of the great metamorphosis which overtook the *seigneurie* between 1100 and 1200 will emerge still more clearly from an examination of the agricultural services.

We can make our comparison exact by reference to a specific example. The village of Thiais, to the south of Paris, remained in the possession of the monks of Saint-Germain-des-Prés at least from the age of Charlemagne right down to the Revolution. In Charlemagne's day the majority of the free tenures owed three days' work a week (two to be spent ploughing as necessary, the third in manual work); in addition each was solely responsible for the cultivation of four square perches (about 120 square yards) of the seigneurial fields sown with winter corn and two square perches of those sown with spring corn; finally there were carrying services, to be performed at the lord's discretion. The number of manual services owed by the remaining free tenures was left to the arbitrary decision of the lord. Each servile tenure was responsible for four acres of the monastic vineyard and for the performance of ploughing and manual work 'as ordered'. In 1250 serfdom was abolished at Thiais, and a charter granted on this occasion sets out the general schedule of services to be observed. The only obligations actually suppressed were the servile ones. The others, now reduced to writing, were held to be ancient custom and date at latest from c. 1200. There is no longer any trace of task-work. Each tenant renders the abbey one day a year for mowing and if he owns draught animals, nine days' ploughing:[22] at most, then, ten days a year. Formerly even those tenants protected by fixed custom owed a minimum of 166 days. Admittedly, presented in this way the comparison is not entirely fair. A tenure could contain several households; but the services detailed in 1250 are clearly those demanded from

---

[22] In addition to its free and servile tenures, Carolingian Thiais also had three *hôtises*, burdened with a variety of obligations; *Polyptique d'Irminon*, xiv. For enfranchisement see *ibid.*, ed. Guérard, i, 387.

the head of each family. Yet even supposing that the average was two households per tenure (which is not the case), the difference is still enormous.

Sometimes the change has progressed further still. Two charters from Beaumont in Champagne and Lorris in Gâtinais which were copied here and there in the twelfth century and ultimately adopted for a large number of places, make no mention of compulsory agricultural services. It is true that at the other end of the scale we find certain local custumals still declaring that the serf 'does what he is ordered', as in Carolingian times; but they are extremely rare and may amount to no more than the assertion of a principle which had little application in practice. As we shall see, most lords would have had no use for labour in such quantity. Thiais undoubtedly represents the norm. Task-work has totally disappeared, day work continues, but on a greatly reduced scale. This state of affairs, reached about 1200, was to be more or less permanent. The system of services in operation under Philip Augustus would be roughly the same under Louis XVI.

There are two possible *a priori* explanations for this remarkable dwindling of agricultural services: either the lord had discovered some other source of labour to assist in the cultivation of the demesne, or else the demesne had itself been drastically reduced.[23]

The facts show the first hypothesis to be untenable. What other source was there to draw on? Slavery was a dead letter and could only be revived by an access of fresh supplies. Certainly there were still wars. But it was now held that no Christian could make a fellow Christian his slave. The religious view was that all members of the *societas christiana* were citizens of one great City, and as such incapable of enslaving one another; the only captives who could be reduced to slavery were infidels and—though there was some hesitation over this— schismatics. Thus slaves are only found in any quantity at

---

[23] The lord could have used his tenants as a source of labour in another way, by forcing their sons and daughters to work for an indefinite period: in Germany, where the system was known as the *Gesindedienst*, it played an important part in the life of some *seigneuries*, particularly in the east and in the late medieval and early modern periods. However it appears to have had little significance in France during the Capetian period, although there are isolated instances of lords demanding forced domestic work from their tenants, or rather from their serfs.

points convenient for the reception of the sorry freight-loads collected in forays beyond the borders of Christianity and Catholicism: the eastern frontier of Germany, Spain in the age of the *reconquista* and the countries washed by the Mediterranean which habitually received cargoes of assorted human cattle— African Negroes, olive-skinned Muslims, Greeks and Russians kidnapped by Tartar or Latin corsairs. The very name *esclave*, slave, which came to replace the older *servus* (whose change of meaning we have already noticed) is ethnic in origin: slave or Slav, it was all one. The origin of the many unfortunates who ended their days in castles on the German marches or the house-holds of Italian citizens is implicit in this word alone. It follows that in France during the twelfth century, apart from some isolated instances, slavery was known only in the Mediterranean provinces. But even there, in contrast to certain parts of Spain, for example the Balearic islands, slaves were too rare and too expensive to be employed on a large scale in the cultivation of the fields. Slaves were used as serving men or women and as concubines. There were practically no farm slaves of either sex.

Hired labour certainly continued to play its auxiliary role and even appears to have increased, thanks to the growth in population. Certain monastic orders, notably the Cistercians after their initial experiment with lay brothers, came to rely quite heavily on hired workers as the solution to their labour problems. But to work estates comparable in size to the vast *mansi indominicati* of former times by this means would have taken a really large rural proletariat which did not, and could not, exist. Although the population of France had undoubtedly increased, there was still no surplus and in the absence of any major technical advance the cultivation of the old-established tenures and of the new lands taken in by the great clearances still occupied many hands. Finally, the general economic situation would have made it very difficult for great entre-preneurs to pay or maintain great masses of employees.

There can be no doubt that the lords only acquiesced in the loss of so many agricultural services because either by default or design they were allowing their demesnes to shrink. The demesne fields which had once been the responsibility of tenants owing task-works were gradually being absorbed into the hold-ings of those who had previously been burdened with working them. Perrin has given a perfect demonstration of how this process worked itself out in Lorraine.[24] Part of the more extensive portion of the original demesne which had formerly been cultivated by task-works had been carved up in the course of the tenth and eleventh centuries to make petty fiefs for the numerous armed vassals which great barons were obliged to maintain;[25] and these men, who were primarily warriors, probably lost no time in dividing their share among the peasants in return for rents. A still larger part was granted out by the lord himself, either to existing tenants or to newcomers. Often the grant was made in return for a proportion of the yield (ranging from a third to a twelfth), the type of tenure known as *champart, terrage* or *agrier*. In Carolingian times very rare, in Capetian France such tenures were quite common. The explanation for the contrast must almost certainly be that most of the parcels involved were newly apportioned land, which would also account for the special legal status often enjoyed by lands held in champarty. At first the lords were unwilling to accept the fragmentation of their demesnes as irreversible. Around the year 1163 the monastery of Saint-Euverte of Orleans was undergoing a reorganisation which embraced both its temporal and spiritual activities. At the time it seemed impossible to cultivate the seigneurial land at Boulay, which was therefore handed over to the peasants. Later the canons thought it would be more profitable to exploit it themselves, and with authorisation from the King and the Pope took back what they had alienated.[26] Champarty, a tenure characteristic of newly apportioned land, was thus often regarded as essentially non-hereditary. The thirteenth century jurists acknowledge that in Touraine, Anjou and Orléanais a lord is entitled to take back into his demesne any lands for which the tenant paid only a terrage.[27] Until 1171 the lands held in champarty at Mitry-Mory, in the *seigneurie* of Notre-Dame of Paris, changed hands as the canons saw fit; until 1193, no lands in champarty at Garches, in the *seigneurie*

[24] *Mélanges d'histoire du moyen-age offerts à F. Lot,* 1925.

[25] I am endebted for this observation to M. Deléage, who is at present working on the agrarian development of Burgundy during the Middle Ages.

[26] Arch. Loiret, H 4: Bull issued by Pope Alexander III, Segni, 9 September [1179; cf. J.W., 13457 and 13468]. Cf. A. Luchaire, *Louis VI,* No. 492.

[27] *Etablissements de Saint Louis,* ed. P. Viollet, I, c. clxx; cf. IV, p. 191.

of Beaudoin d'Andilly, had changed hands by inheritance; the customs of the Valois village of Borest, written down during the thirteenth century, declare that when properties of this type are sold, nothing is owing to the lord 'because in times gone by no-one had the right to inherit them.'[28] But let there be no mistake; as these examples themselves show, the hereditary principle was in fact slowly insinuating itself, whether by explicit agreement as at Mitry-Mory or by prescription as at Borest. The lords accepted the situation, or at least did nothing to alter it. The great estates finally passed into the hands of the peasantry in the form of perpetual tenures, more or less identical with the older type. Many of our present-day villages contain *quartiers*, long since broken up like their neighbours into a mass of small parcels, whose official name, 'Les Corvées' or some such, recalls that long ago they formed part of the demesne and were cultivated by the forced services of the tenants.

Sometimes the demesne disappeared completely. Elsewhere, and more commonly, part of it survived, but so greatly diminished that its whole character was changed. We can form a good idea of what was considered sound demesne policy in the twelfth century from the somewhat self-congratulatory little treatise written by Suger of Saint-Denis. He clearly thinks that each estate should have its own demesne, of moderate size. Where a demesne has vanished, as at Guillerval, Suger revives it; where a demesne is too large, as at Toury, he grants some of it out. But what should the demesne consist of? As Suger describes it the demesne must include: a house 'preferably strongly built, ready to be defended', which will be the residence of the monks charged with management of the estate and a place where the abbot himself can 'lay his head' on his tours of inspection; a garden with a few fields for the sustenance of permanent or temporary guests; barns for storing produce brought in by tithes or from lands held in champarty; stables or sheepfolds for the seigneurial flocks, which no doubt grazed on the cultivated waste so that their dung could manure the gardens and demesne ploughlands; and finally, where possible, a fish-pond and vine to supply the monastery and its dependants with commodities indispensable to their way of life, which it

---

[28] Guérard, *Cartulaire de Notre-Dame de Paris*, ii, 339, No. lv; Arch. Nat., L 846, No. 30; Paris, Bibl. Ste-Geneviève, ms. 351, fol. 132 v°.

was still more satisfactory to produce on the spot than to purchase in an uncertain market. To sum up, this demesne was at once an administrative centre and a farm engaged in a more or less specialised form of husbandry; its work was certainly important, but demanded no more labour than a small staff of servants helped out by a few tenurial services could easily supply; both in size and function it is a far cry from the huge agrarian undertakings of the past.[29]

There is no difficulty in tracing some of the causes which led to the gradual abandonment of seigneurial farming on the large scale. The Carolingian *mansus indominicatus* had certainly brought its master a quantity of produce. But it all had to be housed, and much of it was perishable; such an accumulation was only valuable if it could be used a little at a time, as needed. Here was indeed an agonising problem, which haunts Charlemagne's famous capitulary concerning the imperial *villae*. Some of this produce was needed to feed the *provendiers* working on the demesne; some went to the sustenance of the lord, who might live some distance off, often leading a semi-nomadic existence. Any surplus—and with large properties there inevitably was a surplus—would have to be sold. But this presented enormous difficulties, in view of prevailing material conditions and the low level of education. Exact accounting was essential to avoid waste, losses and mistakes. There is something pathetic in the spectacle of sovereigns like Charlemagne and great abbots like Adalhard of Corbie toiling to instruct their subordinates in the necessity of keeping even the simplest accounts; the fact that the lessons are often so elementary indicates that they were addressed to minds ill-suited to receive them. Another necessity, if the produce was to be properly distributed, was the services of a corps of administrators. But administration proved the stumbling block of the successor kingdoms which issued from the Carolingian Empire, and the *seigneuries* found the problem just as intractable. The *sergents*, or seigneurial officials, who might even be serfs remunerated by tenures, soon transformed

[29] Cf. Arch. Nat., LL 46 for a comparable picture from the thirteenth century presented by the estates of Saint-Maur-des-Fossés and the work of abbot Pierre I, 1256–85. The largest arable demesne—almost abnormally large in fact—is of 50–70 *hectares*, which corresponds to 'large' in the modern official classification but is well below 'very large' (100 *hectares*). The demesnes of most of the *villes neuves* were of the same order.

themselves into hereditary feudatories, like so many miniature counts and dukes; they used the authority entrusted to them to further their own ends, they appropriated part or all of the demesne or its profits and sometimes declared open war on their masters. Suger obviously considered any estate handed over to *sergents* as lost to the demesne. Selling produce, moreover, meant transporting it—but along what roads and at what risks! Finally, where were the markets? In the tenth and eleventh centuries towns were small and more than semi-rural. Villeins were often starving, but since they lacked money could purchase next to nothing. Thus it was clearly more profitable and, above all, more convenient, to increase the number of small-holdings, which would both be self-supporting and a source of fixed revenue, some of it in cash which was easy to collect and store. Moreover, an increase in the holdings would bring profits of another kind: the more portions the lord carved from his demesne, whether for his tenants or for his vassals as petty fiefs, the more 'men' he had to swell his army and his prestige. The process had in fact already started in the last days of the Roman Empire, with the decline in the great slave plantations and the increase in 'hutted' slaves and the growth of the colonate. The heavy services of the Frankish period were simply palliatives which enabled the demesne to remain tolerably large. The great landlords of the succeeding period— of lesser landlords we know nothing, and their demesnes may never have been at all extensive—simply resumed where their Gallo-Roman predecessors left off.

This apparently straightforward interpretation runs into a difficulty whose importance it would be dishonest to gloss over. The conditions of life just described were common to Europe as a whole; but the attentuation in services and the shrinking of the demesne were peculiar at this period to France. There was no similar movement in England, where even in the thirteenth century the situation as reflected in the surveys of estates belonging to St. Paul's cathedral is reminiscent, detail for detail, of the picture presented by the Carolingian inventories. Nor, so far as I can see—the obstacles in the path of comparative studies are among the most vexing incidents of our modest achievement in the human sciences—was anything comparable happening in the greater part of Germany. Both countries would certainly experience this transformation, but a century or two later. Why the contrast? Here I must beg indulgence of the reader. There are times when the first duty of a scholar is to admit that he does not know. The moment for such an avowal of ignorance has now arrived—and with it is coupled an invitation to join in an investigation vital to our understanding of one of the three or four major phenomena of our rural history.

This particular transformation was more decisive than any in the life of the *seigneurie*. From Frankish times onward tenants always owed both rents and services; but at first the scales were weighted on the side of services. Now the balance was reversed. The old rents were augmented by new charges, tallage, tithe, payments for the use of seigneurial monopolies, servile dues; and from the twelfth and thirteenth centuries rents were sometimes exacted in place of ancient services whose futility the lords at last acknowledged but whose loss they were not always able to bear without compensation. Services were now immeasurably lighter. Formerly the tenure had been first and foremost a source of labour. Henceforward its real justification was the 'rent' it produced—rent in this context has no precise legal significance. The lord had abdicated from his position as head of a large agrarian and semi-industrial undertaking. His overseers no longer commanded the services of entire villages for days on end. As time went on more and more lords abandoned direct cultivation even of the home farm, which had often been salvaged from the wreckage of the demesne. There was a growing tendency, especially in the thirteenth century, for the home farm to be alienated, not in perpetuity it is true, but for a term: the distinction is important and had its effects, as we shall discover, but was no obstacle to the master's progressive relinquishment of his land by this means. An analogy will help to give some idea of the transformation in the seigneurial way of life between the eleventh and the thirteenth centuries. Suppose an important manufacturer were to hand over his machines to his employees, to be operated in a number of small workshops; the former boss would become merely a stockholder, or more precisely, for the purposes of our analogy, a debenture-holder (since the majority of rents were or would become fixed), in the enterprise of each artisan family.

Politically speaking the lord was still a leader to his men: he remained their military commander, their judge, their born protector. But his economic leadership had gone—and all the rest could easily follow. He had become a 'stockholder' in the soil.

# CHAPTER FOUR

## Changes Affecting the *Seigneurie* and Landed Property from the Later Middle Ages Down to the French Revolution

### I. LEGAL CHANGES AFFECTING THE *SEIGNEURIE*; THE FATE OF SERFDOM

THE ending of the Middle Ages and the transition to modern times is signalised by a crisis in seigneurial revenues.

The old framework was not shattered all at once. The position of the tenants (by a confusion characteristic of the obscurity overtaking the older notions of personal relations they were now starting to be known as vassals, a term once reserved for dependants of a totally different kind) and their tenures *vis-à-vis* the lord was the same under Francis I, or indeed under Louis XVI, as in the time of St. Louis. The same, that is, with two important exceptions: the importance of seigneurial jurisdictions was declining, and serfdom had either completely disappeared or, where it survived, had been radically transformed.

Seigneurial jurisdictions were still far from extinct—only the Revolution would finally kill them off. Many matters still lay within their competence. But they were far less lucrative and powerful than formerly. Under a legal rule which had gained general recognition in the sixteenth century and was almost invariably observed, the lord could no longer sit to do justice in person. In view of the growing complexity of the legal system he might have been reluctant to do so. He now had to appoint a professional judge, who could no longer be rewarded by the grant of a 'fief' (a form of payment ruled out by changing economic conditions) but had to be paid in hard cash. No doubt, the rules governing magistrates' salaries as laid down in royal ordinances were no better observed than those prescribing their minimum legal qualifications; on many estates the greater part of their profits came from fees paid to them by those who came before the court. But even without this the lord's expenditure was often quite heavy and the total outlay might well exceed the benefits, so much so that lords feared to dispense justice too often. 'The amount received in fines, fees and confiscations,' wrote a Burgundian nobleman in the seventeenth century 'falls short of what is needed for the wages of the officials.' And in 1781 the intendant of the Duchy of Mayenne sent the following report to his masters: 'Poverty in these parts has given rise to many criminal proceedings; I have suppressed as many as I can, apprehending only two or three real rogues who have been holding up travellers pretty well by force.'[1]

But above all, seigneurial justice now had a formidable rival in public justice, dispensed either by the courts of the great principalities or by those of the crown, which from the sixteenth century was almost alone in the field. A large number of causes were removed from the seigneurial courts altogether, in other cases the seigneurial courts were forestalled by the greater despatch of local royal officials; lastly, it was now possible to appeal against their judgments. This appellate jurisdiction of the crown was a source of endless annoyance and expense to the seigneurial judges, whether high or low, since under an old law which was still in force as late as the seventeenth century it was the judge in the court of first instance and not the successful plaintiff who was named by the appellant in his suit; furthermore, the very existence of the appellate jurisdiction represented a loss of power and prestige to the inferior courts. The lords of the tenth and eleventh centuries had augmented their power and revenues by letting their men feel the weight of their judicial authority. This weapon had not fallen completely from their grasp, since as a rule they still had the last word in the matters of rural discipline which touched so many interests; but its force was greatly diminished. One might think that this was a serious threat to the whole seigneurial regime. As we shall see, the danger was in fact averted, thanks to the attitude

[1] J. de la Monneraye, in *Nouvelle Revue Historique de Droit*, 1921, p. 198.

adopted by the public courts. But the judge whose every sentence was in danger of cancellation was further than ever from playing a leading role, however successful he might be in maintaining and even increasing his authority within its legitimate sphere.

The transformation of the social structure which declared itself in the growing activity of the state and its courts was also at the root of the changes affecting serfdom. Eleventh century society can legitimately be conceived of as an essentially vertical structure, consisting of innumerable small groups clustered round superiors who were dependent in their turn on others higher in the scale: groups of serfs or tenants, *mesnies* of vassals. But from the middle of the twelfth century or thereabouts, the human blocks tend to become distributed in horizontal layers. Small *seigneuries* are annexed and stifled by larger administrative units such as the principalities and the monarchy. The commune, which although primarily an urban form of association was sometimes adopted by rural communities, based itself on that most revolutionary of all institutions, the sworn pledge of mutual aid among equals, which replaced the old oath of obedience sworn by an inferior to a superior. And the ties of dependence linking man with man are everywhere becoming less meaningful. Now serfdom, an institution forged from the debris of slavery, the colonate, conditional enfranchisement and the voluntary (or allegedly voluntary) subjection of free peasants, was by its very nature one of the essential elements in the reciprocal system of subjection and protection which ran the whole gamut of the social scale. If the truth be known, this was really the whole essence of serfdom. The serf had always been regarded as a member of an inferior caste. Formerly, however, this inferiority had been but one aspect of his status. Now, from the thirteenth century, as the definition of *servaille* becomes more rigorously exclusive in keeping with the general trend—note particularly that the law begins to insist on the inherent incompatibility between serfdom and knighthood—it is membership of an inferior class that in the common view becomes the dominant feature of serfdom.

It is also precisely because the idea of a bondage 'bred in flesh and bone' is becoming indistinct and dying out that serfdom will in future attach less to the person than to the land.

It is not birth alone, but also the occupation of certain tenures, residence on certain parcels of land, which will turn a peasant into a serf. What is more, these territorial serfs will be regarded as 'attached' to the soil. It would hardly be correct to say that they must never leave their land; but if they depart without their master's permission, their tenures will be forfeit. Opinion on this question was influenced to some extent by academic theories. The lawyers of the twelfth and thirteenth centuries who set themselves to study Roman Law ransacked their venerable authorities, the source of all wisdom, for precedents bearing on the social institutions of their own day, and on serfdom in particular: a very tall order, when one considers that serfdom was the most specifically medieval of all existing institutions. Serf, *servus*: the consanguinity of the words was a standing invitation to compare serfdom with classical slavery. But the gulf between the two conditions was only too patent; and the French lawyers, if we except certain instances of individual aberration, had the sense to refrain from pressing an analogy which was to provide so much capital for their colleagues in Eastern Germany in succeeding centuries, to the great misfortune of their compatriot *Leibeignenen*. To make up for this restraint, the French jurists were less diffident about assimilating serfdom with the colonate, which certainly differed from slavery but resembled it in entailing submission to a lord. In this they were doubtless encouraged by the fact that the serfdom they knew, which was territorial rather than personal in character, had already advanced some way towards becoming inseparably linked with bondage to the soil. But by giving legal definition to this growing affinity they can only have accentuated it. The very terms used most readily by notaries and academic lawyers to designate the new-style serf were those applied by students of Roman law to the colonate: *ascriptus glebae*, or with still greater force, *serf de la glèbe*, serf of the glebe —an arresting contrast indeed with the 'body man' of former days. But we must not overrate the importance of legal theory. Had the excess of land over labour been as great as formerly, the efforts of lords to retain their serfs by threatening to confiscate their 'glebe' would surely have met with little success. Had the great clearances not already been accomplished, the rule of 'attachment' would have been an empty formula.

Most of the old dues and disabilities of the servile condition still obtained, above all those of *mainmorte* and *formariage*. But a new idea was gaining ground, which together with the emphasis on class inferiority and the territorial bond was to form one of the criteria of the new serfdom. It was now generally held that liability to the 'arbitrary' impositions (that is to say, impositions whose terms were not stated in any written agreement nor fixed by firmly established custom, so that they could be exacted at will) was a mark of serfdom: for example, tallage 'at will', the form in which tallage had first made its appearance but which was now a rarity. Admittedly, not all serfs were liable for tallage at will, still less for arbitrary services; but a man suffering one or other of these disabilities was in grave danger of being taken for a serf. In Carolingian times it was the *servi*, at that time actual slaves, who were doomed to work 'as they are told'. Perhaps the idea lingered on in the general mind that subjection to the arbitrary will of a master was somehow incompatible with freedom. Its revival was prompted by the abnormal character of the obligation; and also, no doubt, by comparisons between the serf and the Roman *servus*, which certainly must have had some influence on men's thinking.

If we disregard innumerable local variations which cannot be gone into here, we can fairly say that the disabilities just mentioned were the main characteristics of the servile condition at the end of the Middle Ages and would remain so until its total disappearance at the Revolution. But the number of men actually belonging to this category was becoming fewer and fewer.

The general decline of serfdom started in the thirteenth century and continued until the middle of the sixteenth. No doubt servile obligations sometimes fell into abeyance simply from desuetude. But by and large freedom was obtained by an explicit deed of manumission, duly sealed, which was addressed to individuals or families or sometimes entire villages. This freedom was sold rather than given. It is true that enfranchisement was regarded as an act of piety, a '*grant aumosne*' as Beaumanoir has it, one of those deeds which will tip the archangel's scales towards heaven on the day of judgment. The preambles to charters provided a splendid opportunity for the recital of such eternal verities, with more or less eloquence or verbosity;

one might refer to the teachings of the Gospels, or, if one's notary preferred to look for inspiration in the Codes rather than Holy Writ, to the beauties of 'natural liberty'. Convention demanded this homage to the dictates of morality, and doubtless at times the high-flown phrases enshrined a genuine intent, a piece of ingenuous calculation: after all, earning terrestrial profit from a good deed did not rule out hope of a celestial reward as well. For it was obviously quite unthinkable that the seigneurial class should submit to voluntary pauperism purely out of charity. In practice, then, although there were rare instances of deeds prompted by gratitude or friendship, manumissions were as a rule in the form of actual contracts, whose clauses were sometimes debated at length and bitterly contested. To understand how they came to be granted in such large numbers, we must consider the advantage to both sides.

The lord was renouncing dues which although lucrative were irregular and inconvenient to collect. In exchange he usually received a lump sum, which might perhaps rescue him from one or other of those financial embarrassments which chronically afflicted the landed nobility, or permitted indulgence in some long-desired extravagance, or even opened up the prospect of a profitable reinvestment. A wonderful variety emerged from the transmutation of 'liberty pence' under the alchemy of circulating money. Some found their way directly into the royal coffers, since a lord whose finances were shaky might have been forced to manumit serfs to satisfy the tax collectors. Other sums perhaps went to Florentine bankers, in settlement of a pressing debt, or to swell the booty of a victorious enemy—after the battle of Poitiers not a few French knights and squires had to manumit their serfs to raise the cash for their own freedom. In other instances, we find 'liberty pence' converted into church masonry; the chapel of the Virgin in the monastery of St-Germain-des-Prés, one of the jewels of Paris in the time of St. Louis, was built with money raised from manumissions dispensed by the abbot. More frequently the money was turned into well-favoured properties, fields, meadows or vineyards, fat quit-rents and tithes, presses, houses, mills, all bought, built or repaired thanks to savings accumulated sou by sou in a woollen stocking until the day finally came when a peasant could bear the burden of serfdom no longer.[2] Instead of receiving a lump sum, the manumitter might perhaps settle for a periodical fixed rent, payable in addition to the old tenurial rents, which was an improvement on the servile charges whose receipts had been so uncertain. Later on lords sometimes took their recompense in land; for example, where a whole village was being enfranchised the lord would be given part of the commons in exchange, a deprivation still felt in more than one rural community. We find many examples of such alienations in Burgundy during the sixteenth century, as also in the neighbouring Franche Comté during the seventeenth.[3] They arose from the extreme poverty into which the peasants had fallen on account of the wars, combined with the growing interest of the lords in the consolidation of their estates. On the other hand it was exceptional for a peasant to buy his liberty at the price of renouncing all or even part of his tenure. The boot was on the other foot: in abandoning his claim to *mainmorte*, the lord had effectively lost all hope of enlarging his demesne by eventually inheriting from the serf. In France enfranchisement did not, as in Russia at a later date in comparable social circumstances, directly entail even partial dispossession of the servile population in favour of the lords.

The attraction of all these immediate benefits was sometimes reinforced by a further motive, which is frankly acknowledged in a number of the charters. Suppose that an estate still subject to servile obligations adjoined others where freedom was the rule—*villeneuves*, perhaps, whose success their founder had underwritten with lavish grants of liberty (though this was not

[2] Arch. Nat., J J 60, fol. 23 (1318, 17 Dec.): enfranchisement of a married couple by the abbot of Oyes, negotiated to pay the tenth levied on the monks by the king; cf. the last item of this note. Froissart, ed. S. Luce, v, 1, n. 1; Arch. Nat., L 780, No. 10 (1255, Dec.): the community felt aggrieved not only at the manumissions but also at the use to which the 2460 *livres* was put, contending that it should have been used for purchases which would bring some return, and were only satisfied by a somewhat elaborate compromise; Bibl. Ste Geneviève, ms. 351 fol. 123, a list drawn up for the canons of Ste Geneviève and headed 'Iste sunt possessiones quas emimus et edificia que fecimus de denariis libertatum hominum nostrorum et aliorum quorum nomina inferius scripta sunt'—included among the items relating to acquisitions, buildings and repairs is a payment of 406 *livres* (much too large a sum to be written off as a papal tenth) made to *mercatoribus florentinis*, and a note of 60 l. having been paid *pro decima domini regis*.

[3] There are of course earlier examples: cf. De Vathaire de Guerchy, *Bullet. de la Soc. des Sciences Historiques de l'Yonne*, 1917.

always the case, since in the heyday of serfdom there were serfs even on newly assarted lands), or older places to which freedom had come early. Such an estate was in great danger of gradually losing its population to these better-favoured neighbours. The wisest course was to arrest emigration by an opportune and lucrative sacrifice, paid for by the beneficiaries. Such forethought had everything to commend it in times of crisis; and so we find that the reappearance of vacant lands, brought about by the Hundred Years' War and in many frontier regions by the wars of the seventeenth century, stimulated the masters of the soil to great flights of generosity. When the Hospitallers of the Commandery of Bure in Burgundy enfranchised their men at Thoisy in 1439 they gave their reasons: 'since a certain date the dwellings and granges or a greater part of them at the aforesaid Thoisy were and have been set on fire, burnt down and destroyed . . . and also, because of the aforesaid *mainmorte*, no people wish to inhabit this said township . . . but all have withdrawn and departed to live on free territory'. And in 1628 the lord of Montureux-les-Gray in Franche Comté openly declares his hopes that the enfranchised village would be 'better inhabited and populated' than before and that 'consequently' the seigneurial rights would produce 'greater revenues'. Misfortune sometimes brought freedom in its train.[4]

If any further proof is needed that administrators of wealthy estates generally looked on a well-planned programme of enfranchisement as a sound business proposition, we need only point to the propaganda campaigns mounted by some of the most powerful lords—kings like Philip the Fair and his sons or Francis I and Henry II, great barons like count Gaston Phoebus of Béarn—in an effort to persuade or even coerce their subjects (with mixed success) into changing their status.[5]

And what of the advantages to the serfs themselves? The great twelfth century poet Chrétien de Troyes puts into the mouth of one of the few servile heroes to figure in medieval literature words which must have found a secret echo in the

[4] J. Garnier, *Chartes de communes et d'affranchissements*, ii, 550; J. Finot, *Bullet. de la Soc. d'Agriculture . . . de la Haute-Saône*, 1880, p. 477.

[5] Marc Bloch, *Rois et serfs*, 1920; Garnier, *loc. cit.*, Introduction, p. 207; P. Raymond, in *Bullet. de la Soc. des Sciences . . . de Pau*, 1877–8: inquest of 1387—see Nos. 98 and 119 for mention of two earlier campaigns.

heart of many a 'man of the body': 'Sirs . . . there is nothing I would not do . . . to grow old in freedom with my wife and children free'.[6] Serfdom had always been a 'taint'. But the longing to be free must have become more and more desperate as the original conception of serfdom as essentially a bond between two human beings, providing service in return for protection, steadily gave way to a feeling of acute class inferiority; furthermore, with the daily decrease in their numbers, such serfs as remained felt all the more isolated, more than ever conscious of being outcasts. Little enough trace of their bitterness has survived. But one keenly felt indignity thrusts itself through the smoke-screen of the texts: both male and female serfs found it difficult to marry, so much so that, as one chronicler tells us, for want of a husband many girls 'went to their ruin'.[7] To be fair, so long as the servile population was large, and despite the allegation made by the author of *Renart le Contrefait* that prohibition of *formariage* was responsible for the 'depraved generation'[8] which had grown up since the beginning of the fourteenth century, the difficulty was not insurmountable. Inside a *seigneurie*, serfs belonging to a single master could marry one another—at the risk of multiplying those consanguineous unions which to churchmen were the main reason for condemning not serfdom itself (which they considered almost justified by original sin) but the incidental rule forbidding marriage outside the group. If some independent spirit chose a marriage partner from outside, a fine was paid to the lord (or to two lords, if both parties were serfs) or an exchange of serfs arranged between the two masters, and there was an end to the matter; in the twelfth and thirteenth centuries this was the way most seigneurial official families, usually of servile condition but too important and prosperous to be united with ordinary peasants, contracted suitable marriages. But when each lord had fewer serfs than formerly, and the number over the country as a whole had diminished, prohibition of *formariage* became a real hardship. Prospects of marrying into free society were more

---

[6] *Cligès*, 11. 5502 ff.
[7] Du Cange under the heading *Manumissio, Recueil des Histor. de France*, xxi, 141; Guérard, *Cartulaire de N.D. de Paris*, ii, 177, No. vii. The instances are far too numerous for them all to be cited here.
[8] Line 37203 ff.

and more remote: few men and women born free were prepared to make the sacrifice entailed by such a union, both on
their own account (the 'taint' was contagious) and because of
the children; and if some were willing, their families opposed it,
either from pride or from fear that their patrimony would one
day be subjected to the demands of *mainmorte*. A poor servant
girl of Champagne convicted of infanticide in 1467 pleaded
blighted love as the excuse for her misconduct: her father had
refused to let her marry as she wished, because the object of her
affections was a serf.[9] This stern father was certainly no
exception. Once enfranchisement had been introduced into a
given region it usually spread with great rapidity, not only
because of seigneurial anxiety over the loss of tenants but also
because of the serfs' acute fear of being pegged down, to remain
the helpless victims of old impositions and objects of general
contempt among a buoyant mass of human beings who had
already won their freedom.

But this precious boon had to be paid for. Although the
intensity of the longing for freedom, as it developed from the
thirteenth century onward, may have been fairly uniform
throughout the country, the possibility of its fulfilment varied
enormously according to the region. The only peasants capable
of finding the necessary money were those able to build up a
reserve from the sale of their produce, or with access to money-
lenders prepared to invest capital in the countryside, usually in
a form which was the medieval equivalent of our modern
mortgage: in effect, they were those peasants who lived in a
region where trade was already established, where the urban
markets were capable of absorbing a considerable quantity of
agricultural produce, and where a business mentality, backed
by adequate financial resources, was sufficiently developed to
sustain a class of large or petty capitalists. From the second
half of the thirteenth century these characteristics are found in
combination in the region around Paris; and this explains why
serfdom, formerly the condition of whole blocks of the population, totally disappeared there from the time of the Valois.
Where economic circumstances were less favourable serfdom
survived much longer. In the fourteenth century, Paris

[9] G. Robert, *Travaux de l'Académie de Reims*, cxxvi, 1908–9, pp. 257–90.

churches with not a serf to their name on estates near the city still possessed large numbers of serfs in Champagne; the communities of the Orléanais, who in the days of St. Louis had enfranchised all their body serfs in the Beauce, under Francis I were still enforcing *mainmorte* and *formariage* on their villages in Solange. It is surely indisputable that enfranchisement, a mass phenomenon, is much less explicable as the individual policy of this or that lord than as the result of conditions prevailing among a large social group. In Champagne, the provinces of central France, the duchy of Burgundy and the neighbouring Comté the process of enfranchisement, whose progress was never rapid but followed a curve whose undulations one hopes may some day be traced in detail, continued well into the sixteenth century. Even then it was still incomplete in the two Burgundies and in central France. From the second half of the sixteenth century, as we shall see, the lords became increasingly bent on maintaining their rights, especially those such as *mainmorte* which held a prospect of territorial gains, and were no longer sympathetic towards requests for manumission. Villages which had not yet acquired it found freedom increasingly difficult to obtain. Pockets of serfdom survived until the Revolution—a type of serfdom which, as we have seen, was very different from the original form.

But it was strictly economic causes, rather than the declining competence of seigneurial jurisdictions or the relaxation of the personal bond between the lord and his serfs, which from the fifteenth century produced a crisis and subsequent transformation in seigneurial fortunes.

## 2. THE CRISIS OF SEIGNEURIAL FORTUNES

Throughout Western and Central Europe the last two centuries of the Middle Ages were characterised by rural malaise and depopulation—the price, one might say, of thirteenth century prosperity. The great political creations of the preceding age— that is, the Capetian and Angevin monarchies, and on a slightly lower level, the territorial principalities of the new Germany—had been carried by their own momentum into a number of military adventures, and for the time seemed incapable of discharging their appointed office, the imposition of law and order. Worse still, the denser concentrations of humanity which resulted from the great land clearances and an increase in population offered hideously vulnerable targets to attack from epidemics. England suffered the Wars of the Roses and the great peasant revolts, in Germany more and more villages were being permanently depopulated to become *Wüstungen*, while France was being bled almost white by still greater trials. The France of the Hundred Years' War was the prey of mercenaries, devastated by the rising of the Jacqueries and by the still more terrible destruction accompanying their repression, and finally afflicted by the *grants mortalités*, which were all the more deadly for attacking the forces of potential recovery at their roots.

The partial restoration of peace brought by the victory of the Valois was followed by further troubles under Charles VII and Louis XI, leaving a large part of the kingdom one vast abandoned battlefield. Contemporary texts—now in the form of a mass of humdrum everyday records, inquests, registers of diocesan visitations, inventories, charters of enfranchisement or alienation, rather than chronicles—convey to perfection the chill horror of a countryside where 'neither cock crowed nor hen clucked'. How many Frenchmen then living could not echo the priest of Cahors who said he had never known his diocese free from war! In a time when the slightest alarm sent villagers flying to a refuge in river islets or to cabins of branches hastily put up in the forests, when men were forced to spend long days cooped up behind city walls as the plague redoubled its onslaughts among the unfortunate and overcrowded occupants, some peasants were inevitably uprooted. Farm workers from the region of Cahors fled en masse to the Garonne valley, wandering as far east as the Comtat Venaissin. Everywhere villages were being left completely deserted, sometimes for several generations. Such occupants as remained were usually no more than a handful. The forest was encroaching on fields and vines in the Sub-Alpine regions, in Périgord and in the country round Sens. On countless village lands there was nothing to be seen but 'thorns, thickets and other encumbrances'. The old boundaries were no longer recognisable; when the estates of the monks of Vaux-de-Cernay were being repopulated towards the end of the fifteenth century, 'there was neither man nor woman who could say where their patrimonies lay'.

It took centuries to repair some of these ravages; traces of others have persisted to this day. In Puisaye land which fell out of cultivation at this period was only restored to use in the nineteenth century. Even when fields were at last brought back under the plough, the villages themselves were not rebuilt and settlement became more concentrated. Bessey in Burgundy disappeared altogether from the map, its lands distributed among inhabitants of two adjoining communities. Ten out of the twelve villages destroyed at this time in the county of Montbéliard were never restored. Even so, efforts at reconstruction were widespread, although progress was very slow. At Rennemoulin, south of Paris, two peasants could boast in 1483 that they had been the first to 'clear' the ground, one over a period of twelve to thirteen years, the other of eight or nine. Sometimes the old inhabitants returned one by one, to be joined by former neighbours whose own dwellings, although close by, were still submerged by undergrowth. Elsewhere lords concerned to reinstate their land were importing foreign labour, Italians, Savoyards and Frenchmen from the north or from Burgundy for Provence, Germans for the Valentinois and Comtat Venaissin, men from Brittany, Limousin and Tourangeaux for the Sens region. The day might come when these migrants took root, as for example the three men from Normandy who in 1457 comprised the total population of Magny-les-Hameaux close to Paris. Two of the new arrivals found in 1480 at La Chapelle-la-Reine in the Gâtinais came from Beaujolais, a third from Anjou, a fourth from Touraine. At Vandoue, not far way, one of the earliest pioneers was a Norman, as also at Fromont in the same narrow vicinity. Sometimes settlement was so discontinuous and the foreign element so preponderant as to give rise to what might be described as agrarian amnesia: in the fifteenth century the names of fields and other local landmarks at Recloses in the Gâtinais are almost totally different from those of the fourteenth. This evidence of displacement among the peasant population must surely cast doubt on the validity of the simple antithesis which contrasts the cross-breeding of the towns with the ethnic purity of the countryside. Reconstruction continued into the first two or three decades of the sixteenth century, a piece of obstinate human endeavour which has particular appeal to the men of our generation, evoking as it does memories which are still fresh.[10]

The sufferings of the peasants had been terrible. But reconstruction when it came was not unfavourable to their interests. Anxious to attract settlers for the rents they would bring, lords often made appreciable concessions; some were of immediate application, such as temporary exemption from charges and the loan of equipment and seed, others were more permanent, the grant of franchises of various kinds, and the offer of very low rents. When in 1395 the monks of Saint-Germain-des-Prés made their first attempt at reinstating their vineyard at Valenton they offered the ground at a rent of eight shillings per arpent; they failed to attract tenants. Starting again in 1456, this time the monks were more successful but had to be content with rents mostly less than four shillings, even though the value of the bullion content of coins had markedly declined during the intervening period.[11] The lords were legally empowered to take possession of estates left uncultivated over a long time, and often saw to it that this right was expressly recognised. They wanted not so much to add these waste lands to their own demesnes as to be free to grant them out to new tenants, without having to allow time for the problematical return of the former occupants. At this period there is no trace of any initiative on the part of the lords to replace perpetual tenancies by direct large-scale exploitation or by leases for a fixed term. The reconstruction of the *seigneurie* followed the pattern established by custom and took the form of a cluster of small holdings grouped round a demesne pro-

[10] Much more work needs to be done on both the crisis and the reconstruction. The references given here relate only to facts not mentioned in the monographs listed in the bibliography. H. Denifle, *La desolation des églises*, ii, 2, 1899, pp. 821-45; J. Maubourguet, *Sarlat et le Périgord meridonial*, ii, 1930, p. 131; J. Quantin in *Mémoires lus à la Sorbonne, Histoire et Philologie* 1865 (Sénonais); Roserot, *Dictionnaire topographique du département de la Côte d'Or*, p. 35, and Arch. C. d'Or, E 1782 and 1783 (Bessey); C.D., *Les Villages ruinés du comté de Montbéliard*, 1847; *Bulletin de la Soc. des Sciences historiques de l'Yonne*, 1925, pp. 167 and 184 (Puisaye); C. H. Waddington, in *Annales de la Société Historique et Archéologique du Gâtinais*, xxxix, 1929, pp. 14 ff. (Gâtinais).

[11] Olivier Martin, *Histoire de la Coutume de Paris*, i, 1922, pp. 400-1.

perty, normally only of modest size. Even after the crisis was past, the life of the peasant was still one of great hardship. Fortescue, who has left us a comparison of the lot of the English and French peasant in the days of Louis XI, reserves his darkest hues for the French panel of his diptych. Reasonably enough, he stresses the burden placed on the French countryside by the increasingly heavy demands of royal taxation. But fine jurist though he was, one essential point eluded him: crushed by taxation, ill-nourished and ill-clad, quite indifferent indeed to his creature comforts, the French villager nevertheless still held his land by 'inheritance'.

How was it that the peasantry emerged relatively unscathed from an ordeal which could have been fatal? There can be no doubt that ultimately the peasants benefited from the very disasters whose imprint was left on their fields and from the mortality which thinned their own ranks. Labour was scarce and therefore dear. In the countryside, as in the towns, wages were constantly rising, in defiance of the royal ordinances and local byelaws whose fruitless efforts to check the trend are such eloquent testimony to its existence. It was noted in the reign of Charles V that many labourers had been able to purchase land for themselves, thanks to the increase in day wages.[12] Any lord with an urge to cultivate a large demesne by hired labour would have found the expense prohibitive. To carve up an estate into tenant holdings seemed a better proposition. But since land was once again plentiful and men scarce, tenants would only be attracted if the demands on them were not too heavy and the heritability of their tenures assured, since this was now an accustomed right, not to be surrendered without a struggle.

Yet these arithmetical considerations are not the whole story. In the seventeenth century certain provinces such as Burgundy and Lorraine were once again the scene of fierce fighting, with the same physical consequences: overgrown farmlands, obliteration of field divisions, deserted villages, where a few derelicts maintained themselves among the ruins by a reversion to the most primitive of human pursuits, hunting and fishing. Once again, there followed a gradual rehabilitation, partly at the

[12] L. Delisle, *Mandements ... de Charles V*, 1874, No. 625.

hands of outsiders. This time, however, the lords knew how to take advantage of the chances offered by the restoration. For this was the time when the seigneurial class, rejuvenated and enriched, was becoming conscious of its power and evolving far more sophisticated methods of exploitation than any used in the past. At the end of the Middle Ages the situation was very different, with the seigneurial class, the only one superior to the small-holders, itself in disarray, shaken in its fortunes and mentally ill-prepared for the effort of adapting to an unprecedented situation.

Seigneurial fortunes were menaced first and foremost by the desolation of the countryside itself. It is true that war was not without its benefits, at least for the lay nobility; no knight disdained opportunities for ransom and plunder. It is recorded that when Charles VI assembled an army at Melun in 1382 to subdue a mutinous Paris, the noblemen who gathered round his banner brought waggons they hoped to fill with booty from the big city.[13] But such rewards were capricious and might easily be snatched away by a cruel reversal of fortune. Neither they, nor the court pensions on which the greater and lesser nobility increasingly depended to balance their budgets, could compare with the former expectation of a regular income from quit-rents, tallages and tithes, now reduced to vanishing point by the uncertainties of the times. Stripped for the most part of their reserves and incapable of thrift, as the Hundred Years War drew to a close many lords of ancient family were living from hand to mouth. Ecclesiastical communities were also on short commons, the number of religious they could sustain much reduced.

Nor was this all. Even where the old dues continued to be paid or had been reinstated, any that were paid in cash (from the thirteenth century the most frequent form of payment except in the case of tithes) fell far short in real value of what they had once been. From the end of the fifteenth century the decline was marked, and the dizzy descent continued into the following century. This monetary collapse, which was the prime cause of the temporary impoverishment of the seigneurial class, had two phases, quite distinct in character and timing but whose effects were cumulative; the first saw a decline in the

[13] *Chronique des quatre premiers Valois*, ed. S. Luce, 1862, p. 302.

nominal value of money, the second a reduction of the bullion content of the coinage itself.[14]

In medieval France, which had inherited a complex monetary system codified under the Carolingians, accounts were reckoned in pounds, shillings and pence (*livres, sous* and *deniers*). The ratio between the three remained constant at twenty shillings to the pound, twelve pennies to the shilling. But for a long time past the separate units had ceased to bear any exact correspondence to a stable material entity. For centuries French mints had been producing nothing but silver pennies.[15] Their face value was always the same, but the content of precious metal varied enormously from place to place and time to time, with an overall tendency towards appreciable diminution. By the reign of St. Louis the debased penny piece had become so insignificant that its only useful purpose was as small change, and this was in effect the role henceforth assigned to it by a society in which money circulated much more freely than in the past. Now that the minting of coins had become almost exclusively a royal prerogative, the monarchy began to strike heavier coins of finer quality, both in gold and silver, which in theory had greater value. Ultimately, however, this necessary reform only gave rise to still greater instability in the currency. Following ancient custom, all the new coins were issued without any inscription indicative of their face value; nor were their names—*gros, écu, agnel, franc, louis* etc.—any guide, since they referred to a type rather than to a specific unit of value. The state, as the minting authority, was in the unique position of being able to determine just how many pounds, shillings and

---

[14] Experts will I hope excuse the inadequacies of this sketch of monetary history. The economic history of money is more obscure and less well understood than any other subject, and this is true both of the currency 'mutations' which took place in the later Middle Ages and of the great crisis of the sixteenth century. But there is also no subject more important for building up our picture of French social life, and rural life in particular, before the Revolution. I can only indicate, in summary fashion, the most important features in an evolution itself extremely complex; and since it is summary, the treatment is inevitably over-simplified, a defect which could only be avoided by extended analysis, quite out of place here.

[15] This is not to say, however, that all payments involving money, or at least the notion of money, were made in pennies. Leaving to one side payments in kind which were valued in monetary terms, and ignoring payments made in bullion, large payments were quite frequently made in foreign gold currencies, either Byzantine or Arab. But this had no effect on seigneurial revenues. I hope to be able to deal with these delicate problems of circulation in more detail elsewhere.

pence a coin of a given type was supposed to represent, when measured against the abstract standard of the pound and its fractions. This ratio was so arbitrary that it could and did vary. At times the currency was 'debased', or in other words the same quantity of metal was assumed to be spread out over a larger number of units (whose value therefore 'fell'); at other times the process was reversed and the currency 'reinforced'. The same weight of gold which on 1 January 1337 was the equivalent of exactly one pound was from October 31 of that year held to be worth 1 pound, 3 shillings, $1\frac{7}{9}$ pence: debasement. On 27 April 1346, having been credited in the interval with an even greater value in pounds, this same weight of gold was put back to 16 shillings and 8 pence: reinforcement. These government manipulations were inspired by a variety of motives, some of them difficult to disentangle. They created the necessity for new issues, an appreciable source of profit to the sovereign; they were a means of making opportune adjustments to the public balance sheets; they made it possible to re-establish conformity between the actual price of the two precious metals and their legal ratio, always a problem with a bimetallic currency. A further advantage was that when coins had become so worn in use or mutilated by the snippings of too-clever speculators that their metallic content was obviously inferior to what it had been when they left the mint, 'debasement' could restore the official metal currency to the level of what was actually in circulation. Lastly, at a time when financial expertise, still in its infancy, knew nothing of banknotes and the subtleties of discounting at variable rates of interest, 'currency mutations' were almost the sole means whereby the state could influence circulation. In the long run the oscillations of the curve failed to cancel one another out. The descending trend became dominant and easily carried the day. The extent of the decline is clearly shown by the following figures. In 1258 the value of the pound *tournois*, the basic unit of account, was equivalent in gold to about 112 fr. 22 of our present money; in 1360 it was 64 fr. 10, in 1465 40 fr. 68, in 1561 21 fr. 64, in 1666 9 fr. 39, in 1774 5 fr. 16, in 1793, on the eve of the abolition of the old monetary system, 4 fr. 82. Even so these figures omit the most spectacular plunges: in 1359 the pound had fallen to a metal content—always in gold—

equivalent to 29 fr. 71, and in 1720 to 2 fr. 06. Silver currency followed a very similar curve.[16]

Outstanding obligations, including seigneurial dues, were as a rule always reckoned in money of account (except where expressly stated otherwise, as in certain commercial contracts). The amount owed by each tenant was set down not as a certain weight in gold or silver but as so many pounds, shillings and pence. And this figure, which was unrelated to any material object, was almost universally regarded as unalterable. It was governed in fact by custom, which might still be oral, although there was a growing tendency for it to be written down; but whether written or oral, custom was paramount and when need arose was upheld by the courts. It is worth recalling that in the Middle Ages the dues themselves were known in ordinary speech as *coutumes* and the villein who was burdened by them as the *coutumier*. The result was that the successor of a lord who in 1258 had received one pound was paid the same amount in 1465; but while the lord of 1258 received the equivalent in gold of about 112 modern francs, his heir of 1465 had to make do with 40 francs. A modern parallel would be a debt contracted in 1913, which if settled in francs would mean a loss of four-fifths to the creditor. Through the interplay of custom and the depreciation of the monetary unit, legal and economic circumstances thus combined to produce a gradual alleviation of peasant burdens; moreover any profits peasants earned by working for wages or from the sale of produce kept pace with the new standard, since they were unaffected by customary limitations. The lords were slowly becoming impoverished.

[16] I have taken these figures from N. de Wailly, *Mém. de l'Acad. des Inscriptions,* xxi, 2, 1857, but with the following modifications: (i) the figures relating to the franc are expressed in terms of its present value; (ii) for this reason, I have been obliged to confine my attention to the value of the old units of account in gold; this bias, almost unavoidable in view of our present monometallism, makes for various difficulties of which I am quite aware—silver content did not always vary in the same degree as gold, the legal currency of gold, which was the medium of international trade, was often at a different level from its commercial currency (usually lower), and, lastly, seigneurial dues were almost always paid in silver. However, we are here concerned only with orders of magnitude, fortunately unaffected by these possible occasions of error; (iii) I have discarded any decimals lower than a centime, since their presence gives a totally misleading impression of mathematical rigour. I have naturally taken no account of the short-lived attempt made by the government in 1577 to end the system of reckoning in pounds, shillings and pence.

The impoverishment was certainly gradual and at first went unrecognised. The most convincing proof that this was so is the preference still shown by many seigneurial administrators in the late thirteenth and fourteenth centuries for payments in cash rather than kind, as in the days when the use of money first became widespread; they were in effect bartering the solid substance of produce, always in demand, for the most unstable of all mediums of exchange. In our generation we know only too well that so long as the standard of value remains nominally the same men are blinded to any actual depreciation: the label is what counts. But sooner or later the day of reckoning must dawn. We shall not go far wrong if we settle on the early fifteenth century as the moment when the public mind first became conscious of the general depreciation in rents. It is at this period that royal (ducal in Brittany and Burgundy) ordinances reveal what was happening in no uncertain fashion,[17] as do some writers, none more forcefully than Alain Chartier. In a dialogue written in 1422 he puts the following complaint into the mouth of a knight. 'The common people have the advantage that their purse is like a cistern which has collected and collects the waters and rivulets of all the riches of this kingdom ... for the weakness of the coinage has diminished the amount of dues and rents that they owe, and the outrageous price they themselves have set on victuals and labour has increased the wealth they daily receive and amass.'[18] The date at which an economic trend is first noticed may be something of a landmark, since it is only then that counter-action becomes a possibility. But the discovery and initiation of measures capable of arresting the drain owed nothing to Alain Chartier's knight and his contemporaries. Before battle had been fairly joined, a second cause of depreciation, whose impact was more sudden, was added to the first.

Useful as it is to know the metallic content of a coin, it is more interesting still if we have some means of estimating its purchasing power. So far as the Middle Ages are concerned, the present state of research permits only conjecture on this point. Moreover, in a country whose economy was so frag-

[17] *Ordonnances*, xi, 132; L. Lièvre, *La monnaie et le change en Bourgogne*, 1929, 49. No. 1; Planiol, *La très ancienne coutume*, 1896, p. 386.
[18] *Le Quadriloge invectif*, ed. E. Droz, 1923, p. 30.

mented, the exchange value of coins inevitably varied greatly with the region. Worse still, exchange values in all the fourteenth and early fifteenth century markets for which we have any evidence were subject to sudden and violent fluctuations, easily explained by the 'fortunes of war'. But there is no doubt that around the year 1500 prices had everywhere reached a fairly low level. The lord was certainly receiving less in gold and silver (mostly silver, since gold was used only for the payment of substantial sums) than he had in the past, but this modest amount of metal purchased more goods than it would have in the immediately preceding period. Although insufficient to redress the balance, the compensation was appreciable. During the sixteenth century affairs took on a different complexion. There was a phenomenal increase in the available bullion, first from the intensive working of the Central European mines and later from the still greater influx of treasure and mined bullion from America, particularly after the magnificent silver-ore lodes at Potosi had been opened up. At the same time, as the velocity of circulation increased more money was available for spending. The consequence was a formidable rise in prices. This phenomenon, generally speaking common to Europe as a whole, first made itself felt in France about 1530. M. Raveau has estimated that in Poitou the purchasing power of the pound fell from the equivalent of about 285 fr. of our money in the reign of Louis XI to 135 fr. under Henry II, reaching about 63 fr. in the time of Henry IV. The metallic debasement of the artificial unit, the pound, worked together with the rise in prices to produce a decline in purchasing power of more than three-quarters in the course of one and a half centuries. This revolution had widely divergent effects on the various classes who lived directly or indirectly off the land. The producers suffered scarcely at all. But two classes were seriously affected. These were the day-labourers, whose scarcity value was diminished now that the population was rising, who found their wages lagging far behind the soaring prices; and the lords, since they lived primarily on rents. In 1550 the *seigneurie* of Châtillon-sous-Maîche in Franche-Comté brought in to its master 1673 francs; in 1600 the figure was 2333, an apparent increase of almost 150 per cent. This may have been partly due to careful management, but the chief explanation must be that in this long economically backward area the lord was still obtaining fairly substantial amounts of produce, either from the payment of seigneurial dues in kind or from his own demesne, which he was able to sell. At first sight he seems not badly placed. But between the two dates mentioned the price of wheat in this same area had risen by 200 per cent. So even where the figures seem to indicate a gain (and this is unusual), viewed in their economic setting they actually show a loss.[19]

Seigneurial fortunes were not all equally affected. Most of the ecclesiastical foundations had accumulated tithes, whose handsome profits continued without alteration. In certain provinces remote from the mainstream of economic developments the changeover from payment of dues in kind to payments in cash had never made much headway; and the lords in these parts, above all perhaps the small fief-holders, had preserved a relatively large portion of their demesnes. By a curious reversal of fortune, these noblemen suffered less than their counterparts in the traditionally prosperous regions, where everything had been reduced to money. In other instances the accumulation of large amounts of silver brought in by rents (which made their depreciation less damaging), the possession of tithes or champarts, and the additional income from public or court offices, all helped to tide some families over lean times and gave them a chance to recoup their losses. The passing bell had not yet tolled for the old nobility. But many houses of ancient lineage were now entering on their decline. Some avoided catastrophe only by a temporary renunciation of their social rank, seeking to recruit their strength by engaging in commerce. Others, more numerous, were carried from one crisis to the next until in the end they were forced to sacrifice part of their patrimony in order to survive.

Imagine then a gentleman of ancient birth who finds himself in financial difficulties. Often his first reaction will be to raise a loan, pledging or mortgaging his land. But how to redeem it? In the long run he must resign himself to the sale not merely of a

---

[19] A further contributory cause of the decline in seigneurial wealth was the custom of partition; it seems that primogeniture was not so widely prevalent as was once thought: cf. Y. Bezard, *La vie rurale dans le sud de la région parisienne*, 71 f.; Ripert-Montclair, *Cartulaire de la commanderie de Richerenches*, 1907, p. cxxxix f.: and for Provence the example given *infra*, p. 139 (Lincel).

few fields but of whole *seigneuries*, either to his creditor or to some other buyer whose cash will meet his most pressing debts. And what social class will produce the new master? The class which has money. The lord's castle, his squire's pew in the parish church, the forked gibbet which is the insignia of higher jurisdiction, the quit-rents, tallages and rights of *mainmorte*, in a word all the glories and rewards of the old hierarchical system will almost invariably go to swell the patrimony and prestige of some wealthy business-man and office holder, either already or about to be ennobled, by birth a bourgeois but in process of becoming a lord. Over a wide area around Lyons, extending as far as Forez, Beaujolais and Dauphiné, baronies, castellanies and fiefs of all descriptions were accumulating in the hands of great patrician families enriched by cloth and spices, mining and banking: families of French origin, the Camus, Laurencin, Vinois and Varey, Italians and Germans such as the Gadagne, Gondi and Cléberg. Only three out of the forty *seigneuries* sold by the Constable of Bourbon or liquidated on the confiscation of his properties went to nobles of ancient birth. Even if the story is true that Claude Laurencin the money-broker, son of a draper and grandson of an innkeeper, only secured the homage of his new vassals in the barony he had purchased from the daughter of Louis XI with the greatest difficulty, what did it matter? His wife still became lady-in-waiting to the queen, his son chief almoner to the king.[20] The seigneurial regime was certainly not extinct; on the contrary, it was soon to take on a new lease of life. But seigneurial property had to a large extent changed hands.

We must however resist the suggestion sometimes made that the bourgeoisie was only now making its appearance on the rural scene. From the first, many burgesses had been acquiring rural properties in districts surrounding their towns, while the more eminent among them had gradually infiltrated the world of the nobility. Renier Acorre, chamberlain to the counts of Champagne, was bourgeois; so was the d'Orgemont family, whose wealth was no doubt derived from the administration of the Lagny fairs; so was Robert Alorge, wine-merchant of Rouen, tax-farmer and usurer. Yet all of them, Acorre in the

---

[20] A. Vachex, *Histoire de l'acquisition des terres nobles par les roturiers dans les provinces du Lyonnais, Forez et Beaujolais*, 1891.

thirteenth century, the others in the fourteenth and early fifteenth centuries, had acquired landed estates which the Camus and Laurencin, contemporaries of Francis I, would not have despised.[21] But it is true that such penetration *en masse* was confined to the sixteenth century, never to be repeated. By the seventeenth century the nobility was already a semi-closed caste. Some fresh entrants were still being admitted, but their total number was much reduced and their initiation more prolonged. This advance by the bourgeoisie, followed by such rapid entrenchment, was the most decisive event in French social history, especially in its rural aspect. The fourteenth century had been marked by a violent reaction against the nobility. In the 'war of the non-nobles against the nobles', to use a contemporary description, the burgesses and peasants had often found themselves allies. Étienne Marcel had made common cause with the 'Jacques'; the feelings of the worthy merchants of Nîmes towards their local chivalry had been no more tender than those of the 'Tuchins' who took to the maquis in Languedoc. Move on a century or a century and a half, and we find the Étienne Marcels of the day transformed— by royal decree into nobles, by the processes of economic change into landlords. The whole weight of the bourgeoisie, or at least of the higher bourgeoisie and those aspiring to enter its ranks, is now directed towards maintaining the seigneurial structure. But new men, new manners. As merchants, tax-farmers, money-lenders to kings and princes, these men were accustomed to handling considerable liquid assets with caution, skill and even boldness; as the new proprietors of the soil their ambitions and habits of mind remained unaltered. It was as business-men that they addressed themselves to the management of their recently acquired properties, giving the lead to such gentry of more authentic pedigree as had managed to retain their estates; their daughters were in demand among impoverished noblemen as a fruitful match, on occasion welcomed as business-women into the old-established families whose patrimony was so often to be rescued by the skill of a managing woman. These were men and women with the habit of calculating gains and losses,

[21] Bourquelot, in *Bibl. de l'Ecole des Chartes*, 1867 (very inadequate); L. Mirot, *Les d'Orgemont*, 1913; Beaurepaire, *Notes et documents sur l'état des campagnes en Normandie*.

the capacity to look ahead and to risk some not directly profitable outlay for the sake of future benefits. In short, they had acquired the capitalist mentality. Such was the leaven which would transform seigneurial methods of exploitation.

### 3. THE SEIGNEURIAL REACTION: LARGE AND SMALL SCALE FARMING

The depreciation of rents was a European phenomenon. So was the effort of the more or less thoroughly rejuvenated seigneurial class at re-establishing its fortunes. In Germany, England and Poland the same economic drama unfolded as in France, posing the same problems. But the differing social and political conditions of the various countries imposed different lines of action.

In Germany east of the Elbe, and in the Slavonic lands which were its eastward continuation, the old seigneurial system was completely transformed, to give way to a new regime. Rents and dues were by now quite unproductive. But instead of resigning himself to bankruptcy, the squire took on the job of producing and selling corn. Peasants were deprived of their fields, which went towards the creation of a huge consolidated demesne surrounded by just enough small-holdings to ensure an adequate supply of labour, most of it compulsory; the continuance of this source of free labour was guaranteed by the increasing stringency of the ties binding peasants to their master; the demesne had swallowed up the tenures, or at least sucked them dry. In England the course of development was noticeably different. Although it is true that here too direct exploitation made considerable inroads on peasant holdings and on commons, the squire remained largely dependent on income from rents. But the majority of rents were no longer pegged. In future small-holdings would be granted out for a limited term at best, more frequently merely at the lord's will. Each renewal of the lease thus provided a golden opportunity for fixing a rent in harmony with the economic conditions of the moment. At either end of Europe we find the same abandonment of the perpetual tenures which had been the main cause of the crisis.

In France, however, the solution could not take this crude form. It will be simplest to ignore Eastern Germany and Poland, whose institutions were so very different from our own monarchical structure in that they allowed greater latitude to the seigneurial class, and concentrate on a comparison between France and England. If we place ourselves towards the end of the twelfth century we shall see that the situation was much the same on either side of the Channel; the custom of *seigneurie* or manor protected the peasant and in practice guaranteed the heritability of his tenure. But what authority was responsible for seeing that custom was observed? It is here that the two paths noticeably diverge. In England from the twelfth century onward royal justice made itself felt with exceptional force. The king's courts now stood above the old courts of free men and the tribunals held under seigneurial jurisdiction, with the whole country acknowledging their authority. But this unusual maturity had to be compensated for. In the twelfth century the ties of dependence were still too strong to accommodate the direct intervention of a third party, even if it were the king himself, between a lord and his subjects. Under the Plantagenets the lords refrained from the punishment of crimes against life and limb perpetrated within their manors, since these offences came under public jurisdiction. In such cases villeins —men that is who held land from a lord in exchange for rents and services—were usually justiciable before the king's courts. But over all matters affecting their tenures the lord himself, or the lord's court, was the sole judge. It was of course assumed that the seigneurial court delivered its judgments in accordance with custom, an assumption shared, not always incorrectly, by the courts themselves. But unless committed to writing, in the last resort a customary rule becomes simply a matter for rule of thumb jurisprudence. It is no surprise to find the manorial judges bending precedents to suit the interests of the master. In the fourteenth and fifteenth centuries they become more and more reluctant to recognise the heritability of villein tenure (known as copyhold because evidence of title was proved from an entry on the manorial court roll). There was one brief period, towards the end of the fifteenth century, when the king's judges at last broke through the old barrier and started to intervene in manorial affairs. But they too could not but base their judgments on the customs of the various estates, in the form in which they were presented to them. In most cases the change to non-permanent tenures was already complete, and where this was so the judges had to admit it as accepted custom.

In France the evolution of royal justice lagged a good century behind that of England and followed a totally different course. The French royal tribunals started their piece-meal erosion of seigneurial jurisdictions in the thirteenth century, annexing here a cause from one, evoking there appeals from another, all as occasion arose. There were no great legislative acts to set beside the Plantagenet Assizes, and little attempt was made to view the scheme of justice as a whole; but neither were there any prohibited boundaries. In theory law-suits between lords and tenants had at no time been exempt from royal intervention. Given the opportunity, royal officials were always ready to hear them. Naturally they based their judgments on local custom, and in the process helped to establish it; in consequence their decisions were often disadvantageous to the peasants, whose burdens they perpetuated or, where abuse had hardened into precedent, even increased; but the principle of heritability was always upheld. With this juridical support, inheritance of tenures had become so firmly rooted by the sixteenth century that it could not be contested. Once the Code of Justinian had become part of the legal curriculum, the lawyers were faced with a difficult semantic problem. They saw the land burdened with a whole hierarchy of superimposed property rights arising from the seigneurial system and its feudal superstructure; founded on custom or contract, all these rights were perfectly legitimate in their proper spheres, yet none possessed the absolute, overriding character of ownership as defined in the Civil Law. For centuries past all suits relating to mastership of the soil or its revenues had in practice turned on seisin (possession protected and sanctioned by tradition), and never on ownership. But the Roman categories demanded a definite answer to questions never before raised: who was the owner of a fief, the lord or the vassal? who was the owner of a tenure, the lord or the villein? The lawyers urgently needed to know. We shall not here concern ourselves with fiefs, nor with all the various mixed systems elaborated over the years (those for example which drew a distinction between two 'dominions', direct dominion and useful dominion.) Academic teaching long remained undecided in its identification of the true proprietor. But from the thirteenth century there were practising lawyers who were prepared to regard the tenant in this light, and from the sixteenth century this was the view disseminated by a number of legal writings, including those of the illustrious Dumoulin. By the eighteenth century it had become received opinion.[22] In the terriers or registers which were kept by seigneurial officials to facilitate the collection of rents, it is not uncommon to find the names of land-holders subject to such charges listed under the prophetic heading *'propriétaires'*. The word was indeed fraught with meaning; it confirmed and reinforced the idea of perpetuity which was already implicit in the right of real property traditionally exercised by the tenant over his house and fields. By a curious historical paradox the slow-moving advance of French royal justice had proved more beneficial to the peasantry than the daring innovations carried through by the Norman and Angevin kings of England.

Since they were legally barred from engrossing the soil, it might seem that the French lords had no choice but to surrender in the face of the catastrophic threat presented by changing economic conditions. But to believe this would be to misjudge the state of mind induced among them by fresh entrants to their class, the new fief-holders who had been schooled in the disciplines of bourgeois prosperity. All that was needed was the adoption of a subtler and more insidious tactic. Seigneurial rights proper were still far from being worthless, although the revenue from them had fallen steeply. Stricter

---

[22] Early examples from actual practice: R. Merlet, *Cartulaire du Grand-Beaulieu*, 1907, No. CCCXXI, 1241 (where 'proprietor' is clearly synonymous with 'perpetual tenant'); Arch. de Seine et Oise H., *fonds de Livry*, 1 (1296). For the sixteenth century, see J. Legras, *Le Bourgage de Caen*, 1911, p. 126, n. 1, and p. 220, n. 2; R. Latouche, *La vie en Bas-Quercy*, p. 72. A trend in this direction can be traced in the legal literature from J. d'Ableiges onwards (see especially II, c. XXIV): Dumoulin, *Oeuvres* ed. of 1681, i, 603; Pothier, *Traité du droit de domaine*, § 3. Cf. Championnière, *De la propriété des eaux courantes*, 1846, p. 148. Admittedly it would not be difficult to cite still more numerous cases in which the tenant is shown as possessing ownership not of the land itself but of rights in the land; and it is true that medieval ideas of real property largely took the form of allowing for rights over the property rather than property itself.

management should surely make possible a better return. In the long run the system which had made the lord live from his rents rather than directly from his estates had proved disastrous; why not try to put the machine into reverse and tenaciously, skilfully (but without force, for force was not allowed), set about the reconstruction of the demesne?

Towards the end of the Middle Ages many of the ancient dues were no longer being regularly collected, partly because their profit was so meagre, but also because many noble houses were in a state of chronic confusion. In consequence, the lord was losing not only his annual rent, usually of little value, but also the chance to prove his right to the succession tax when the land changed hands through death or conveyance; this loss was the more serious, since although also fixed by custom, the amount of the tax was relatively high. Sometimes, particularly in the sixteenth century, no-one any longer knew for certain to which *seigneurie* a particular parcel belonged. The tenurial network had become so involved and the boundaries so difficult to determine that this uncertainty sometimes continued into the succeeding centuries, although it became increasingly rare, since by this time seigneurial management had been penetrated by sound business practices: strict book-keeping, for example, and the use of inventories. The wisdom of making periodic surveys and keeping a written record of seigneurial rights had doubtless been recognised from the first; the Carolingian *polyptiques*, which probably continued a Roman tradition, are early evidence of this prudence, represented later by the '*censiers*' and terriers which start to multiply once the troubled tenth and eleventh centuries are past. But it is in the period of reconstruction following the Hundred Years' War that these documents really proliferate, so that we find the same estate being surveyed at increasingly shorter intervals and with ever greater system and precision. There was one drawback. Such records were quite costly to produce; who was to foot the bill? Now it was possible to maintain that there was a legal duty on the tenant, as on his social superior the enfeoffed vassal, to make 'recognisance' to his lord of his properties and obligations when required to do so at certain times and for good reason. From this it was a short step to the definition of a terrier as a collective recognisance; and what could be more fitting than that those bound to make it should bear the cost? So far as tenants were concerned, however, recognisance had always been an exceptional formality; the compilation of a terrier, which constantly needed to be brought up to date, threatened to become a much more burdensome affair. In other words, an old legal principle was being used as an excuse for a new charge. Judicial opinion was apparently indecisive; it was never unanimous and under the *Ancien Régime* was rarely the same from one Parlement to another. From the seventeenth century, however, it was acknowledged that over a large part of the kingdom the lord had indeed the right, every twenty or thirty years, to claim from his men all or part (the amount varied with the region) of the costs incurred in revising the awesome volumes which confirmed their subjection.[23] What lord would now refrain from an undertaking which cost little or nothing to execute and was so certain of reward? A whole technique was evolved for the purpose, its methods codified during the eighteenth century in a body of professional literature and applied by a corps of specialists or 'commissioners' who were adept at finding their way among the thickets of seigneurial rights. Before long there was scarcely a château or monastic library without its long parchment or sheepskin bound row of *terriers, lièves, arpentements, marchements* (their names and forms are various in the extreme), the earliest volumes written usually in a miserable scrawl, the most recent in an elegant and legible hand. From the late seventeenth century it is increasingly common to find them accompanied by 'geometrical plans' or a folder of maps. Mathematics was now being put to economic use, to show the lie of the land. Thanks to these surveys, made in each generation or at even more frequent intervals, the meshes of the seigneurial web visibly tautened. There was no danger that even the most modest right would henceforth be overlooked.

All this collating of old titles and thorough rummaging of the seigneurial archives made it very tempting to go even further, to revive ancient rights which had fallen into abeyance, to burden an estate with an obligation which although customary in the region it had so far escaped, to discover in some usage a

---

[23] Guyot, *Répertoire*, under *Terrier*. For the evolution of jurisprudence cf. O. Martin, *Histoire de la coutume de Paris*, i, 406.

legal implication hitherto unnoticed, or even to insinuate some entirely new charge into the tangle of existing rights. Any feudal or seigneurial official who made his employer such a gift could not fail to cover himself with glory and enhance his professional reputation. There was also the incentive of a direct profit, since the commissioners were normally entitled to the arrears resulting from their 'discoveries'. 'They found out many things'.[24] 'The picture at Brieulles is completely altered' wrote the representative of the Prince de Condé in 1769 on the completion of his survey of the estate. He had, it is true, been shown a more ancient record, patently less favourable to His Most Serene Highness; but this, being 'of no account and full of mistakes' should never in future be communicated to anyone, 'no matter who he is'.[25] These feats of legerdemain were possible because traditions were so uncertain. They were indeed a jungle, where even the best-intentioned of men might find it difficult to know any longer what was and was not an abuse: we should remember that the disappearance of some of the older charges had itself been a breach of the law and an offence against the established order, so that the lords were not always wrong when they accused their peasants—'thoroughly sly creatures' says a noblewoman from Auvergne[26]—of shedding their admitted obligations whenever they had the chance. These legal misapprehensions are inevitable when social classes are in conflict. Then again, standards of measurement were ill-defined and in the absence of invar and platinum easily altered. Holdings in champarty and tithes could be made to produce a few extra sackfuls simply by adjusting the volume of the bushel, as was done by a Breton monastery during the eighteenth century. Ingenious manipulation, aimed at producing greater profits in a form adapted to the changed economic situation, was even more successful when applied to the subsidiary charges. The peasants of the duchy of Rohan had from time immemorial brought the grain they owed to the

[24] Report of the civil commissioners for Lot, 15 March 1791, in *Arch. Parlementaires* xxv, 288.

[25] Letter (dated 2 December 1769) inserted at the beginning of the 1681 terrier: Chantilly, reg. E 41. The terrier which was so slighted is the sole survivor of the first series of Clermontois terriers. One wonders if the others were deliberately destroyed by the prince's agents.

[26] *Revue d'Auvergne*, xlii, 29.

lord's granary. In the seventeenth century, when the seigneurial economy in Brittany entered—or re-entered—the general current of trade, the noble duke reacted like any Baltic junker and turned himself into a corn merchant. Under a series of judgments handed down by the Parlement of Rennes the peasants were now obliged to carry their wagon-loads directly to the port, often a much longer haul. In Lorraine there were lords who from medieval times had claimed the privilege of '*troupeau à part*', which meant they were not obliged to send their livestock to join the village herd at the seasons when the arable waste or commons were opened to collective pasturage, and thus escaped irksome restrictions on the number of beasts allowed and the places where they grazed. Up to the end of the sixteenth century the number of lords possessing this right of exemption was very small. In the two succeeding centuries, with an expanding market for wool and meat and the involvement of the seigneurial economy in the general cycle of trade, the privilege became more attractive and the circle of the select few expanded to include all lords with rights of higher jurisdiction and many more besides. In law the privilege extended only to those exercising it on their own behalf. Yet, despite explicit texts to the contrary, the courts of Metz and Nancy (already lavish with their grants to any who claimed it) allowed the privilege to be farmed out to commercial stock-rearers. In Béarn, at the other end of the kingdom, the Parlement of Pau was also accepting without a qualm the unfounded claim of many fief-holders to possess the analogous privilege known in those parts as *herbe morte*.[27]

It is not by chance that the word Parlement figures in nearly all these example and in innumerable other cases which could be cited. As a result of the invasion of the nobility by the office-holding bourgeoisie and the conversion of the judiciary into a separate caste (an effect of the hereditary principle combined with official corruption), the royal courts of justice were manned at every level by landed proprietors. In future even the most upright of magistrates could scarcely avoid looking through class-tinted spectacles. In both Germany and England

[27] L. Dubreuil, in *Revue d' histoire économique* 1924, p. 485; Du Halgouët, *Le duché de Rohan*, 1925, ii, 46—cf. M. Sauvageau, *Arrests et reglemens*, 1737, livre I, ch. 289–91; *Annales d'histoire économique*, 1930, pp. 366 and 516.

133

the main support for the seigneurial regime was entrenched in the elective institutions, the junker-dominated German Estates and the English Houses of Parliament, which were composed largely of the gentry who as Justices of the Peace were also responsible for law and order in the countryside. In France the inferior tribunals of the bailiwick and seneschal's courts, the presidial courts and above all the Parlements were all entrenched supporters of landed property. Although they never went so far as to sanction eviction—a legal revolution literally unthinkable, which no-one even dared to demand—the courts nonetheless permitted a host of petty encroachments whose accumulated mass was considerable.

It was fortunate for the French peasants that although the landlords had captured the judiciary, as a class they lacked full command of the levers to power so firmly in the grasp of their English and German counterparts, namely political authority and control of the main administrative organs. From the seventeenth century each province had its direct royal representative in the person of the intendant, himself in all likelihood a member of the squirearchy yet committed by his function to permanent rivalry with the official judiciary. Moreover, since the intendant was primarily a fiscal agent, it was up to him to protect rural communities, ripe material for taxation, from intemperate exploitation by their landlords. In more general terms his brief was to maintain the link between the king and his subjects. In England the end of absolute rule had enabled the gentry to profit from the spread of the Enclosure movement, which although it brought a transformation of agrarian techniques was also directly or indirectly the means of bringing ruin or dispossession on countless tenant farmers. In France, where political events took the diametrically opposite course, the victory of absolute monarchy kept the 'feudal reaction' within bounds. But it was only a containing movement, not annihilation. The servants of the crown always respected the seigneurial regime as one of the mainstays of the state and the social order. They failed to perceive the danger implicit in the paradox already noted by Fortescue on the eve of the modern era, by which the peasants were increasingly subjected to public taxation without receiving any adequate relief from their old obligations towards their landlords, who were now reduced by the advent of the monarchical state to the status of private individuals.

We have already seen some landlords taking steps, by means of stock-rearing (in which they were assisted by their privileges of *troupeau à part* or *herbe morte*) towards winning a direct share in the profits of the soil. A still more efficacious means was the reconstitution of the demesne.

Among the first to suffer were the village commons; a detailed account of the great battle which raged with ever-increasing bitterness over possession of these uncultivated lands will be given in a later chapter. At the moment we need mention only the outcome, which was that many of these ancient grazing grounds were converted either into pasture for the exclusive enjoyment of the landlord or else to profitable tillage.

The inroads on the tenures were perhaps more considerable still. Sometimes the lord found his opportunity in an ingenious reinterpretation of ancient customs. In the past a patrimony or *échoite* burdened with *mainmorte* had almost invariably been sold, usually to close relatives of the deceased holder; this practice was so common during the thirteenth century that it had acquired the force of law on some *seigneuries*. Now, however, we find that lords who still possess serfs (and with them rights of *mainmorte*) are more likely to keep the *échoite* for themselves. It was generally accepted that a landlord had the right to take any masterless properties back into the demesne. Now suppose a landlord has ordered his tenants' parcels to be surveyed, perhaps in the course of compiling a terrier or to facilitate the repopulation of an estate after a period of war. It may be found that some parcels exceed the area laid down in the title-deeds. These additions may perhaps represent illegal acquisitions, though the discrepancy is more likely to be due to inaccuracies in the earlier methods of surveying or to a subsequent adjustment to the standard of measure. But however the discrepancy had come about, these field-ends were indisputably vacant and as such a lawful prize. Another artful trick, denounced by a seventeenth century moralist, was the manipulation of arrears. A landlord anxious to round off his demesne omits to collect any rents for twenty-nine years (thirty years was the normal period of limitation); at the end of this time he cracks the whip. Lulled into false security, the 'poor wretches' have naturally failed to set aside the huge sum now suddenly needed; insolvent, their properties are confiscated. When he died this landlord might indeed find himself 'owner of nearly all the holdings in his parish'.[28]

But in the main landlords refashioned their great estates by a process of slow accumulation, using only orthodox methods such as purchase, exchanges etc. In this respect their achievement deserves to be bracketed with that of their contemporaries in other prosperous social segments, middle class men who were still below the moving line which separated the nobility from the general ruck, and more affluent peasants, always ready to adopt a middle-class way of life.

Let us look at one of the village maps produced in such quantity from the seventeenth century onward, which provide an eloquent likeness of the shell of rural society and, if we use our imagination, of the living organism it once housed. Suppose our plan is of a village in a region of fragmented fields—if we make it long-furlong fields the results will be more significant still. Everywhere the ground is seen to be furrowed by the familiar long strips. But here and there the rectangles broaden out, sometimes becoming quite large, to appear as white patches among the maze of threadlike lines. These patches have been formed from the progressive amalgamation of parcels of the more normal type, sometimes in considerable quantity. The plan made in 1666 of the village of Bretteville-l'Orgueilleuse in the plain of Caen clearly exhibits several such fields, which appear in striking contrast to the rest of the village lands. (Pl. XVI). Luckily enough a *marchement* made nearly two centuries earlier, in 1482, provides an exact point of reference: from this, or rather from a comparison we owe to an eighteenth century antiquarian familiar with local history, we know that the ground covered in 1666 by the four huge fields was occupied in 1482 by bundles containing respectively 25, 34, 42 and 48 parcels. In this instance the phenomenon is unusually clear-cut and easy to observe; but the same pattern is repeated in a thousand different places. Leaving the maps, let us turn to the terriers for information they can give about the title and

---

[28] *Annales d'histoire economique*, 1930, p. 535; Père Collet, *Traité des devoirs des gens du monde*, 1763, p. 271.

standing of the fortunate owners of these unusually extensive fields. With striking regularity we are confronted with one of the following: the landlord himself, which is the commonest case; a gentleman living in the neighbourhood, usually a member of the official nobility with one foot still in the bourge-oisie; a bourgeois from one of the nearby towns or larger villages, who might be a merchant, petty official or lawyer but in any case a *Monsieur* (the terriers are usually very particular to reserve this honourable appellation for persons above the level of rustic tradesmen); and sometimes, though more rarely, an ordinary cultivator whose holding in land was already con-siderable and who often combined his farming with a sideline in moneybroking or innkeeping, not to mention the less creditable but more profitable activity of lending money on short term at heavy rates of interest. (Plates VII, XIII and XIV).

These four categories often represent different stages of attainment in the same social ladder: the sons of well-to-do peasants will become *Messieurs,* and their sons perhaps rise to become gentlemen. The men who first started building up estates in the fifteenth century were most typically petty capitalists from the villages and smaller towns, merchants, notaries, usurers; their contribution to the reviving economy, increasingly dominated by the sovereign power of money, although less obvious than that of the great captains of trade and banking, was no doubt just as efficacious: they acted, in a word, as leaven. Rarely hindered by scruples, they knew how to look ahead and size up a situation. Every province had its representatives of the type: whether it was Jaume Deydier, the lawyer from Ollioulles in Provence, 'sire' Pierre Barbisson, merchant of Plaisance in Montmorillonais, or Pierre Cécile, counsel to His Majesty Philip II in the Parlement of Dole, all were inspired by the same tenacity of purpose. The lords were rather slower to follow suit and their land acquisitions often merely rounded off gains made by humbler-born forefathers. Alexandre Mairetet, lord of Minot in Burgundy where he had large estates and counsel to the Parlement of Dijon under Louis XIV, was the descendant of a small trader from the same village who had started accumulating properties there in the sixteenth century. In 1666 the Perrotte de Cairon, a family originally from Caen or its environs, owned nearly all the large, compact arable fields to be found at Bretteville-l'Orgueilleuse. The branches of the family abandoned the title of esquire, and tacked the name of a *seigneurie* onto their patronymic: de Saint-Laurent, de la Guère, de Cardenville, de Saint-Vigor, de la Pigassière. Their noble rank goes back at most a couple of centuries and they had made their fortunes in commerce or office, promptly converting them into a solid stake in the country. From 1482 Nicolas de Cairon was already in possession of the field at the entrance to the village known at that time as 'le grand clos'; 'and', says the *marchement*, 'this was acquired from several people, whether by purchase or exchange or some other means'.[29] Often, as with the Mairetet at Minot, the assumption of the seigneurial title followed some way after the acquisition of the property. Between 1527 and 1529 the attorney-general of the Parlement of Burgundy built up the estate of Vault to an extent of sixty odd hectares, pieced together from twenty-two separate lots acquired by purchase from ten different owners; this done, the new landlord then set about acquiring a share in the seigneurial rights and jurisdiction.[30]

The tradition of acquiring landed property persisted among the families of the higher bourgeoisie into the seventeenth and eighteenth centuries. It also became an ingrained characteristic of aristocratic families. The newly prosperous merchant who joined meadows to fields and vines to woodland was intent on establishing the wealth of his posterity on a surer basis than the shifting sands of commerce: as Colbert observed, 'families can only keep up their position if they are backed by substantial properties in land'. It was also a means of enhancing dynastic prestige; the acquisition of land, and of the seigneurial rights which sooner or later almost automatically followed, brought esteem to their possessor and prepared the way for ennoblement. The families of authentic pedigree who bought up land were insured against the risks attaching to dependence on fixed rents. In the seventeenth century, the scarcity of opportunities for

[29] Aubert, in *Comité des Travaux Historiques (Bull. hist.)* 1898: text relating to 33 Arch. Calvados, H 3226 fol. 271. The Archives of Calvados possess a cartulary of the de Cairon family, starting 13 February 1460; this would repay a detailed study, which I have not had time to undertake.

[30] A. de Charmasse, *Cartulaire de l'église d'Autun*, part iii, 1900, p. CXIV.

sound and lucrative investment was a further reason why anyone with money to spare, whether gentlemen of the old or new
nobility or plain commoner, preferred to sink his capital in the
land. Men bought up fields as they would later invest in
government stock, railway debentures or oil securities. It was
an undertaking that required endless patience. Antoine de
Croz, an advocate from Aix, devoted almost a lifetime to the
reconstitution of the *seigneurie* of Lincel, which had been split
up among so many interested parties that the first portion he
acquired, from an insolvent debtor, amounted to only one
forty-eighth of the whole; it took the lords of Lantenay in
Burgundy seventy-five years to piece together the plot of
ground known henceforth by the characteristic name '*la grande
pièce*', 'the big field'; and a hundred and sixty years had passed
before the land on which they finally built their château was
all in their hands. But the effort was justified by the reward.

In some regions this concentration of estates was so successful
as to affect the distribution of population. In areas of large
villages the cultivated land was too extensive and the inhabitants too numerous to permit the replacement of a small army
of peasant-farmers by a single master. But where enclosure was
the rule, where settlements were much smaller and holdings less
fragmented, as in the central regions and to some extent in
Brittany, where clearance was recent and the assarters lived in
small hamlets, it was by no means impossible for a proprietor
blessed with good fortune to annex by gradual stages the lands
of an entire village. One can point to more than one tiny
ancient settlement which was supplanted at this period by a
single farmstead standing in isolation among its newly acquired
fields: examples may be cited from the region of Montmorillon,
from Limousin and from the hillsides of Montbéliard.[31] One of
the effects of the rehabilitation of landed property at the hands
of the bourgeoisie and the nobility of the *Ancien Régime* was the
fresh impetus it gave to dispersed settlement.

Where some portion of the old seigneurial demesne still
survived, almost its sole function was to serve as a basis for

---

[31] For Montmorillonnais, see Raveau, *L'agriculture . . . dans le Haut-Poitou*, p. 54;
for Limousin I rely on information kindly communicated by M. A. Petit, archivist
of Haute-Vienne, and on material I have collected myself; for Montbéliard see
C.D., *Les villages ruinés*, 1847; cf., for La Combrailles, pl. XII.

future expansion whose limits eventually far exceeded the original nucleus. Here and there estates were rounded off by convenient exchanges, but it goes without saying that the main method was by purchase. How did it happen that so many small peasants were persuaded to part with their ancestral holdings? In other words, why were they so badly in need of money?

Their plight was sometimes due to extraneous events. It is significant that the Burgundian villages with the smallest number of hereditary tenants in the late seventeenth century were also those where the ravages of invasion had been most frequent and the fighting at its fiercest. Some of the former inhabitants had departed and never returned. In disposing of these vacant tenures the average lord acted more prudently than his predecessors of the period following the Hundred Years' War; he was also better favoured by prevailing economic conditions. No new perpetual tenures were created; where holdings were granted out again, it was for a definite term. It is true that many copyholders had either remained on their holdings or returned; but lacking ready money, desperate with hunger and often in debt, they were forced to sell their properties, and at a low price.

But it did not require such drastic blows of fate to involve the mass of the rural population in the toils of financial difficulty. The problems of adaptation to a changed economic environment were sufficient in themselves. The time was past when the small producer could live comfortably (or more often uncomfortably) directly from the fruits of his own labours. Now he was always having to put his hand in his pocket: to pay the tax-collector, the functionary of a state whose needs had been increased a hundredfold by the economic revolution; to pay his landlord's agent, also forced by the necessities of the time to act with greater stringency; to pay his suppliers, for now even the humblest could hardly exist without making purchases of one kind or another. True, there were still the fruits of the earth, and in a good year at least part of the produce could be sold. But to make any profit it was necessary to sell when the time was ripe; this meant being able to wait and to exercise judgment, feats only possible to a man with some reserves and the right mentality. But these were qualities in which the small peasant was normally deficient, since he lacked both capital and the skill to calculate the most favourable conjuncture. Some handsome fortunes were indeed made in the corn-trade between the sixteenth and eighteenth centuries; but the beneficiaries were merchants and cornmongers, sometimes the more prosperous peasants, inn-keepers and carriers. The 'average' countryman's share was very much smaller. Under the *Ancien Régime* his need of ready money became so great that in many regions he was forced to supplement his income by a manufacturing wage, earned by working in his own home. More frequently still he resorted to loans.

It is hardly necessary to say that the loans were made at crippling rates of interest. There was no systematic provision for agricultural credit. Equally, there was no limit to the ingenuity of the money-dealers. The loans might be of money, seed, or livestock, made against the land or the harvest to come and often disguised as harmless-seeming contracts (especially in the sixteenth century when the old prohibition on interest was theoretically still in force): the lenders might ring the changes on all these in varying combinations but the burden on the debtor was equally heavy. Even supposing he was lucky enough to escape the confiscation or forced sale of his land, once a peasant had become caught in the toils of debt and unable to satisfy the simultaneous demands of tax-collector, bailiff and village usurer, he could scarcely hope to avoid selling some portion of his fields or his meadows or his vines by private treaty. The lender, who dealt in property as well as money (*moyenneur* they called him in Poitou during the sixteenth century), was often also the purchaser; perhaps he had only made the loan with this eventuality in mind. He might keep the land and become a proprietor in his own right, as the first step along the road to social prestige and eventual ennoblement; or he might sell at a profit, to some higher placed bourgeois or gentleman. Other vendors, in urgent need of money, might apply directly to some important merchant or even to their own landlords. None of these potential purchasers was likely to take any risks; they knew the price they were prepared to pay so long as a property was 'well-defined', if possible adjacent to 'the close attached to the dwelling'[32] and, most important, consisted

---

[32] Rapin, *Les plaisirs du gentilhomme champêtre*, quoteed P· de Vaissièr, *Gentil-hmmoes campagnards*, 2nd ed., 1928, p. 205.

of a few large fields belonging to a single tenant. When, as it should be, a minute study comes to be made province by province of the revival of the large estate at its point of origin and of the sources which fed the numerous handsome properties spreading themselves over the countryside, one of its chief revelations will surely be a prolonged and serious crisis of credit in peasant finances.[33]

Naturally, the intensity of the drive towards the reconstruction of large estates varied greatly with the region. For the moment we can glance briefly at only a few of these divergent streams, seen most clearly if we place ourselves at the vantage point of the late eighteenth century.[34] If we consider 'property' as a whole (perpetual tenures, allods or fiefs), whether under direct or temporarily indirect cultivation, we can see that the way it was distributed among the social classes varied enormously from province to province. In Cambrésis and Laonnais ecclesiastical landlords had contrived to preserve, or more likely reassemble, considerable estates; in Toulousain their efforts had met with less success or had perhaps been less skilfully deployed; in the wooded country of the West they had drawn a complete blank. The bourgeoisie possessed little landed property in Cambrésis but owned half the land in Flandre Maritime; around Toulouse, a great commercial centre with a strong official element and linked with a nobility which probably contained many families of bourgeois origin, the great majority of landed properties was also in bourgeois hands. This uneven distribution has had a lasting effect, noticeable even in our own day; although the sale of properties at the time of the Revolution meant that many estates changed hands, they were not as a rule much broken up. (Pl. XV.) Today, as in the past, the plain of Picardy is characterised by its numerous large estates, just as the wooded country of Normandy or Oisans is predominantly a region of small peasant holdings. The key to

[33] The alleviation of the crisis at the end of the eighteenth century may have led to the renewal of peasant purchases which Loutschisky claims to have observed, at least in Limousin; but the actual nature of the phenomenon described by Loutschisky still remains pretty obscure, cf. G. Lefèbvre, *Revue d'histoire moderne*, 1928.

[34] References collected and interpreted with great acumen by G. Lefèbvre, *Revue d'histoire moderne*, 1928, p. 103. The fiscal immunities enjoyed under law or in fact by the privileged orders made the augmentation of aristocratic or ecclesiastical estates a danger to the finances of the crown; in this sense therefore the revival of the large estate contributed to the monarchichal crisis.

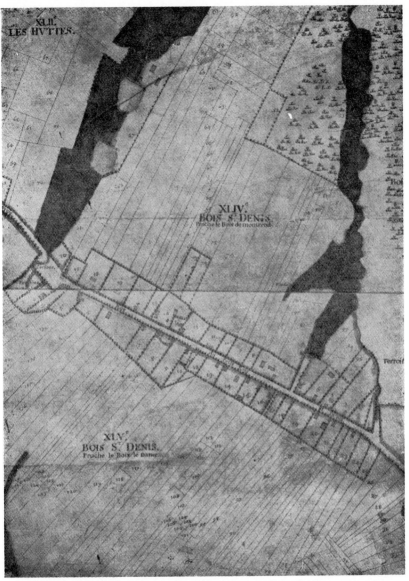

I. FOREST CLEARING ILLUSTRATING FIELDS ARRANGED IN FISH-BONE PATTERN. Map of the hamlet of Petit-Bois-Saint-Denis, taken from the map of the *seigneurie* of La Flamengrie (Aisne, cant. La Capelle), 1715. (Arch. Seine et Oise, D, fonds St. Cyr.)

## II. 'VILLENEUVES' ON THE ROAD BETWEEN PARIS AND ORLEANS

⫻⫻   Existing road. Between Etampes and Paris the general line
is as it was in the twelfth century.

- - - ·⸍   Old Roman road.

•   *Villeneuves* established from scratch.

o   Citadels set up beside older settlements.

TORFOU: Royal villeneuves (*pariages* included)

*Rouvray St. Denis:* Ecclesiastical *villeneuves*

*Brief guide to sources:*

Acquebouille, 1142-3: Luchaire, Louis VII, no. 98.

Les Bordes, 1203-1225: *Cartulaire de St. Avit d' Orléans,* nos. 50-55.

Bourg-la-Reine, originally Préau Hédouin, founded before 1134:
Luchaire, Louis VI, no. 601.

Chalou-Moulineux, before 1185: Arch. Nat., S 5131.

Etampes, Marché Neuf, 1123: Luchaire, Louis VI, no. 333.

La Forêt-le-Roi, 1123-1127: Luchaire, Louis VI, no. 601.

La Forêt-Sainte-Croix, 1155: *Cartulaire de Ste Croix d'Orléans,* nos.
75 and 115.

Longjumeau, before 1268: Arch. Seine et Oise, H, fonds Longjumeau.

Mantarville, c. 1123: *Cartulaire de Saint Jean en Vallée,* no. 33.

Le Puiset, between 1102 and 1106: *Liber Testamentorum Sancti
Martini,* no. 56.

Rouvray-Saint-Denis, 1122-1145: Suger, *De rebus* c. XI.

Torfou, 1108-1134: Luchaire, Louis VI, no. 551.

Villeneuve-Jouxte-Etampes, 1169-1170: Luchaire, Louis VII, no.
566; cf. J. M. Alliot, *Cartulaire de Notre-Dame d'Etampes,* no. xiii
and ci.

Villeneuve (near Angerville), before 1244: Arch. Seine et Oise,
H, fonds Yerres (founder unknown).

Villeneuve (near Artenay), before 1174: Arch. Loiret, G 1502
(under the name Essart).

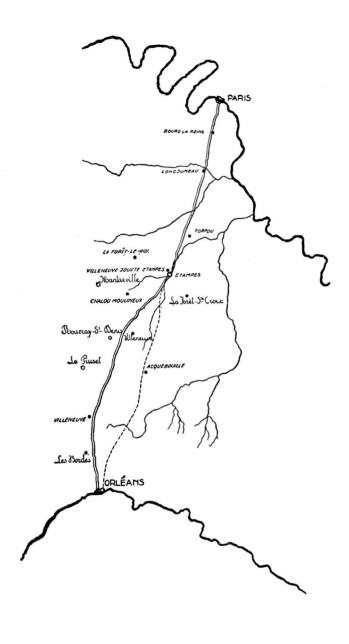

PARIS

BOURG LA REINE

LONGJUMEAU

TORFOU

LA FORÊT-LE-ROI

VILLENEUVE JOUXTE ETAMPES
Montarville
ETAMPES

CHALOU MOULINEUX
La Forêt-Ste Croix

Brouvay-St-Deny
Villeneuve

Le Pusel
ACQUEBOUILLE

VILLENEUVE

Les Bordes

ORLÉANS

III. LONG OPEN-FIELDS IN THE PLAIN OF CAEN, SHOWING
FRAGMENTATION

Map of Bras (Calvados, commune Ifs) and Hubert-Folie (Calvados, Bourguebus). 1738. (Arch. Calvados, H 2503). Bras is shown on the left and Hubert-Folie on the right.

The shaded parcels ▨ belong to Claude Vanier, a relatively prosperous tenant. There is a noticeable tendency towards plot amalgamation. The parcels blocked out in black ▮ belong to a less prosperous tenant, Jean le Febvre (see the extent, H 2489); he has 17 parcels against Claude Vanier's 16 (one has not been identified, which explains why the shaded parcels only add up to 15), but they are more scattered and the total area of his holding is considerably smaller. Enclosures are marked in here and there; they occur in places very close to the village centres and are often planted as apple orchards: cf. Chapter VI and the remarks made there concerning agrarian changes in the plain of Caen during the sixteenth century.

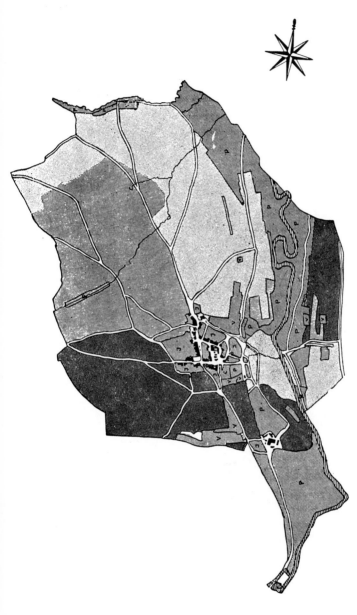

IV. MAP SHOWING CROP ROTATION: I. Seasonal map of Monblainville (Meuse, cant. Varennes), 1769, after the map in the Cabinet des Titres, Chantilly, E reg. 35. Note that in this instance the same rotation is observed over large blocks of land.

Houses.

Gardens (J), Vines (V), Oak plantations (C), Meadows (P).

*Couture* or *roye* under the control of Cour or Noyer, wheat.

*Couture* or *roye* under the control of Sugnon or Oserois, spring-sowing.

*Couture* or *roye* under the control of Perchie, fallow.

Communal meadows or rough grazing.

The odd snippets of fields visible to the east probably represent clearances of relatively recent date.

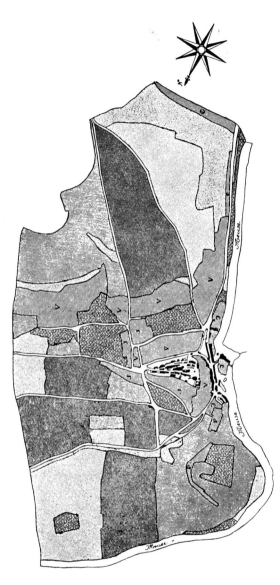

V. MAP SHOWING CROP ROTATION: II. Seasonal map of Dun sur Meuse (Meuse), 1783, after the map in the Cabinet des Titres, Chantilly, E reg. 39. Note that in this instance the rotations are not observed over large continuous blocks as in Plate IV, and that some lands are altogether 'out of course'.

Houses.

Gardens and orchards (J), Vines (V), Oaks (C), Meadows (P).

*Couture* under wheat.

*Couture* under spring sowing.

*Couture* under fallow (*versaine*).

Lands out of course and sown at will.

Communal grazing.

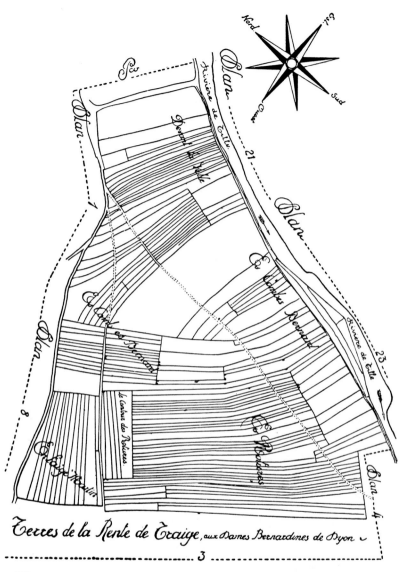

*Terres de la Rente de Traige, aux Dames Bernardines de Dyon*

VI. LONG OPEN-FIELDS ORIGINATING FROM A MEDIEVAL CLEARANCE.
From an item in the atlas for Spoy (Côte d'Or, cant. Is-sur-Tille), compiled
between 1782 and 1786. (Côte d'Or, E 1964, map 2). The name *Rotures*
given to one of the *quartiers* signifies that this was an assart. The little
triangular-shaped *quartier* of Bas de la Rochette (the name is omitted
from this map), situated on the edge of the river, paid tithe to the priest
under the heading *novales*, an indication that this too was a later clearance,
made after the parish had come into being and its tithes appropriated
by the patron of the church. Here we have a very clear example of additions
being made to the cultivated area round an ancient village. Spoy is first
mentioned in 630.

VII. IRREGULAR OPEN-FIELDS IN BERRY. Sheet 9 of the map of Charost (Cher), 1765, copy made in 1829: Arch. Cher, non-classified maps. The shaded parcels belong to a sieur Baudry, obviously one of those bourgeois land-gatherers mentioned in Chapter IV.

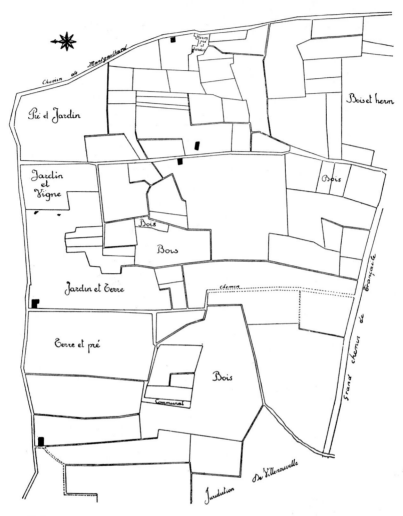

VIII. IRREGULAR OPEN-FIELDS IN THE MIDI, LANGUEDOC. After
an extract from a map of Montgalliard (Haute-Garonne, cant. Villefranche),
eighteenth century. (Arch. Haute Garonne, C 1580, map 7). The types
of cultivation are shown according to the key marked on the map. Where
no special type is indicated the land is under tillage.

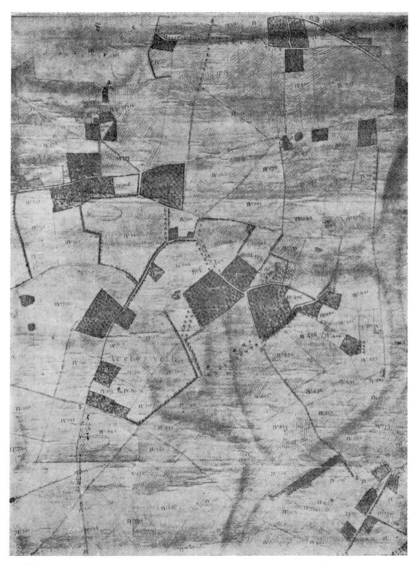

IX. IRREGULAR OPEN-FIELDS IN THE PAYS DE CAUX. Part of a map of Bréauté (Seine Inf., cant. Goderville), 1769. (Arch. Seine Inf., maps, no. 165.) The presence of some enclosures will be noted. These were a consequence of the post-medieval changes in the agrarian regime of Normandy mentioned in Chapter VI.

X. ENCLOSURE IN THE 'BOCAGE' COUNTRY OF NORMANDY. Part of
a map of St. Aubert sur Orne (Orne, cant. Putanges), c. 1700. (Arch.
Calvados, H 3457.) Note the enclosures fencing off several contiguous
parcels, e.g. 1336-1339, 1340-1342, 1332-1334. Plots 1340 and 1342 belong
to a number of different parties deriving their title from the same original
owner. On the later map appended to the terrier of 1758 (H 3458), plots
1332 and 1333 are separated by a hedge, as are plots 1097 and 1098,
near the top edge of the map.

XI. ENCLOSURES AND HAMLETS IN BRITTANY. Map of Kerhouarn
(comm. of Marzan, Morbihan), 1777. (Arch. Nat., N II, Morbihan. 8.)

XII. ENCLOSURE IN CENTRAL FRANCE (COMBRAILLES). Map of
the hamlet of Joberts and the *locaterie* of La Boire (comm. St. Sauvier,
Allier), 1785. (Arch. Cher E 717, *plan* 59.) It will be seen that in 1785 a
large part of the land belongs to François Belat, *bourgeois*, and his wife,
whereas in 1603 it is divided among various tenants (cf. the terriers E 693
and 690).

XIII. EXTENSION OF A SEIGNEURIAL DEMESNE. Map of a *quartier* of Champs-Potots, part of Thomirey (Côte d'Or cant. Bligny-sur-Ouche), drawn up between 1754 and 1764. (Arch. Côte d'Or, G 2427 map R.) In 1635 the lord of the place owned 7 *journaux*, a quarter of a perch, a twenty-fourth of a perch and five perches (terrier G 2414). In 1754-64 (terrier G 2426) the canons of Notre-Dame of Autun, who had acquired the *seigneurie* on 25 May 1652, held 22 *journaux* and seven-twelfths (shown in black). The demesne had thus nearly tripled in size over the space of about a century and a half.

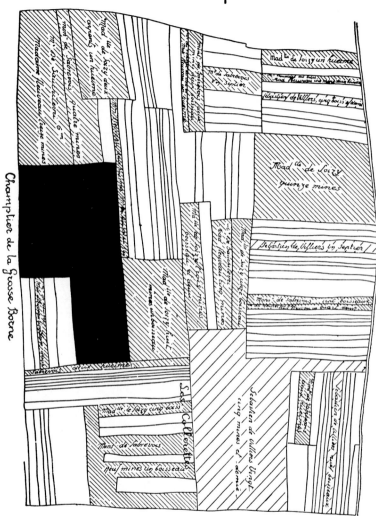

XIV. FORMATION OF LARGE-SCALE PROPERTIES IN THE BEAUCE: I.
After part of the map of Monnerville (Seine et Oise, cant. Mereville),
1699-1702. (Arch. Seine et Oise D, fonds St. Cyr.)

Seigneurial farm, attached formerly to the *mensa* of the Abbot of
St. Denis, transferred with the *seigneurie* to the house of the Dames
de St. Cyr.

Noble estates
{ heirs of Mme Fleureau, lady of Millourdin
Mlle de Choisy or Soizy
M. de Sabrevois, squire of Bleury

Sebastien de Villiers, '*marchand et laboureur*', living at Monnerville.

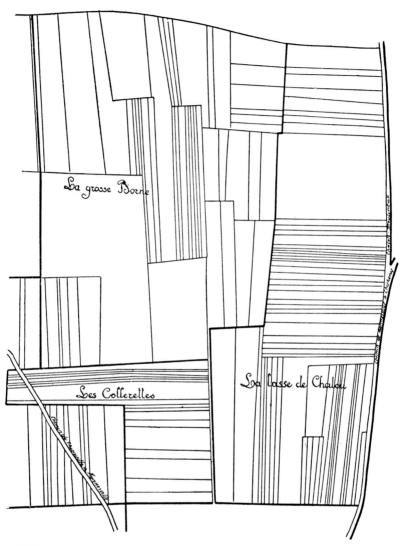

La grosse Borne

Les Colletettes

La Casse de Chalou

Chemin de Monnerville à Monnerville

Chemin de Saint-Martin à Châtenay

XV. FORMATION OF LARGE-SCALE PROPERTIES IN THE BEAUCE: II.
The same portion of Monnerville shown in Plate XIV, after a map drawn
up for the Land Registry in 1831, section A, sheet 3. Apart from the
parcel numbered 163-170 in the preceding map (near the southern end)—
land belonging to Sebastien de Villiers and since divided up—all the
large plots shown in 1669-1702 are still in being.

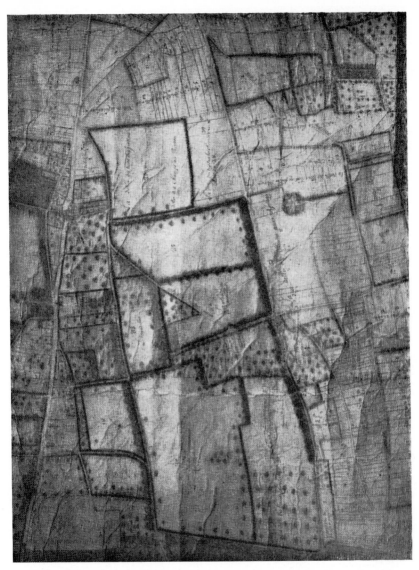

XVI. AMALGAMATION OF PARCELS AND ENCLOSURES IN THE PLAIN OF CAEN. Part of a map of the barony of Rots, 1666, showing the village of Bretteville-l'Orgueilleuse (Calvados, cant. Tilly-sur-Seulles), and the land immediately adjacent to the south. Arch. Calvados, H 3222; cf. the terrier of 1666, H 3229; the *marchement* drawn up in 1482, H 3226; and the comparison made of the two documents in 1784, H 3351. The enclosures numbered 18, 29, 31, 33, 34, 35 and 36 belong to the de Cairon family; they are all under tillage and 31 also includes gardens. In 1482 plot no. 30 was occupied by 42 parcels grouped into 5 *delles*, no. 35 by 25 parcels, no. 36 by 34 parcels. No. 33 was already in existence prior to 1482, pieced together by the de Cairon from acquisitions or exchanges; it was already known as the Grand Clos, a name at that time fully justified since it appears to have been the only existing enclosure of any size.

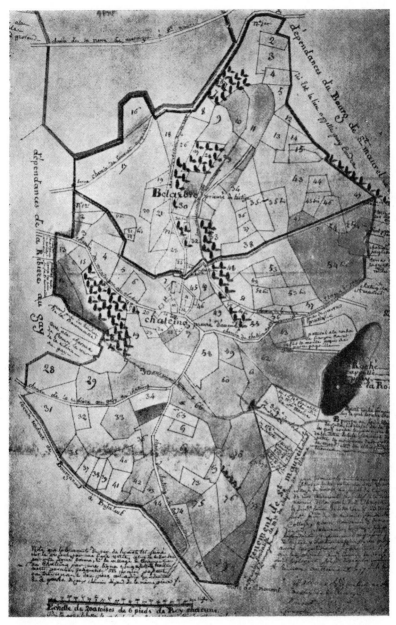

XVII. 'MAS' TYPICAL OF LIMOUSIN AND MARCHE. 'Plan du village, mas et tènement' of Chateing, and of the *'tènement'* of Belarbre (Creuse, comm. St. Moreil), 1777. (Arch. Haute Vienne, D 587, map 2.) The 'Mansum qui vocatur lo Castaint' is mentioned for the first time c. 1100 (*Cartulaire d'Aureil*, printed in the *Bullet. soc archéologique du Limousin*, xlviii, no. CXLV).

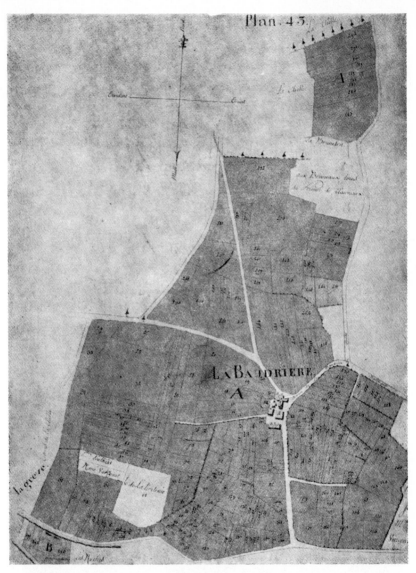

XVIII. 'FRÉRÈCHE' IN CENTRAL FRANCE, GIVING RISE TO A HAMLET.
Map of the *frérèche* of La Baudrière (now part of the commune of Scorbé-
Clairvaux, Vienne), 1789. (Arch. Vienne, E 66 bis., map 43.) The portion
marked B at the bottom of the map belongs to a neighbouring *frérèche*,
that of Baudets, whereas the portion marked A belongs to La Baudrière.

this pattern must undoubtedly be sought in the divergent paths towards rehabilitation followed in the centuries after the Hundred Years' War; unfortunately we still lack the detailed studies which would alone enable us to knit the present to the past.

Whether noble or bourgeois, how was a new master of the soil who was unwilling to act the part of absentee landlord to organise its exploitation? Some proprietors had no hesitation in cultivating their land directly, hiring farm-hands for the actual work. Here was a social revolution indeed. Although the medieval lord (except in the Midi) had always been a country-dweller by preference, he had taken little interest in the work of the fields. There is no reason to disbelieve the thirteenth century poet who tells how the lord of Fayel went out early in the morning 'to survey his corn and his fields'. It is always pleasant to contemplate the tender green of young shoots or the golden ears of ripe corn, whose harvest will be chinking coin. But farming was no proper occupation for a gentleman. The function of the lord in his castle was to watch over the collection of his rents, mete out justice, and see to building work; these, together with war, politics, hunting and the enjoyment of heroic or lighthearted tales made up the sum of his pursuits and pleasures. A story-teller who introduces a gentleman-farmer into his recital is at pains to point him out as a ruined man. And although we are told that an early twelfth century Archbishop of Dol, Baudri de Bourgueil (a good humanist who had doubtless read his *Georgics*), supervised the reclamation of the marshes in person, this can only have been a passing whim since he proceeded to allocate the land as perpetual tenures.[35] But in the sixteenth century a new figure emerges in literature as in life, that of the gentleman farmer. We have already encountered a Normandy squire of the latter half of the century, the sire de Gouberville, whose position and way of life belonged to the nobility although his descent was from townsmen and legal officials. Not content with maintaining an active correspondence with his agents, he sold his

[35] *Le Châtelain de Coucy*, line 6387; C. V. Langlois, *La vie en France au moyen-âge*, ii, 1925, p. 154, n. 1; J. Allenou, *Histoire féodale des marais de Dol*, 1917, p. 57, c. 17 and p. 63, c. 20.

beef cattle himself, supervised the building of dykes or fences and the digging of ditches and led out the farm-hands of the neighbourhood to pick stones off the fields. Women, both noble and bourgeois, also had their finger in the pie. There was Mademoiselle Poignant, wife of a king's councillor, who in the sixteenth century supervised the hay-mowers and grape-gatherers on her property in the Île-de-France and was present when the fields were manured. In the seventeenth century there was the Countess of Rochefort in Provence: in the absence of her husband she saw to the planting of the vines and the threshing and garnering of the corn. In 1611 official notice was taken in Artois of the advances made by direct exploitation.[36]

Nothing brought greater advantage than direct exploitation of his property, provided that it was intelligently pursued, by the landlord himself. But to be successful the master had to live on the spot, a condition which also applied where the estate was wholly or partially let out to tenants: to get the most out of such property, the master had to be there to supervise the tenant-farmers, to consume some of the produce (which formed a proportion of the rent) and arrange for the sale of the remainder. Bussy-Rabutin wrote to Madame de Sévigné: 'relatively speaking, I derive more benefit from my estates than you do from Bourbilly, because I am close at hand while you are far away. . . Get yourself exiled—it is easier than you think.'

But exile was after all a desperate measure and many great proprietors, noble or bourgeois, had neither the leisure nor the inclination to bury themselves in the country; in any case the estates of wealthy landlords were usually too numerous and too scattered for them all to be directed in person. The solution was to lease them out, naturally for a fixed term, since hereditary tenures were now quite alien to the masters' way of thinking. There were two choices open. The estate could either be split up into a number of small units, each entrusted to a different lessee, or it could be leased as a whole. Where the latter happened and the estate comprised a seigneurial demesne,

[36] A. Tollemer, *Journal manuscrit*, 2nd ed., 1880; *Mém. de la Soc. des Antiquaires de Normandie*, xxxi and xxxii; *Lettres missives de Charles de Brucan*, ed. Blangy, 1895; A. de Blangy, *Génealogie des sires de Russy*, 1892; Y. Bezard, *La vie rurale dans le sud de la région parisienne*, 108; C. de Ribbe, *Une grande dame dans son ménage . . .* 1890; C. Hirschauer, *Les Etats d'Artois*, i, 1923, p. 121, n. 3. For all this see P. de Vaissière, *Gentilshommes campagnards de l'ancienne France*, 2nd ed., 1928.

the rents and sundry charges owed by the tenants normally went to the lessee, in accordance with a practice widespread from the thirteenth century. These two methods matched the two social types from which lessees were drawn. The small tenant-farmer was a peasant, who often already possessed a tenure and would require only a small amount of working capital. It was in fact precisely because he lacked both ready money and the aptitude for acquiring any that rents in many provinces were payable either wholly or partly in grain. But the large-scale tenant-farmer, who was required to possess much greater capital, qualities of salesmanship and judgment and to fill the position of head of a substantial household (to which the *seigneurie* itself was added) was within his sphere a powerful personage, in economic terms a capitalist, in outlook and way of life most usually a bourgeois. We have a list of the lessees between 1641 and 1758 of the *seigneurie* and demesne of Thomirey in Autunois; while there are twenty-one 'merchants', one butcher, one notary, one barrister, and one man described simply as a bourgeois, all from Thomirey itself or neighbouring towns or larger villages, and all more or less related, there is mention of only one family (represented by two contracts) drawn from the local farming community, and they were obviously people in easy circumstances who had also married into business families.[37] One must allow for some vanity in this choice of titles, since merchant was long considered a more dignified appellation than cultivator. Many of these so-called merchants probably derived the greater part of their revenues from the land and would not have thought it beneath them to set their own hands to the plough as need arose. But it still remains true that farming was not the end of their activities, that they set their sights beyond the narrow circle of village life. It was not unheard of for a rich leaseholder to supplant his master. In the eighteenth century, when agriculture throughout the country was becoming more and more an undisguisedly capitalist undertaking, many landlords who had hitherto found it more convenient to split up their estates now set about re-integrating the holdings in favour of a few large leaseholders, at the expense of a host of smaller men. The *cahiers* returned in 1789 from Northern France are full of protests from the

[37] Arch. de la Côte d'Or, G. 2412 and 2415.

peasantry against this practice, which had recently become widespread. The reconstruction of large estates, which in some places had hitherto operated in support of a regime of small holdings, now at this late hour, and by an indirect route, led in France, as it had already done elsewhere, to actual evictions.[38]

Inevitably some small farms were in the hands of recent purchasers whose resources would not stretch to a larger estate or who had had to sell most of what they had bought. Such holdings held no attraction for capitalist proprietors, nor was it always easy to find a peasant-farmer with enough money in hand to buy them. Moreover, recent experience of monetary instability, above all in the sixteenth and early seventeenth centuries, had given landlords a wholesome distrust of money rents which remained fixed for the period of the lease, however short the term might be. It was for these reasons that the form of lease known as *métayage*, in which a proportion of the produce (usually half) formed part of the ground rent, made such rapid headway.

The practice whereby the cultivator paid over a proportion of the produce as a means of discharging the ground-rent on a piece of land, already recognised in Roman Law, was no novelty to France. One has only to think of those champarty tenures which became prevalent in the tenth and eleventh centuries as demesnes grew smaller. Subsequently this form of tenure became less frequent, as the landlords of the later Middle Ages favoured the substitution of money rents for payments in kind. Where champarty tenures survived they rapidly became hereditary; and at the same time the amount due, far short of half the total produce, became invested with that immutable character which the landlords of the *Ancien Régime* found so distasteful. Even so, the word *métairie* applied to the custom of fixing the lessor's share at half the produce or thereabouts is met with in certain provinces from an early date; it is found throughout the West between Maine and Perche from the eleventh and twelfth centuries, and appears at much the same

[38] It is true that in Brittany the creation of large leaseholds did not necessarily lead to the suppression of small holdings; often those 'rich individuals' who annexed 'nearly all the farms' of a community had them cultivated by 'sub-farmers'; E. Dupont, *Annales de Bretagne*, xv, 43. But in many other regions—the northern plains, Picardy and Beauce for example—small holdings were genuinely replaced by large. On peasant opposition see *infra*, p. 195.

time in Artois. Were these leases permanent or temporary? The sources often allow of no definite answer, nor is it possible in every case to decide whether this was a genuine tenure, subject to the whole nexus of seigneurial obligations, or a simple agreement between the parties which did not create any bond of dependence; it is moreover doubtful whether a real property contract of this latter purely private type was clearly recognised before the thirteenth century. What is certain is that throughout the Middle Ages the institution of *métayage* was either completely unknown in many regions or was normally applied in practice only to particular categories of land, notably vineyards: the townsman or ecclesiastic who acquired some vines was thinking more of his cellar than of his money bags and so preferred a share-cropper to a tenant-farmer. From the sixteenth century *métayage* showed a sudden increase, which was maintained at least until the eighteenth century: formerly restricted to a few regions, and even there a rarity, it came to cover the whole of France. No safer remedy against monetary fluctuations could have been devised. The first people to realise its merits were the subtle financiers who ran Italian city governments: there were cities where every citizen of the commune who leased land to the subject and downtrodden inhabitants of the *contado* was obliged to employ this type of lease—at Bologna the law to this effect was passed in 1376. French landlords were not slow in following their example.

At first, in the period immediately following the Hundred Years' War, these contracts were sometimes made in perpetuity. The masters of the soil were seeking to recoup their fortunes from a depopulated countryside. Money rents were discredited in their eyes; many were neither willing nor able to cultivate their estates themselves; and there was little hope of attracting tenants prepared to clear overgrown fields in return for a merely temporary lease. The hereditary *métairie* was of benefit to both parties: the lessee was protected against eviction, the lessor against a fall in the value of money. In some regions, Central France in particular, the system was a notable success.[39]

But as large-scale proprietorship became more firmly re-established, *métayage* for a limited term (against a half, a third

[39] A. Petit, 'La métairie perpetuelle en Limousin', in *Nouvelle Revue Historique de Droit*, 1919.

or a quarter of the produce) became by far the most usual form. Under Henry IV Olivier de Serres came out strongly in its favour, as the next best thing to direct exploitation. Although found nearly everywhere, geographically speaking *métayage* was associated above all with impoverished regions, where the peasantry was totally without reserves of capital; socially speaking, it was the type of lease preferred by landlords of the petty bourgeois type. It was not merely that their estates were too meagre to attract leaseholders from among the capitalists; it was also, and above all, because for many reasons this type of lease suited their outlook and way of life. The small town merchant or notary liked to eat food grown on his own land; he delighted in the crusty bread and golden *galettes* made in his domestic bakehouse with flour from corn grown on his *métairie*; his wife could produce unrivalled delicacies for his table from the eggs, poultry and pork which were the minor incidents of the lease, set out in great detail in the contracts. Whether he was living in town or in his house among the fields, he found it pleasant to see the *métayer*—his *métayer*—coming to him cap in hand, obliged to render him the various services, not far removed from *corvées*, so carefully stipulated in the agreements, and the subject of his condescension. In law an 'associate', in practice the *métayer* was a client, in the Roman sense. A lease '*à demy fruits*' concluded in 1771 on behalf of Jérôme de Rimailho, honorary counsel to the presidial court of Toulouse and a usurer of the deepest dye, declares that the lessees are to owe the lessor 'loyalty, obedience and submission'.[40] Under the system of *métayage* a whole section of the urban population was kept in direct contact with the soil, linked by genuine ties of personal dependence with the men who tended it; and this is a matter of quite recent history.

The whole movement just described had two effects; one was transitory, the other has lasted into our own day.

The slow apparent trend towards the emancipation of the peasantry from the clutches of seigneurial control was halted. The lords were energetic in tightening up the diffuse burden of charges. Often newcomers to their role, they were all the more conscious of their position as masters. When terriers came to be

[40] J. Donat, *Une communauté rurale à la fin de l'Ancien Regime*, 1926, p. 245.

revised, a highly significant stress was laid on obligations which implied the honour due to a master. 'When the Lord or Lady de Bretennières or their family are entering or leaving the church, all the inhabitants and parishioners of the said place shall keep silence and make their respects.' So says a Burgundian terrier of 1734. There is no mention of any of this pomp in the previous version.

Everyone knows how the seigneurial edifice crashed in ruins between the years 1789 and 1792, taking with it a monarchical régime with which it had become identified.

For all that he liked to see himself as the head of his peasantry, the new-style lord had really reverted to being a large-scale manager; as such he was more than a simple bourgeois. If we can imagine, which is of course absurd, the Revolution breaking out around the year 1480, we should find that land relieved of seigneurial charges was reallocated almost without exception to a host of small occupiers. But the three centuries between 1480 and 1789 saw the rehabilitation of the large estate. It was not, as in England and Eastern Germany, all-embracing. Large tracts of land, in total larger perhaps than those covered by the great estates, were still left under peasant proprietorship. But the victory was a sizeable one, though its completeness varied noticeably with the region. The Revolution was to leave the large estate relatively unimpaired. The picture presented by the rural France of our own day—which is not, as is sometimes said, a land of petty proprietors but rather a land where large and small properties coexist in proportions which vary considerably from province to province—is to be explained by its evolution between the fifteenth and eighteenth centuries.

# CHAPTER FIVE

# The Social Groupings

## I. THE *MANSE* AND THE FAMILY COMMUNITY

EARLY societies were made up of groups rather than individuals. A man on his own counted for very little. To earn his bread and protect himself he needed the association of other men; moreover, those in authority, masters, lords and princes, were accustomed to count and tax men in groups of every size.

At the time when our rural history first begins to emerge from the mists in the period we call the Early Middle Ages, the primitive cell (contained within the relatively more complex organisms of village and *seigneurie*) was a unit at once territorial and social. This unit, a dwelling with its allotted fields, was occupied and cultivated by a small group of men; it is found nearly everywhere in Frankish Gaul and under a variety of names, of which the most usual is *manse (mansus)*[1]; it may also be described as *factus, condoma* or *condamina*. All these expressions are relatively late in appearing; *mansus* is not found before the seventh century,[2] nor (in Gaul) is *condamina*, an expression which is most frequent in the Midi, though the first text in which

[1] I am aware that *manse* is a barbarism. In good *langue d'oil* the expression should be *meix*, although in Provençal it would be *mas*; and there are other dialect forms which should be taken into account. Furthermore, as we shall see, in their present applications (which have the sanction of long usage) *meix* and *mas* relate to something quite different from what was understood by the Frankish *mansus*. Since the forms are so various and the changes in meaning so considerable, there seems every excuse for abandoning the search for a modern equivalent and for retaining —with a good conscience for once—the Latin word we historians have adopted with a fine disregard for phonetics, the *mansus* of Guérard and Fustel de Coulanges.

[2] Cf. M. Prou and A. Vidier, *Recueil des chartes de l'abbaye de Saint-Benoît-sur-Loire*, i, 1907, p. 16; Zeumer, in *Neues Archiv*, xi, 331; L. Levillain in *Le Moyen Age*, 1914, p. 250. Naturally we are not here concerned with texts in which *mansus* clearly has (or can be construed to have) the meaning 'dwelling', as in *Formul. Andecav.* 25.

it occurs happens to come from Maine;[3] *factus* does not appear until the ninth century. Our knowledge of early agrarian terminology is virtually non-existent, which accounts for these tardy references; the institution itself was certainly much older. The name *factus* defies explanation. We do not even know what language it derives from; there seems little to connect it with Latin *facere*. *Condamina* is suggestive of community (the rudimentary community sharing the same house) and in practice is applied, with little apparent discrimination, either to the small group of men living off a plot of land or to the land itself. *Mansus* originally signified the house alone, or the house and its agricultural outbuildings. This meaning was never completely lost sight of and is the only one to survive, as the Burgundian *meix* and Provencal *mas* still current in our own day. The related expression *masure*, treated in old documents as a synonym for *mansus* in all its senses, was used in the Île de France, as it still is in Normandy today, to describe a country dwelling with its close. The agrarian unit thus took its name from the house inhabited by its occupants; as the Scandinavians said, 'is not the house the mother of the field?'.

As with most other social categories of this period, study of the *manse* must start from the *seigneurie*: not because we wish to prejudge the issue by crediting the *seigneurie* with some factitious pre-eminence in the role of universal matrix, but simply because seigneurial archives are the only sources full enough to permit a preliminary survey. The essential function of the *manse* on the early medieval *villa* is clear enough: it was the unit of assessment. Rents and services were not reckoned by individual parcels, households or dwellings. In recording what was due from that part of the estate which was divided up into *manses* (as we shall see, one small portion was excluded), the inventories recognise only one unit of contribution, the *manse*. It was immaterial that fields grouped under this heading were worked by several families in common. The tax fell on the *manse*; it was for the *manse* to produce the required sums of money and bushels of corn, the stipulated number of hens and eggs and days of work.

---

[3] *Actus pontificum Cenomannensium*, ed. G. Busson and A. Ledru, 1902, p. 138. It is first mentioned in Italy in the sixth century, Cassiodorus, *Variae*, v. 10. For the meaning (and the doubts expressed by Mommsen) see the judicious remarks of G. Luzzato, *I servi nelle grande proprietà ecclesiastiche*, 1910, p. 63, n. 3.

The various occupants—associates, *socii*—were left to share the burden among themselves as they pleased. There can be little doubt, however, that they were held jointly responsible and had no right to rupture this joint responsibility by partition. As the basic unit of seigneurial taxation, the *manse* was regarded as indivisible and immutable. If for some reason fragmentation was permitted, the division had to be into some simple fraction, halves or much more rarely quarters; once established these new units were immutable in their turn.

The *manses* within a *seigneurie* were not as a rule all of equal value and dignity. They usually fell into various categories, each of which carried different obligations. Within each category, however, the burden of charges was much the same for every *manse*. The basis of classification varies. It is frequently legal in character, with personal status as the major criterion. As we have seen, *manses* might be free (i.e. reserved for free men, *coloni* in particular) or servile; there was also the *lidile* category, *manses* occupied by *liti*, men enfranchised under Germanic law. For the record we should add the manses known as '*censile*', which were leased out for a term under contract and were thus in a class apart from the three other groups mentioned, all customary and in practice hereditary. In other instances the classification depends on the type of service owed, for example carting or labouring, *mansi carroperaii*, *mansi manoperaii*. In practice the contrast between these two methods of classification was more apparent than real. In the Frankish period, as we know, there was no longer any strict correspondence between a man's personal status and that of his land; a *manse* occupied by free men was still called servile if its earliest, perhaps very remote, incumbents had been slaves. The imprint left by the original occupants was so strong because custom decreed that their status, rather than that of the present tenant, determined the obligations attaching to a *manse*. However they might be labelled, for day-to-day purposes the various grades of *manse* were distinguished primarily by the duties with which they were charged. Labouring *manses* had originally been 'servile', and the *polyptiques* apply either term to them indiscriminately.[4] The traditional label, which struck a jarring note when taken in conjunction with the actual status of the present occupants,

---

[4] *Polyptyque des Fossés*, in B. Guérard, *Polyptique de l'abbé Irminon*, ii, 283.

was gradually abandoned in favour of the more realistic descriptive epithet. But, and this is important to notice, the initial classification appears to have been based on human groupings.

One would naturally expect variations in size between the different categories of *manse* on the same *seigneurie*. Taking only the two principal types, we do in fact find that the servile *manse* is always smaller than the free one. It would be equally reasonable to expect no differences between *manses* in the same category belonging to the same estate, since they were all on the same footing as taxable units. Often this was indeed the case, as on most of the estates of St. Bertin's (northern Gaul) during the ninth century. It seems that where the size of the *manse* was concerned, local standards prevailed: in 1059 Saint-Florent de Saumur received a grant of woodland from which seven *manses* were to be created, 'of the kind usual among men living close to this estate'.[5] But there were also some glaring inequalities. Minor discrepancies can be accounted for by differences in the fertility of the soil: parity in surface area could not always guarantee parity of return. But some *manses*, two or three times greater than the norm, are altogether too large to be explained in this way. The only conclusion to be drawn is that in the distribution of the *manses* certain occupants were favoured at the expense of others. It is difficult to say whether this was so from the beginning or the result of evolution. But it is worth noting that from the ninth century these divergences were a particular feature of the region around Paris, where, as will be seen, the decomposition of the *manse* apparently set in at a very early date. On the other hand, there is nothing at all mysterious about the variations in the size of *manses* between one *seigneurie* and another, and one region and another, where on average the differences are even greater. In Picardy and Flanders, where population was relatively sparse, the ninth century *manse* was generally larger than in the Seine valley. But if we take Gaul as a whole, the disproportions were not so flagrant that the area covered by a *seigneurie* would be much affected by the number of tenurial *manses* of any particular type it contained, or even, generally speaking, by the sum total of tenurial *manses*. This helps to fix the size of our basic territorial unit. It will

[5] Bibl. Nat., nouv. acqu. lat. 1930, fol. 45 v° and 46.

simplify matters if we concentrate on free *manses* which, anomalies apart, range in area from between 5 and 30 hectares. This gives an average of about 13 hectares, slightly lower, as might be expected, than the minimum $16\frac{1}{2}$ hectares which Carolingian legislation, always solicitous for the interests of the country clergy, laid down for the *manse* supposed to be attached to each parish church. Everything points to the same conclusion. In size the *manse* was equivalent to a small or medium-sized holding of our own day; but in view of the low level of cultivation at this period, as a unit of production it would rank very near the bottom of our scale.[6]

Most of the tenures were *manses*; but on many *seigneuries* there were some holdings which, although subject to rents and services, escaped this classification. They were known by a variety of names, *hospitia, accolae, sessus, laisinae*, or, as in many regions at a somewhat later date, *bordes* or *chavannes*. These anomalous tenures were always much fewer and smaller than the *manses* and far from uniform in size; they seem to have been unaffected by the rule of indivisibility. Sometimes the holder of a *manse* (*mansuarius*) annexed one of these oddments, perhaps a fragment detached from the demesne or an assart reclaimed from the waste, to add to his principal tenure. More frequently they were occupied by people who had no other land. They were minor deviants within the *villa* organism. But suppose such a holding were to grow, enlarged by a grant from the master or an assart from the waste or by some other means. The next step was obviously to raise it to the dignity of one of the typical cells of the *villa* organisation. Once the holding had become a *manse*, it was easier for the seigneurial officials to collect the dues systematically and the cultivator also no doubt benefited by being admitted to the unrestricted enjoyment of collective privileges (pasture, wooding etc.) which was accorded only to full tenants. We find the monks of Saint-Germain-des-Prés declaring that they have turned the land of Augart and Auri into a *manse*, 'so that in future they may pay the full charges'. On another occasion these monks took back a fragment of their demesne which was on temporary lease to one *mansuarius*, combined it with sundry lands granted to another and let the whole as a *demi-manse* to yet a third. Changes of this

---

[6] Cf. F. Lot, *Le tribut aux Normands*, in *Biblioth. de l'Ecole des Chartes*, 1924.

nature were more than merely nominal; they required an explicit deed, emanating from a qualified authority. The *manse* was thus a genuine institution, since it contained an element of intention, something deliberately contrived.

Since the most obvious feature of the *manse* is its utility as a unit for seigneurial taxation, the temptation to regard it as a seigneurial creation is strong. On the face of it nothing could be simpler: at some moment in the dawn of history the master of the village shared out the land among his men in units of more or less equal size, which he declared indivisible. Yet on reflection any such hypothesis presents formidable difficulties. Was there ever really a time when the population of Gaul was composed of two classes to the exclusion of all others, the one a handful of all-powerful dynasts, the other a flock of docile slaves, eager to accept whatever portion of virgin soil their master saw fit to give them? There are any number of possible objections, starting with the 'master' himself. Exhaustive discussion of this myth is quite pointless, since it can be demolished by reference to one set of facts alone. We know from various regulations concerning military service that there were free men in Carolingian Gaul whose whole estate consisted of a single *manse* or even a *demi-manse*. Were they tenants? It is quite clear from the texts that they were not, that their land was unencumbered by any superior right of real property. Were they then lords? Hardly: how could a solitary *manse*, let alone a *demi-manse*, support a landlord and his family in addition to the men who cultivated it? These insignificant people were small peasant proprietors who had for the moment escaped the clutches of the aristocracy. If their land, which was not held in tenure, was nevertheless classed as a *manse*, then the word must denote a unit of cultivation quite independent of any idea of seigneurial charges.

Moreover, the state also found the *manse* very useful as a unit, both for military purposes and for assessing taxes. From the reign of Charles the Bald down to 926 the kings frequently resorted to a general levy to raise the huge sums needed to buy off Viking attacks. Their regular procedure was to tax lay and ecclesiastical landlords according to the number of their dependent *manses*. It is true that only tenurial *manses* were included in this reckoning. But suppose we go still further back in time. The Merovingians had inherited the Roman land tax; this they continued to levy, mostly on the basis of old registers though a few new ones were drawn up. But after a long period of decline the day came when this bureaucratic weapon finally eluded their inexpert grasp. Although unparalleled among the institutions of the Later Empire for its obscurity, this land tax possessed at least one feature of which we can be certain: it rested on the division of the soil into small taxable units— *capita, juga*—each of which roughly corresponded to a single agricultural holding. Even though the nomenclature is different, the resemblance to the *manse* is obvious. But we know that the Roman fiscal unit went by other names in popular usage, names which varied with the province and have now largely disappeared.[7] There seems no reason why *condamina*, which appears in Italy as early as the beginning of the sixth century, *mansus*, and *factus* should not have been among them.

All the same, even if we think the Frankish *mansus* was descended from the Roman *caput*, or rather represented the Roman *caput* under another name, we are not necessarily obliged to regard the reality underlying these terms as the abstract creation of imperial officials working without a register to guide them. I have so far treated this problem as though it applied only to France, but in fact it affects much of Europe, and not only the Roman parts. Italy was not the only place where the land was divided into agrarian units analogous in every respect to those of Frankish Gaul and, what is more, often designated by the same terms. The Germanic countries present a similar picture; we find the German *Hufe*, English hide and Danish *bool* all readily translated into Latin as *mansus*, while the institutions they denote display unmistakable affinities with the French *manse*, a unit at once agrarian and fiscal. Would anyone be so bold as to explain these similarities as borrowings? Can we seriously imagine barbarian kings deliberately extending the system of land divisions they inherited from the Roman fisc to vast territories where it was hitherto quite unknown? Any such hypothesis is surely ruled out by the well-attested administrative weakness of barbarian kingdoms. Are we then to assume that the *manse-Hufe* was a

[7] C. Th., XI, 20, 6; cf. A. Piganiol, *L'impôt de capitation*, 1916, p. 63.

Germanic invention, introduced into the countryside of the
*Romania* by uncouth conquerors? Even if we had not already
identified the *manse* as the successor of the Roman *caput,* indulgence in such fantasies would founder on our certainty that the
barbarian invaders, rare exceptions apart, aimed at conquest
rather than settlement. The *manse* must therefore be something
more than the superficial creation of administrative regulation,
and older than historic national boundaries. The use of the
*manse* for fiscal purposes by Roman, Frankish and seigneurial
administrators profoundly affected its history. But its origin lay
elsewhere; to penetrate its mysteries we must once again return
to the land itself, and to the types of agrarian civilisation whose
ages are measured in millennia.

Before doing this there is a terminological difficulty to be
cleared away, of the kind inflicted on historians by the vagaries
of everyday language, and medieval language in particular.
The lord had his own fields, distinct from those of his tenants,
which constituted his demesne. When Carolingian governments raised a levy from large estates the tax fell not only on the
dependent tenures *pro rata* but also, as a rule, on the demesnes;
but although demesnes varied enormously among themselves,
they were arbitrarily credited with a uniform and fictitious
value, so that although quite unstandardised, the seigneurial
demesne became a fiscal unit on its own. Now taking a general
view, what was a *manse* at the Frankish period other than a unit
of cultivation which also served as a basis for taxation? In
England the demesne, which was exempt from taxation, is never
given the name hide; but in the lands forming the Frankish
empire the demesne is called *manse* or *Hufe.* In order to distinguish seigneurial *manses* from the rest, the term *mansus
indominicatus* was for a time adopted in these countries (it
disappeared again quite soon, some time around the eleventh
century). But this was not the true *manse.* The true *manse* was
in the hands of tenants or independent peasants; it was the cell
of rural life, made up of dwelling, fields and a share in the
collective privileges; in theory it possessed perfect stability, and
its order of magnitude was so well-defined that a man known to
hold a whole, half or quarter *manse* could immediately be placed
by contemporaries in his appropriate social group.

But in its actual setting the *manse* appeared under various guises, which varied according to the prevailing type of cultivation.

In regions of dispersed plots and nucleated settlement—above all in regions of long-furlong open-fields—the *manse* was very rarely all of a piece. The buildings were huddled in the village with those of the other *manses*; the widely scattered parcels of land lay interspersed with those of other *masoyers* over the *quartiers*. Yet these *manses* were stable, if purely fictitious, units; and if they were not all equal, their classification by size made them readily comparable. The discussion of field-plans in a previous chapter has already led to the conclusion that the successive phases in the occupation of the soil obeyed some over-all plan, conceived on a more or less comprehensive scale. How this plan was arrived at and imposed, whether by chieftain or lord or by the free operation of the collective will, is one of the secrets of prehistory. What we can say is that the village and its fields were the creation of a large group, perhaps—though this is only conjecture—a tribe or clan; the *manses* must have been the portions assigned—whether from the beginning or only at a later date is impossible to say—to smaller sub-groups, communities within the community. The organism which had the *manse* as its shell was very probably a family group, smaller than the clan in that it was restricted to members whose descent from a common ancestor was a matter of only a few generations, yet still patriarchal enough to include married couples from several collateral branches. The English 'hide', rendered in Latin *terra unius familiae*, is probably descended from an old Germanic word meaning family.

The portions thus distributed (often unequal among themselves by reason of circumstances beyond our power to explain, yet always conforming to the same type of cultivation) did not account for the total arable of the village. Where there was a chieftain, his share was doubtless larger. And at the other end of the scale were sundry occupiers whose position was inferior to that of the main families (perhaps they included later arrivals) and whose lots were more meagre. These were the *hospitia*; judging from the Italian evidence, the *accolae* at least must have represented fragments detached from the communal lands at a later date, by small-scale assarters approved by the group.

Such then was the ancient institution later adopted by governments as the basis of their land registers and by lords (in so far as they had power over villages) to serve their own ends. When seigneurial demesnes came to be broken up, *manses* were created for the slaves now being settled on the land; in all probability these servile *manses* were established in direct imitation of the free *manses*, which on aggregate were far more numerous. The same pattern was followed when an enterprising lord started a new foundation from scratch.

The existing documentary evidence and the present state of research makes it impossible to arrive at any precise idea of the form taken by the *manse* in regions of irregular open-fields. Nevertheless certain indications suggest that it was often, though by no means always, all of a piece.[8] For the enclosed regions, however, the picture is clear, and the contrast with long-furlong country as striking as one could wish.

Here, as elsewhere, the term *manse* signifies an agrarian holding worked by a small group, probably a family. But we are no longer dealing with an abstract legal entity made up from fields dispersed over a huge terrain, to which was added a proportionate share in the collective privileges of the community. This *manse* was a self-contained block. In old documents the *mansi* of these regions are usually identified by reference to their four adjacent boundaries, which proves that they were all of a piece—such descriptions are rarely found in areas of long-furlong fields. In Limousin, where the course of this development is particularly easy to trace, we find that the Carolingian *manse* nearly always gave rise to a hamlet, which may first be mentioned by name very early in the Middle Ages. Some of these names have survived into the present; the two *manses* of Verdinas and Roudersas, mentioned in a deed of partition dated 20 June 626, still retain their identity as dependencies of a small commune in the department of Creuse.[9]

---

[8] There is an interesting and important piece of work waiting to be done on *manses* situated en bloc (identifiable by reference to four adjacent boundaries). Somewhat to my surprise I found one at Oscheret in Burgundy: Pérard, *Recueil de pièces curieuses*, 1664, p. 155.

[9] F. Lot, in *Mélanges d'histoire offerts à H. Pirenne*, 1926, p. 308. For an example of a *manse* lying all in one piece from western France, see *Cartulaire de la cathédrale d'Angers*, ed. Urseau, No. XX. There is need for a study of the Breton *ran*, which was perhaps analogous to the *manse*.

In these areas of poor soil and light settlement, the family cell emerged as a separate entity instead of mingling with the rest as part of an amorphous mass. (Pl. XVII).

The antithesis between two types of *manse*, the one fragmented, the other all of a piece, is reflected in their contrasting fortunes.

If we ignore regions of enclosure, it can be said that from the beginning of the Middle Ages the *manse* was already in a state of dissolution. It was no longer indivisible, which in practice meant that it was ceasing to exist. Everywhere portions were being detached by alienation or by some other means. This process may have started as early as the sixth century, when we find Gregory of Tours remarking that 'the division of possessions' made it difficult to levy the land tax. It was certainly in full swing by the time of Charles the Bald; an edict of his reign dated 25 June 864, complains that the *coloni* have taken to selling the lands of their *manses*, retaining only the dwelling-house. Evidently the alienation of the unit as a whole would not have been considered grounds for reproof. The evil came from breaking up the *manse*, to the 'destruction' and 'confusion' of *seigneuries*; rents could no longer be levied in due form. The edict goes on to enjoin the restoration to the *manses* of any portions detached without seigneurial consent. Vain hope! At much this same period, there was a *villa* in the Parisis where 11 out of the 32 men sharing in the cultivation of the 12 free *manses* were living outside the *seigneurie*.[10] It was probably this erosion, and the subsequent increase in the number of tenures which were not *manses*, which in 866 prompted the government to make its first attempt at taxing the *hospitia*, hitherto regarded as negligible. There had already been some tentative efforts at raising certain extraordinary levies by households (*casatae*) rather than *manses*.[11]

From the eleventh century the *manse* was so fragmented that it gradually vanished altogether. Admittedly the timing of its disappearance varied with the region and place, and no doubt these differences will one day emerge even more clearly, as a

[10] *Polyptyque des Fossés*, c. 14.

[11] The meaning of *casata*=household is pin-pointed for us by a letter of Pope Zacharias, in which it is used explicitly as a synonym for *conjugio servorum* (*servus* here has the general sense of a dependant of a *seigneurie*); cf. E. Lesne, *Histoire de la propriété ecclésiastique*, ii, 1, 1922, p. 41 ff.

result of more detailed investigations. In Anjou a clear distinction was being made between *manse* and *borde* as early as 1040; the same can be said of Roussillon in the twelfth century, although there the meaning of the distinction seems to have remained less clearly understood. In 1135 there is mention of a *demi-manse* at Villeneuve-le-Roi in the Parisis. In 1158 rents at Prisches in Hainault were being assessed by the *manse* or *demi-manse*, as they were at Limoges and Fourches (to the south of Paris) between 1162 and 1190. At Bouzonville and Bouilly (Orléanais) the rule was upheld in 1234 that *masures* could only be divided into equal fractions, never more than five; *masure* is here equivalent to *manse*, since it denotes the entire holding, including the fields. As late as the fifteenth century the Burgundian Castellany of Sémur still harboured the vague tradition that the *manse* was something indivisible.[12] But such cases were by now exceptional, and had been for some time past; soon they would disappear altogether. In future—broadly speaking this had been so from the twelfth century—every separate parcel would be saddled with responsibility for its own rent, every house with its own poultry dues and every man or household with his own services. By the same token, there was an end to stability and fixed relationships between the tenures, which could now be increased or subdivided at the will of their possessors, subject only to the rule that alienation required seigneurial assent, now more and more rarely withheld.

This progressive disintegration of the primitive agrarian unit, under whatever name, was to some extent a European phenomenon. But in England and Germany the process was far more gradual than in the open countryside of France. When the English hide finally disappeared (mentions of it are still fairly frequent even in the thirteenth century) it left behind a graduated system of tenures based on the virgate and bovate, a quarter and eighth of a hide respectively. In Germany the *Hufe* also survived into the thirteenth century and in some places later; it was often succeeded by tenures which although

---

[12] Bibl. Nat., nouv. acqu. lat. 1930, fol. 28 v° (Anjou); Tardif, *Cartons des rois*, No. 415 and Arch. Nat. S 2072, No. 13 (Villeneuve-le-Roi); *Revue belge de philologie et d'histoire*, 1923, p. 337 (Prisches Arch. Loiret, H. 30², p. 438 and Arch. du Cher, *fonds* Saint-Benoît-sur-Loire, unclassified cartulary, fol. 409 v° (communicated by MM. Prou and Vidier; Bouzonville and Bouilly); Flour de Saint Genis, in *Bullet. du Comité des trav. historiques, Section des sc. écon.*, 1896, p. 87 (Semur).

more disproportionate amongst themselves were still indivisible, produced by the operation of inheritance laws (some of which are still in force) which secured the succession on a single claimant. In France peasant tenures knew no such restrictions, except on certain Breton *seigneuries*, where they operated in favour of the youngest son.[13] In short, over much of France from the twelfth century the *seigneurie* and the rural community were no longer beautiful well-ordered structures, arranged in neat compartments. Broadly speaking it could be said that the *manse*, under all its different names, was a European institution; it was only in France that its demise was premature and without issue.

The reasons for the metamorphosis must be deep-seated, touching the life of society at its roots. We know all too little of the history of the medieval family. However, it is possible to discern a slow evolution, starting in the early Middle Ages. The kindred, that is to say the group related by blood, was still a powerful factor. But its boundaries were becoming blurred, while the legal obligations binding on its members tended to become mere moral constraints, little more than habit. Prosecution of a vendetta was still expected by public opinion, but there were no precise laws detailing joint responsibility in criminal matters, whether active or passive. There was still plenty of life in the habit of preserving the family holding intact, to be worked in common by fathers and sons, brothers, or even cousins; but it was nothing more than a habit, since individual ownership was fully recognised by law and custom and the only established right enjoyed by the kindred was the privilege of pre-emption when a holding came on the market. This loss of definition at the edges and the sapping of its legal force hastened the disintegration of the kindred as a group. Where communal life had once been broadly based on the vast patriarchal family, there was now an increasing tendency to concentrate on the conjugal family, a narrower community formed from the descendants of a married couple still living. It is hardly surprising that the fixed territorial framework of the old

[13] There are similar examples from the Netherlands. Cf. G. des Marez, *Le problème de la colonisation franque*, 1926, p. 165. For some tentative and not altogether successful attempts at establishing fixed tenures in Lorraine see C. Guyot, 'Le *Lehn* de Vergaville', in *Journal de la Société d'archéologie lorraine*, 1886.

patriarchal community should have disappeared at the same time. From the Carolingian period onward it is common to find *manses* in the occupation of several households who each kept their own hearths and may have had no connection with one another apart from the joint fiscal responsibility imposed on them by their lord: on the *seigneurie* of Boissy, a dependency of Saint-Germain-des-Prés, we find as many as 182 hearths for 81 *manses*. This is evidence of a disintegration from within. But at this period the *manse* was still maintained as an indivisible entity, after a fashion, by the use made of it by state and seigneurial authorities. The first of these props was soon to be removed. In contrast with England, where a system of taxation based on the hide was in force until well into the twelfth century and must have contributed to its survival, in Gaul all attempts at public taxation ceased at the beginning of the tenth century. As for the lords, their failure to keep alive the old unit of assessment can be explained by the decisive changes introduced into their methods of exploitation between the tenth and twelfth centuries as a consequence of the decline in labour rents, in itself something peculiar to France. There was no point in adhering to the system of assessing dues by *manses* when the substance of the charges had so greatly altered. The old *polyptiques* bristled with antiquated regulations whose very language had now become well-nigh incomprehensible, as was noted by the monk who copied or summarised the *polyptique* of Saint-Père de Chartres in the late eleventh century; since they were no longer consulted, these inventories ceased to perpetuate the norms of a past age. To sum up, it seems that a number of weighty if slightly mysterious happenings lie behind the superficially trivial fact that in the eleventh century estate surveys are arranged by *manses*, in the thirteenth or seventeenth centuries by fields or households: the reduction of the family to a narrower and more changeable compass, the total disappearance of public taxation, and a radical transformation in the internal organisation of the *seigneurie* must all have played their part.

These remarks, however, apply primarily to regions where the *manse* was made up of a multiplicity of scattered fields and had no clear definition on the ground. Essentially arbitrary, such units were naturally fragile. But in enclosed regions, where the *manse* was all of a piece, its division into separate holdings did not necessarily entail its disappearance. The evidence from Limousin again illustrates the point: the *manse* of Carolingian times, standing alone in open country, was the progenitor of a number of equally isolated hamlets, since each conjugal family built its own dwelling and claimed its own share of the land. The same is true of Norway, where nucleated settlements were also unknown; here too it can be shown that the dispersal of the primitive patriarchal community was in more than one instance followed by the dissolution of the *settegaard*, the huge ancestral estate, into a number of independent homesteads.[14] Even so, the Limousin hamlet retained its ancient designation, *mas*, which has lasted into our own times. In the eyes of the seigneurial administration this was still its correct title, since the occupants were collectively responsible for the charges (Pl. XVII). In the same way, the mountainous region of Languedoc until quite recently still possessed its *mas* or *mazades*, hamlets whose *parsonniers* had remained for centuries in joint possession of the soil. But even here disintegration finally set in. By the time we reach the eighteenth century communal ownership seems as a rule confined to the woodland and waste; the arable has been divided up. And although joint responsibility for the Limousin *mas* was kept alive from above, the actual economic unit was henceforth the family in the narrower meaning of the word.[15]

We have seen that the familial community had nearly everywhere made the transition from *manse* to simple household, an association often described as 'implicit', since it came into being without any written instrument; such associations were also known as *'freresche'*, meaning an association of brothers. The children continued to live with their parents even after marriage and on their parents' death frequently remained together, sharing 'hearth and home', working and possessing the land in

---

[14] Magnus Olsen, *Farms and Fanes of Ancient Norway*, 1928, p. 48.

[15] The information about the *mas* of Limousin is based on notes communicated by M. A. Petit and on my own researches. On the *mazades* see the article (otherwise very inadequate) by J. Bauby, *Recueil de l'Académie de legislation de Toulouse*, xxxiv. Brittany also appears to have its hamlets of 'parsonniers'; but they may have had their origin in ordinary family communities of the type to be studied *infra*; little attention has been given to this question, but see *Annales de Bretagne*, xxi, 195.

common. Sometimes friends formed an association of this kind, under a contract of fictitious brotherhood (*affrairement*).[16] Several generations lived together under the same roof: a deputy to the Estates-General in 1484 cited an instance of ten couples and seventy persons living in a house in the region of Caen, which was in any case a thickly populated area.[17] This habit of living in common was so widespread that it became the basis of *mainmorte*, one of the fundamental institutions of French serfdom. Conversely, it was the thought of *mainmorte* that deterred servile families from dividing their properties; if the community was broken up, there was all the more danger that the inheritance would devolve on the lord at some future date. Where taxes were levied by hearths, fear of increased contributions to the fisc also acted as a restraint on the multiplication of separate dwellings. Yet although so firmly established, these small collectives contained no element of coercion or immutability. Individuals of an independent turn of mind could, and did, detach both themselves and their fields; in the Middle Ages they were known as *foris familiarii*, 'dismissed from bread and board'; sometimes this was a punishment, but often it was done of a man's own free will. It was inevitable that the day should come when the hive separated out into a number of different swarms. The 'implicit' community lacked the supporting framework of land whose indivisibility was protected by law.

In time the habit of communal living also disappeared, slowly, as is the way with habits, and at dates which differed widely according to the region. Around Paris the practice appears to have virtually died out before the sixteenth century. In Berry, Maine and Limousin and in a whole sector of Poitou it was still very much alive on the eve of the Revolution. A comprehensive study which did justice to these contrasts would throw a flood of light on a subject of burning interest, as yet too little understood, namely the regional diversities of French social structure. Even as things are, one feature emerges in clear relief: like the *manse*, the familial community maintained itself with marked tenacity in regions of dispersed settlement. There are seigneurial maps from Poitou, on the outskirts of the Massif Central, which show the soil divided into *frereches* as late

[16] C. De Ribbe, *La société provençale*, 387; R. Latouche, *La vie en Bas-Quercy*, 432.
[17] Jehan Masselin, *Journal des Etats Généraux*, ed. A. Bernier, 1835, pp. 582-4.

as the eighteenth century.[18] In a few cases fragmentation has resulted in the birth of separate hamlets, since the dissolution of these older associations always brought about an increase in the number of dwellings, each couple wishing to live under their own roof.[19] In districts with no experience of large villages family holdings have sometimes survived into our own day. It is no accident that the Agrafeil and Arnal who figure in the novels of Eugene Leroy and André Chamson are respectively natives of Périgord and the Cévennes.

To return to the open-field regions. Here the emergence and eventual disappearance of groups working in common had an important influence on the actual make-up of the fields. The ritual chorus of complaint against fragmentation as the scourge of effective husbandry in this country, which was first raised by eighteenth century economists to be taken up by their successors in the nineteenth and twentieth centuries, is familiar enough. Over the past hundred years it has usually been accompanied by scathing denunciation of the naked ineptitude of the *Code Civile*, regarded as the root of all evil because it countenanced the division of inheritances into equal parts. Had heirs been content to distribute an estate among themselves in complete parcels, the consequences would not have been so serious. But in their thirst for equality, each demanded his share of each field, so there was no end to the process of fragmentation. There is no denying the serious inconvenience caused by breaking up the land in this way, nor that it has been one of the greatest stumbling blocks to the rationalisation of French agriculture. But the practice of division among heirs cannot be made to bear the full responsibility. Fragmentation goes back to the earliest days of the occupation of our soil; the farmers of the Neolithic Age may well have been its first practitioners. Successive partitions certainly aggravated its effects. But the *Code Civile* introduced no innovations, since it merely followed the old provincial customs in which heirs were usually on an equal footing; in contrast with the practice in England, in France the right of primogeniture applied only to the nobility, and even then was

[18] See the very odd maps of Oyre and Antogne (perhaps eighteenth century?) in the Archives of Vienne, *série de plans*.

[19] For some excellent observations on this subject see L. Lacrocq, *Monographie de la commune de La Celle-Dunoise*, 1926.

far less overriding than is sometimes supposed. Moreover, there was no part of France where property could be freely devised by will, and wills were in any case a rarity in country districts. There can be no denying that the break-up of holdings has made considerable progress in more recent centuries, nor that the pace has increased with the approach of more modern times. But this has not been the result of legal changes, for the laws altered nothing. The responsibility must rest with changes in the social order. In the days when heirs lived together as a *freresche* they had no reason to divide up the fields constituting their patrimony, which were already narrow and scattered enough. It was the gradual dissolution of the old familial associations which brought about an increase in the number of parcels on the arable and of dwellings in the village. The point is once again brought home to us that changes in the material aspects of rural life are always a reflection of changes in human societies.

## 2. THE RURAL COMMUNITY: THE COMMONS

The individuals and families who cultivated the same ground and whose houses stood close to one another in the same hamlet or village were not separate individuals and separate families, living side by side. They were neighbours, *voisins*—in Frankish times this was their official title, as it has always been in Gascony—linked by economic and sentimental ties and forming the small society of the 'rural community' which was the ancestor of most of the communes—or communal subdivisions —existing in our own day.

Admittedly, the word 'community' is rarely found in any document prior to the thirteenth century. These older records have much to say of *seigneuries* as collective units, but hardly ever refer to the inhabitants as a body. Can this be taken to imply that there was a period when the *seigneurie* completely stifled the collective life of the group? Some have thought so. But negative evidence is of value in historical matters only on one condition: that the silence of the texts is caused by the absence of facts rather than witnesses. In this case it is the witnesses who are lacking. Nearly all our sources are seigneurial;

few communities kept any records before the sixteenth century. What is more, for centuries the mainstream of community life ran parallel with that of public law; these were *de facto* associations long before they acquired a legal personality. As Jacques Flach has said, the village was for centuries 'an anonymous actor' in the midst of our societies. But there are plentiful indications that it was alive and vigorous.

The territorial limits of a rural community were those containing the land subject to the various rules of communal husbandry (which dealt with temporary cultivation, grazing on the commons, dates of harvests etc.) and to the performance of collective services for the benefit of the group as a whole; its boundaries were especially clear-cut in unenclosed regions where nucleated settlement was the rule. The *seigneurie* consisted, amongst other things, of the land subject to the payment of rents and services to a single lord, and over which he exercised his rights to aid and his power to coerce. Were the two coterminous ? Sometimes, as in the new settlements, they must have been. But this was not always or even most frequently the case. Naturally our information is fullest for more recent periods, when very many of the older *seigneuries* had already been broken up by alienations and, still more frequently, by subinfeudation. But even in Frankish times a *villa* often contained *manses* dispersed over different villages. The same is true of all the countries of Europe where the seigneurial regime was in operation. If it is true that we should regard the Frankish and French lords as the latter-day heirs of the ancient village chieftains, we should add that it was apparently possible for a number of separate authorities to flourish side by side in the same place. This simple topographical observation is in itself sufficient refutation of the idea that the rural community could ever have been completely absorbed by the *seigneurie*. Conscious of its unity, the rural group could react just as vigorously as any urban community to the break-up of a *seigneurie*. For example, the lands and village of Hermonville in Champagne came to be divided among eight or nine sub-fiefs, each with its own court; but from 1320 at latest the inhabitants appointed their own communal officers to enforce agrarian discipline, irrespective of *seigneurie*.[20]

[20] G. Robert, in *Travaux de l'Acad. de Reims*, cxxvi, 257.

It was above all in dealing with its enemies that the small rural collective not only became more conscious of its own identity but also gradually forced society as a whole to accept it as a viable and living institution.

The principal targets for opposition, which was often accompanied by violence, were the masters. 'How many serfs have killed their lords and burned their castles!' exclaims Jacques de Vitry in the thirteenth century. Flemish[21] 'slaves' whose plotting was denounced in a capitulary of 821, Norman peasants massacred around the year 1000 by the ducal host, peasants of the Sénonais who in 1315 elected a 'king' and 'pope' as their commanders, Jacques and Tuchins in the time of the Hundred Years' War, the peasant leagues in Dauphiné massacred at Moirans in 1580, the '*Tards Avisés*' of Périgord under Henry IV, the Breton *croquants* strung up by 'the good Duke' of Chaulnes, the incendiaries of castles and archives in the blazing summer of 1789—all were so many links (and many have been omitted) in a long and tragic chain. Shocked and surprised, Taine described the last act of the drama, the upheavals he witnessed in 1789, as 'spontaneous anarchy'. But there was nothing novel about this 'anarchy'. What appeared a newly-minted outrage in the eyes of the ill-instructed philosopher was little more than the recurrence of a traditional phenomenon which had long been endemic. The forms rebellion took (and they were nearly always the same) were also traditional: mystical fantasies; a powerful preoccupation with the primitive egalitarianism of the Gospels, which took hold of humble minds well before the Reformation; lists of grievances in which precise and often far-reaching proposals were mingled with a host of petty complaints and often quite ludicrous suggestions for reform (the Breton *Code päisant* of 1675 called indiscriminately for the abolition of tithes, to be replaced by a fixed stipend for parish priests, for limitations on hunting rights and seigneurial monopolies and for the distribution of tobacco with the blessed bread at Mass, purchased with money raised from taxation, 'for the satisfaction of the parishioners.')[22] Finally, at the head of these 'stiff-necked' yokels as the old texts describe them, as leaders of this stubborn people who were

[21] Jacques de Vitry, *Exempla*, ed. Crane, 1890, p. 64, No. cxliii.
[22] La Borderie, *La revolte du papier timbré*, 1884, pp. 93 ff.

'unwilling', as Alain Chartier said, 'to suffer the subjection of the *seigneurie*', one nearly always finds a few country priests, whose plight was often no better than that of their parishioners but whose minds could better encompass the idea that their miseries were part of a general ill; in a word, men well-fitted to play the time-honoured role of the intellectual by acting as leaven in the long-suffering masses. None of these traits is specifically French; they are common to peasant revolts all over Europe. A social system is characterised not only by its internal structure but also by the reactions it produces; a system based on authority at times may result in the sincere performance of mutual obligations, at others in a brutal outbreak of hostility on both sides. To the historian, whose task is merely to observe and explain the connections between phenomena, agrarian revolt is as natural to the seigneurial regime as strikes, let us say, are to large-scale capitalism.

Almost invariably doomed to defeat and eventual massacre, the great insurrections were altogether too disorganised to achieve any lasting result. The patient, silent struggles stubbornly carried on by rural communities over the years would accomplish more than these flashes in the pan. During the Middle Ages the consolidation of the village as a group and its recognition by the outside world was a constant preoccupation of peasant life. These goals were sometimes achieved by concentrating on the village in its ecclesiastical aspect. The parish, whose territory in some places was co-extensive with that of a single community although in others it might embrace several, had one or other of the local lords as its master; he was in the habit of appointing the priest, either directly or by nomination to the bishop, and of appropriating some part of the dues which should have gone towards the maintenance of church services. But it was precisely because the lord was more concerned to profit from these dues than to employ them for their proper ends that the parishioners were able to take his place and undertake what he neglected, in particular the up-keep of the church. The church was the only really large and solid structure in the village, towering above the huddle of dwellings; might not the House of God serve also as a house for the people? Meetings for the discussion of communal affairs were held in the church—except when men preferred to gather under the shade of the elm tree at the crossroads or among the grass of the cemetery; at times the church was used for the storage of surplus produce, to the great indignation of academic theologians; in time of danger it was the place of refuge, a centre of resistance even. The men of the Middle Ages found it easier than we do to treat sacred things with a familiarity from which reverence was not excluded. Many places started, at latest in the thirteenth century, to elect 'parochial church councils' or 'fabrics', which had official ecclesiastical sanction; here was yet another opportunity for the inhabitants to meet and debate their common affairs, in short, to become aware of the solidarity of their common interests.[23]

These parochial organisations were formed to serve well-defined ends and were frankly official in character; the religious confraternity, more spontaneous and more flexible, was an even better training-ground for communal action. For the confraternity not only provided for the spiritual needs of its members but also directed their attention towards common courses of action, which might include quasi-revolutionary activities for which the confraternity was a kind of 'front'. An association of this kind was formed about 1270 by the people of Louvres, to the north of Paris. Even in its avowed aims, which were innocent enough, this confraternity went well beyond simple acts of piety: in addition to their irreproachable intention of building a church and paying off the parish debts, they aimed to maintain the roads and wells of the parish. But this was not all. They also promised to 'preserve the rights of the village', by defending them against the lord's bailiffs (their lord was in fact the king). The members were bound together by oath, possessed a communal chest which was fed by contributions paid in corn, ignored seigneurial justice and elected 'masters' to settle disputes. Disregarding the fact that law enforcement was also a seigneurial monopoly, they issued their own police regulations, whose contravention was punished by a fine. Any inhabitant who jibbed at joining the association was

[23] In 1660 treasurers of parish fabrics in Normandy took part in the election of deputies to represent the Third Estate in the provincial Estates; cf. M. Baudot, *Le Moyen Age*, 1929, p. 257. We find parishioners taking part in the financial administration of the church even before parochial councils were formally constituted, for an example see B. Guérard, *Cartulaire de Saint-Père de Chartres*, ii, 281, No. xxi (early twelfth century).

boycotted; men refused to work for him, a time-honoured weapon in village hostilities.[24]

But these were devious methods. Essentially secular by nature, it was only as a secular group that the rural community could hope to achieve the status of a corporate person.

Such medieval villages as reached this goal were inspired by a movement of urban origin. During the eleventh, twelfth and thirteenth centuries there were many towns where the burgesses had joined together under an oath of mutual aid: as we have already noted, this was a truly revolutionary step, whose implications had not escaped notice by upholders of the hierarchical order. For this was a new type of bond, a departure from the old oaths of fidelity and homage in that it created an obligation among equals, instead of perpetuating ties of dependence. This sworn association or *amitié* took the name *commune*; where its members were sufficiently powerful and adroit (and favoured by circumstances) the group and its rights received recognition under a formal charter granted by the lord. Now town and country were by no means separate worlds. The links between the two were numerous: there are instances both of intervention by individual townsmen in rural affairs, as in the case of the burgesses of Paris who negotiated the enfranchisement of the rural serfs belonging to the Chapter of Notre Dame in the time of Louis VII, and of group action, as when the liberation from serfdom of the royal villages in the Orléanais and of the city of Orleans itself, in the reign of Louis VII, was effected under the same charter and no doubt at common expense. Moreover, the dividing line between town and village was usually far from distinct: we have only to think of the many small market towns and centres of industry which were more than semi-agricultural. In their turn, not a few purely rural settlements tried to turn themselves into *communes* —more, probably, than we shall ever know, since most of the attempts foundered and so escape notice. We only know of the tentative efforts at forming rural *communes* in the Île de France during the thirteenth century because they were forbidden by the lords. A handful of peasants planted in open country lacked the numbers, the resources and the unyielding solidarity of a

[24] *Layette du Trésor des Chartes*, v, No. 876.

merchant community packed shoulder to shoulder behind its town walls. Yet here and there a few villages, or leagues of villages—federation was a means of compensating for numerical weakness—won for themselves a charter of recognition as a *commune*. In the lands of the *Langue d'Oc*, where *communes* were always more of a rarity, towns which had achieved a measure of autonomy were known from the thirteenth century as *consulats*. Among the *consulats* (especially in the fourteenth and fifteenth centuries) we find a large number of communities which were more rural than urban, sometimes even pure villages: these were often of the type so common in the Midi, villages arranged round a public square and possessing the aspect and outlook of a small town.[25] The community which achieved the status of *commune* or *consulat* became a permanent body, which did not die with its members for the time being; when jurists of the thirteenth century started to reconstruct the theory of legal personality on the Roman model, they recognised the *commune* as a collective entity, a *universitas*. The *commune* had its own seal, which was the mark of its legal identity, and its own magistrates, appointed by the inhabitants under more or less effective seigneurial control. In short, the *commune* as an association had won a place for itself in the legal sun.

But most villages never rose to this height. The charters of enfranchisement granted by lords in fairly large numbers from the twelfth century onwards were not charters setting up a *commune*. What these charters did was to fix ancient custom, often with some modification in favour of the peasants; they did not result in the birth of a corporate person. There were indeed jurists such as Gui Foucoi, afterwards Pope Clement IV, who could maintain, as he did in 1257, that 'every collection of men inhabiting the same settlement' should necessarily be regarded as a *universitas*, capable of electing representatives.[26] This liberal interpretation was not generally followed. For a long time to come, communities without a charter of incorporation

[25] Village *consulats* were largely peculiar to Languedoc; but many Provençal rural communities early attained corporate status under the name '*syndicat*'. The village of the Midi,—the *oppidum* of Mediterranean lands—was very different from the Northern type.
[26] E. Bligny-Bondurand, *Les coutumes de Saint-Gilles*, 1915, p. 183; for the towns cf. the argument put forward in the name of the citizens of Lyons, *Olim*, i, 933, No. xxiv.

had to be content with an ephemeral existence in the eyes of the law. Suppose the inhabitants of such a village had some common business to transact—the negotiation of a franchise from their lord, for example—or felt aggrieved by some injury. In such cases it was recognised (officially from the thirteenth century at latest, in practice much earlier) that they had a right, by a majority decision, to conclude an agreement, authorise expenditure or embark on a legal action—which even when directed against seigneurial justice might well have a friendly reception in the royal courts—and that they were entitled to elect proxies known as proctors or syndics for any of these purposes. Logically, both decisions and mandates should have affected only those who voted them. However, Beaumanoir, the most illustrious of the thirteenth century jurists, was prepared to accept that the will of the majority was binding on the whole community. But always on one condition: that the majority included some of the wealthier members. This was no doubt partly so that the poor should not be in a position to oppress the '*mieus soufisans*', the 'better-off'; but it was also in line with the policy of linking representation with a property qualification which was generally adopted by the monarchy in its dealings with urban groups and was to determine the attitude of the government towards rural assemblies down to the end of the *Ancien Régime*. This lack of precision in the law is reflected in the difficulty of finding a proper name for these temporary associations. There was a parish in Champagne, comprising five villages, whose inhabitants were in the habit of acting in concert; in 1365 four of these villages fell out with the fifth and found themselves in serious difficulties because they had been rash enough to describe their association by the words *corps* (meaning corporate body) and *commune*. They had to explain to the Parlement that their purpose in using these words, which were not meant to be taken literally, was simply to underline as best they might that their association was something more than a collection of individuals.[27] All the same, from quite an early date we find legal records in the habit of designating the 'companies' who were a party to a suit by a special name, instead of merely referring to them as 'X, Y and Z,

[27] G. Robert, *L'abbaye de Saint-Thierry et les communautés populaires au moyen-âge*, 1930 (extract from *Travaux de l'Acad. Nationale de Reims*, cxlii, 60).

residents of such and such a place', which would have implied a complete absence of any legal personality; they are described not, indeed, as *communes*, but as the 'community' of the place, a formula already pregnant with meaning. But once the action was concluded, the proctors or syndics fell back into their place among the crowd and the group lost its external identity—or at least went into hibernation.

Gradually, however, these representative institutions—assemblies of inhabitants, proctors or syndics—acquired a more permanent form. In many cases the initiative came from seigneurial officials, who found it convenient to enlist peasant help in such tasks as apportioning the payment of tallage and similar taxes among the various households. Royal tax officials followed suit; a central authority was almost bound to rely on local groups if it was to avoid being held to ransom by the lords. In the days before the final triumph of feudal anarchy the Carolingian monarchy had already tried to make locally elected *jurés* responsible for surveillance of the coinage and of weights and measures.[28] When the monarchical government was once again re-established in France, as the administrative authorities developed they came increasingly to rely on the local communities for help in matters concerning police, militia and finance. This meant that the activities of these local bodies had to be regulated from above. Under the *Ancien Régime*, particularly in the eighteenth century when the history of our bureaucracy properly begins, a whole series of ordinances was issued (many of them directed to particular regions and enforced with variable efficiency) which laid down rules governing assemblies, usually in a sense favourable to the more prosperous peasants, and provided for permanent representation. There were now two authorities in charge of the local bodies, the lord and the intendant. The lord still had some say in whether local inhabitants were allowed to hold a meeting, though the legal position varied with the region: custom in Basse-Auvergne decreed that his consent was necessary, in Haute-Auvergne that it was not. The former rule was the more usual—except in cases where the king's representative had already given his consent, a solution already foreshadowed in the jurisprudence of the later Capetian period.[29] It was often the rule that decisions could only be carried into effect after they had been ratified by a court of law or, again, by the intendant. Where so much uncertainty prevailed and the different authorities conflicted, the village was often the gainer. But it is also true that by insinuating themselves into the official legal structure the villages subjected themselves to some fairly narrow limitations. This was the price they had to pay for full membership of the honourable society of bodies corporate.

It had taken centuries for the rural community to force open this door. But they had not waited for anyone's permission before forming a community: indeed, some sort of clearly visible community was implicit in the whole tenor of medieval agrarian life. All that remained was to reveal its existence.

Consider, for example, the pressure brought to bear in open-field regions by the discipline of collective obligations such as communal grazing, compulsory crop rotation, and prohibition on enclosure. Admittedly, when these rules were infringed the case was not judged by the villagers. After the disappearance of the Frankish judicial system, medieval France knew only two sorts of tribunals, those of the king and those of the lord. But until the moment arrived when judgment by peers was finally recognised as a privilege confined to the nobility, there can be no doubt that peasants frequently sat in judgment in seigneurial courts: even well into the thirteenth century, when the trend towards single judges was already pronounced, the *maire* of the Chapter of Paris at Orly was not allowed to give judgment until he had taken the advice of 'good men', and these must have been workers on the estate.[30] But these *ad hoc* judges were acting on

---

[29] In March 1320 the Parlement anulled the appointment of proctors by the villagers of Thiais, Choisy, Grignon, Antony and Villeneuve-Saint-Georges on the ground that they were neither corporation nor commune and should therefore first have obtained the consent of their lord, the abbot of Saint-Germain-des-Prés; at the same time the Parlement reserved the right of the court to act in place of the lord in such a situation if the lord had defaulted—a decision which clearly opens the way for quite large-scale interventions. (Arch. Nat. L 809, No. 69). It is much to be hoped that a legal historian will one day trace the history of this aspect of the law; there is no lack of documents, but until they have been worked over it is only possible to venture on vague and probably erroneous generalisations, while this a subject where fact and theory intertwine. Cf. another episode involving Saint-Germain-des-Prés, dated 1339, Arch. Nat., K 1169A No. 47 bis.

[30] B. Guérard, *Cartulaire de Notre-Dame de Paris*, ii, 17.

behalf of the lord, not the community. At places and periods where the ancient custom of private distraint was still observed there was general agreement that a group which had suffered damage of a specified type was entitled to take reprisals. As late as the thirteenth century, if the inhabitants of Valenton (near Paris) found an alien flock of sheep trespassing on their water-meadows, they were allowed to impound one of them, slit its throat and eat it.[31] But as time went on these violent distraints came to be replaced by the taking of pledges, as the first stage in a legal action which would be concluded before the regular tribunals. In law, with the exception of certain villages enjoying unusual privileges, the right to punish was reserved to the lord whose authority over the place was paramount, though he was sometimes required to release part of the fine to the injured community, whose natural inclination (as in many of the more rudimentary urban societies) was to drink up the money at the local tavern.[32]

We have spoken of rules: but who made the rules? The truth is that they were 'made' by no-one; they were customary, received by the group as tradition. Moreover these customs were so ingrained, so much part of a fully articulated system at once legal and material, that they were accepted as belonging to the nature of things. However, there were occasions when the old order stood in need of amendment or additions: for example, the arrangements for grazing, by which different *quartiers* in turn were reserved for the draught-animals; settling the order of the courses on a sector newly won from the waste, or the rotation over a whole precinct; fixing the dates, necessarily variable, for harvest and vintage. Whose was the decisive voice?

It is impossible to give an answer which will be consistently valid even for any single period or region. It is true that in law the final authority, the *ban*, rested exclusively with the lord. The towns had with great difficulty managed to arrogate part of this authority to themselves; the villages were rarely, if ever, so successful. But in practice, perhaps simply as a matter of convenience, the lord often allowed the group certain initiatives;

---

[31] Arch. Nat., L L 1043, fol. 149 v° (1291). Cf. the ruling of 1211 for Maisons, S 1171, n. 16 (taking pledges as a substitute for slaughter).
[32] Arch. de la Moselle, B 6337 (Longeville, 18 Dec. 1738; Many, 8 Sept. 1760).

and this concession was no doubt of such antiquity that it had taken on the force of law, simply from having been countenanced for so long. The distribution of functions between the lord and the community was dictated by local conditions. In 1536 the monks of Cîteaux tried to change the customary date for grazing the meadows at Gilly; the villagers went to court and refused them permission. In 1356 the squire of Bruyères-le-Châtel near Paris settled the date of the vintage by his own unaided decision. At Montévrein, not far away, the date was fixed by the peasants, on condition that the lord's consent was obtained; and at Vermenton in Auxerrois in 1775 the lord's agent (the lord was the king) was unsuccessful in his attempt to wrest this right from the assembly.[33] The customs governing the appointment of certain officers are especially significant. Occasionally we find peasants even taking a share in appointing the officials who acted for the lord in collecting their dues and meting out justice; but although common in England, in France this arrangement was very unusual. Much more frequently the peasants were allowed a say in the choice of the petty rural officials. We find the villagers of Champhol near Chartres choosing the baker for the seigneurial bakehouse from the beginning of the twelfth century; in 1307 the villagers of Neuilly-sous-Clermont appointed the communal cowherd; at Rungis, in May 1241, the lord's bailiff had the appointment of vine-wards, but he first consulted both the lord and the villagers. At Pontoy in Lorraine during the eighteenth century two out of the three rural policemen were chosen by the villagers, the third by the lord. To make up for this, the lord and abbot of Longeville, very close to Pontoy, insisted that it was his right to 'appoint the fiddlers for the feasts of all the villages in the *seigneurie*'.[34] To sum up, while the principle of seigneurial authority was preserved, notwithstanding quirks of the kind just mentioned, in practice group action in these petty but very

[33] *Revue bourguigonne d'enseignement supérieur*, 1893, p. 407; L. Merlet and A. Moutié, *Cartulaire de Notre-Dame des Vaux-de-Cernay*, ii, 1858, No. 1062; Arch. Nat., L 781 No. 12 and LL 1026, fol. 127 v° and 308; *Bulletin de la soc. des sciences historiques . . . de l'Yonne*, xxx (1876), Pt. i, p. 93.

[34] L. Delisle, *Etudes sur la condition de la classe agricole*, 105, and *Olim* III, 1, p. 98, No. xlvii; *Cartulaire de Saint-Père de Chartres*, ii, 1307, No. liv; Arch. de Seine et Oise, H. Maubuisson, 54; Bibl. de Ste Geneviève, ms. 356, p. 154; Arch. de la Moselle, B 6337.

important questions of rural discipline was always a powerful factor.

Nor, when occasion arose, did the group hesitate to go beyond legal precedent or even to act in direct contravention of the law. This was particularly so in the regions of long-furlong fields, committed by ancient tradition and their own agrarian make-up to a communal way of life which could easily become tyrannical. We have already seen that the weight of public opinion, buttressed when necessary by more violent measures, must often have been a major factor in the enforcement of collective obligations. But what must be quite the most significant expression of this truly indomitable spirit of solidarity among the rural proletariat is a custom of relatively recent origin, in its purest form confined to the plains of Picardy and Flanders, although there are traces of something similar elsewhere, especially in Lorraine: this is the custom known sometimes as *droit de marché* (a 'right', that is, for the peasants, a violation in the eyes of the law) and sometimes by less complimentary names, such as '*mauvais gré*' or '*haine de cens*' ('ill-will', 'rent-hatred') of which the Flemish equivalent is *haet van pacht*.[35] This practice worked counter to that of granting temporary leases; while the temporary lease was a product of economic evolution, *droit de marché* was a reversion to the old notions of perpetuity and heritability, which in the past had secured the customary permanence of tenures. A landed proprietor might be hoping to conserve his estates by concluding contracts for a limited term. But when a lease expired he was in for trouble if he refused to renew it in favour of the former tenant, and on almost the same conditions. Even worse trouble was in store for the new tenant, if such could be found: he was usually a stranger to the village, since the natives neither wished nor dared to play the part of 'interloper'. Both landlord and tenant were likely to pay dearly for their infringement of what

[35] In addition see the regional monographs by J. Lefort, 1892; F. Debouvry, 1899; C. Boulanger, 1906. I have taken some phrases from the memoranda and edicts published by Boulanger, others from E. de la Poix de Fréminville, *Traité— général du gouvernement des biens et affaires des Communautés*, 1760, pp. 102 ff., and *La pratique universelle pour la rénovation des terriers*, iv, 1754, p. 381 (cf. Denisart, *Collection des décisions*, iii, 1786, under 'Berger'.) For Lorraine cf. an ordinance of duke Charles IV, 10 June 1666, directed against the 'monopolising intentions' of leaseholders: François de Neufchateau, *Recueil authentique*, 1784, ii, 144.

the peasant community regarded as their rights: whether it was boycott, theft, murder, 'fire and sword', no punishment was considered too great. Nor was this the limit of popular demands; leaseholders claimed the privilege of first refusal when their property was being sold, and even farmworkers considered themselves permanent, with a hereditary right to their positions as 'harvesters, threshers, shepherds, woodsmen',—there is a notable example in the shepherds of Laonnais and the region of Guise who during the reign of Louis XV 'by threats, by taking the law into their own hands, and by murder' had secured what amounted to a monopoly for their 'tribe'. From the seventeenth century royal ordinances shouted themselves hoarse, all to no effect, in denouncing these practices which, to quote an official report, were making 'a fiction' of 'landed proprietorship' in the crown bailiwicks of Péronne, Montdidier, Roye and Saint-Quentin (Picardy). Even the threat of the galleys was no deterrent: in 1788 the intendant of Amiens, faced with a proposal for yet another edict, doubted whether the mounted constabulary of his *généralité* could provide 'enough of the horsemen who will be needed to contain a resisting mob'. In dealing with this problem the prefects and courts of modern France were to fare little better than their predecessors, the intendants and parlements; for *droit de marché* survived throughout the nineteenth century, when it was chiefly exercised, with characteristic regard for tradition, on certain large properties which corresponded almost field for field to estates formerly in the possession of lords or land engrossers of the *Ancien Régime*; no doubt the practice still survives.

The bond created by collective obligations in the cultivation of the arable was strong; but stronger still was the bond uniting a village group which possessed common lands, no matter what agrarian regime prevailed over the rest of the fields. As Rétif de la Bretonne observed, writing at the end of the eighteenth century: 'the little parish of Saci, since it has commons, governs itself like a large family'.[36]

The commons had multifarious uses. Waste or woodland supplied livestock with the additional grazing which was

---

[36] *La vie de mon père*, 3rd ed. 1788, ii, 82.

normally indispensable, even where there was access to meadows and fallow land. Woodland was also a source of timber and of the many other useful products found in the neighbourhood of trees. Marshland provided peat and rushes; from heathland came brush for bedding, turves, and broom or bracken for mulches. Last but not least, in many regions the commons acted as a reserve of arable, used for temporary cropping. It goes without saying that the use of the commons was subject to regulation; otherwise agrarian life would have come to a standstill, especially in the earlier periods when agriculture offered little scope to individuals working on their own account and few goods could be purchased from the minimal proceeds of small independent holdings. What we have to discover is not whether rules existed but how they were applied at different times and in different regions.

The exploitation of these valuable possessions sometimes led to the formation of a group larger than the village. So we find an extensive tract of heath or forest (such as the forest of Roumare in Normandy), and more frequently still the slopes of a mountain, in the joint occupation of several communities; these might be products of the break-up of a larger grouping, or communities which had originally been independent, but were persuaded by necessity to co-operate with their neighbours over the use of intervening territory. One example is the confederations of the Pyrenees *vallées*, where pasturage was the cementing bond. In most cases, however, commons were exclusive to a single village or hamlet and formed an adjunct to the arable.

In legal terms, the ideal 'commons' would be land unencumbered by any property rights other than those of the group, the type of land known to medieval law as 'allodial', although in this instance possessed by the inhabitants jointly. Although examples of collective allods exist, they are extremely rare.[37] It is far more usual to find the commons, like the rest of the village lands, subject to a complex tissue of rights claimed by a whole hierarchy of interested parties: the lord, the lord's lord

---

[37] B. Alart, *Cartulaire roussillonnais*, 1881, p. 41 (1027); cf. for another example from the former Spanish March, M. Kowalewsky, *Die ökonomische Entwickelung Europas*, 1901 ff., iii, 430, n. 1; A. Berbard and A. Bruel, *Recueil des chartes de l'abbaye de Cluny*, vi, No. 5167 (1271).

and the body of the peasantry. The exact limits of these rights long remained unclear, far longer in fact than was normally the case with individual holdings. Definition was achieved only as the result of bitterly contested litigation.

This battle over the common lands was to be expected. The commons had always been a cause of dissension between the lord and his subjects. A Frankish legal formula from the ninth century (it was actually written down at the Swabian monastery of St. Gall, but could just as easily have come from Francia) refers to litigation between a religious community and the occupiers over the exploitation of a forest.[38] Over the centuries, encroachment on common land figures as one of the oldest and most constant grounds for agrarian revolt. William of Jumièges says of the Norman peasants who revolted about the year 1000 'they sought to bend the customs concerning ponds, rivers and forests to their own laws'. Under the pen of the poet Wace, writing a little later, this becomes a fiery challenge: 'In numbers we are many—let the knights then feel our strength—then we can go to the woods as we will—to cut the trees and take our pick—to catch the fish as they swim—to chase the deer through the forests—to do there what we please—in the clearings, waters and trees'. The feeling that wild places and water, untouched by human hand, could not lawfully be appropriated by an individual was deep-rooted in man's primitive social conscience. A religious of Chartreuse, writing at the end of the eleventh century, says of a lord who had violated custom by making the monks pay grazing rights: 'against all justice, he withheld grass which God ordained the earth to produce for the nourishment of all beasts'.[39]

However, so long as unoccupied land was plentiful, the struggle over waste and woodland was not very acute. Nor was there any urgent need to define the legal status of the commons. The lord usually enjoyed the same rights over grazing land and forest as he did over the arable: rights, that is to say, which were superior but not necessarily supreme, since he was himself usually the vassal of another baron and bound by ties of homage on his own account, so that over and above

[38] A diploma of Lothair III concerning Larrey in Burgundy appears to deal with commons: Pardessus, *Diplomata*, ii, No. cccxlix.
[39] Guérard, *Cartulaire de Saint-Père de Chartres*, i, 172, No. xlv.

his rights might tower the edifice of a whole feudal hierarchy. Let us concentrate, however, on the immediate lord of the village, the first link in the chain of vassalage. The users of the uncultivated ground, that is to say the villagers, were obliged (either individually or collectively) to pay the lord rent in recognition of his superior right. Can we then say that the commons belonged to him? If we do, we shall be speaking recklessly: for peasant customs—to which the lord himself, in his capacity as producer, also subscribed—were in their own way as powerful as any laws. They had all the authority and protection of tradition; in medieval speech the lands subject to communal use were popularly referred to as the '*coutumes*' or 'customs' of the village, a highly revealing expression. A perfect manifestation of this outlook is to be seen in the inventories of the Frankish period, which in listing the appurtenances of a *villa* rarely fail to mention the presence of *communia*. Here indeed is a seeming paradox: why should anyone include 'common lands' among the possessions of a private individual who was free to alienate, sell or enfeof his properties at will? The reason is that the *seigneurie* covered more than the demesne directly exploited by its master. It also embraced territories which were merely under his dominion and from which he could exact charges, that is to say, the lands held in tenure (even where they were hereditary) and the commons: and these last were the subject of collective rights which had to be respected just as scrupulously as the individual seisin of each tenant. The *Customs of Barcelona*, which applied at this period to Roussillon, declare c. 1070 that 'the public highways and byways, running water and springs, meadows, pastures, forests, heaths and rocks . . . are not to be held by lords as though they were '*in alodium*'—that is to say without regard to rights other than their own—'nor are they to be maintained on their *dominicum* in any other way than that that their people may always be able to use them'.[40]

Then came the great clearances, which meant that uncultivated land became scarcer; and a new, more acute phase of the conflict began. The lords were not as a rule tempted to

[40] Cf. the discussion of Brutail's commentary on this text in P. Lacombe, *L'appropriation du sol*, 1912, p. 379. I agree with Lacombe over all the most essential points, but must reserve judgment over his interpretation of *alodium* and *dominicum*.

encroach on the commons so as to increase their own arable—
demesnes were everywhere dwindling; when seigneurial officials
ordered the ploughing up of grazing used by the common herd,
it was because the ground was wanted for allocation to tenants.
The fields thus won brought great gains to their cultivators and
to the lords who benefited from their rents; but the community
as a whole lost both its rights of usage and the unrestricted
opportunity for making assarts. In other instances the lord's
invasion of the commons was prompted by the desire to exploit
them directly, usually by converting them into grazing reserved
exclusively for his own stock: in this period of diminishing
demesnes, seigneurial husbandry was concentrated far more on
sheep-farming, with its minimal demands on labour, than on
tillage. Alternatively, there was the possibility of exploiting a
particular commodity produced by the waste. We have an
example of this from about the year 1200, reported by the cleric
Lambert d'Ardres: 'about this time Manasse, the elder son of
the count of Guines . . . ordered that the peat be dug out and
cut into blocks from a marshy pasture which had formerly been
granted to all the inhabitants of the parish of Andres as common
land'. The lords appear at their most covetous where the
common land happened to be planted with trees; for as we have
seen, timber was becoming more and more valuable. How did
the law stand in all these cases ? The truth is that the boundaries
of legal definition were so uncertain that even the most scrupu-
lous of men could feel at a loss; more than one nobleman no
doubt found himself justifying his usurpation of common land,
at least in his own sight, by the thought expressed with such
candour in 1442 by the squire of Sénas after he had seized the
waste in his Provençal village: 'reason shows that there must be
a difference between the lord and his subjects'.[41] But the
peasants did not suffer in silence. Often the dispute was concluded by a '*cantonment*', a partition between the lord and the
villagers. This meant that the lord gained full control over part
of the formerly undivided commons, while the community,
usually in return for a rent, retained the use, '*aisement*', of the
rest. In many places, therefore, the crisis had the effect of
securing official recognition for the rights of the group over at

[41] 'Car reson monstra que differencia sia entre lo senhor et los vassalhs.' Arch.
Bouches-du-Rhône, B 3343, fol. 342 (28 January 1442).

least a part of the ancient *communia*: and a fair number of our existing townships can trace the origin of their lands back to agreements of this kind.

With the sixteenth century a new and still graver crisis was precipitated. This was the time when the rejuvenated seigneurial class was concentrating all its energy and skill on the reintegration of great estates. Townsmen and prosperous peasants followed their example in accumulating properties. The revolution in legal thought came just at the right moment to support these ambitions. The jurists were now hard at work constructing a clear concept of ownership to replace the tissue of superimposed rights over property. Commons, like other land, had to have a *dominus*, in the Roman sense. In general the *dominus* was identified as the lord. This purely theoretical notion was backed up by a hypothesis concerning the origins of the lord's ownership, a theory which has even been advanced, surprising though it may seem, by historians of our own day. It was asserted that at first the commons had belonged to the lords alone; the inhabitants only enjoyed the use of them in virtue of concessions made down the centuries—which is to say that the village must always be younger than its lord! These theorists had naturally no intention of sacrificing whatever rights communities had won for themselves. But, in keeping with a line of jurisprudence which had been developing from the thirteenth century,[42] they were in general only prepared to accept as valid those rights which had been sanctioned by the payment of a fee: 'concessions' made out of pure generosity unsupported by any formal deed appeared insubstantial and, what is more, left room to doubt whether there ever had been any 'concession' or merely a usurpation on the part of the villagers. This progress towards definition was attended by many hesitations and qualifications. Professors of law, practising lawyers, administrators —all were engaged in unconcerted and not very successful attempts at classifying the mass of communal properties in a manner which took account of the conflicting rights, unequal in force, claimed by the lord and his men. Imbued with this spirit and armed with doctrine, the lords, their legal advisers and

[42] *Olim* i, 334, No. iii and 776 No. xvii (in this case however it turned out that the men were not *'levants et couchants'* of the lord in question, so no judgment was entered on the point of law). L. Verriest, *Le régime seigneurial*, pp. 297, 302, and 308.

even the courts (strongly influenced by respect for rank) felt entitled to adopt a simpler and cruder view. In 1736 the Procurator-General of the Parlement of Rennes adopted the seigneurial thesis in its most unequivocal form: 'all the heaths, *galois* and empty and waste spaces in Brittany are within the demesne of the Lords of the Fief'. Under a deed dated 20 June 1270 the lord of Couchey (Burgundy) was forbidden to alienate 'the commons of the village' without the consent of the inhabitants given in due form; yet notwithstanding this explicit prohibition, from 1386 the Duke's Council, followed at a distance of some three and a half centuries (1733) by the Parlement, held that 'the squares, streets, by-ways, footpaths, grazing grounds ... and other common places' of the village could be treated by the lord as he willed, since they were his. In 1777 the Parlement of Douai refused to register an edict in which there was mention of properties 'belonging' to the communities; the phrase should have run: 'properties used by the communities'.[43]

To sum up, from the sixteenth century the attack on common lands was renewed with unprecedented vigour, as is only too evident from the stream of complaints from villagers, carried up to the Provincial Estates or the Estates General.

The attack took a variety of forms; the first to be noticed is barefaced usurpation. The lords were abusing their authority and judicial powers, as we learn from the deputies of the Third Estate in their address to the Estates of Blois in 1576. 'There are those who have made themselves judges in their own cause, who have seized and apprehended the customs, empty places, heaths and commons which are enjoyed by the poor subjects, and who have even taken away the papers by which their good right is shown.' Rich proprietors, peasants among them, were quick to take advantage of this favourable conjuncture, whose influence, according to an eighteenth century agronomist, could be seen triumphantly at work all over the country. In 1747 the people of Cros-Bas in Auvergne complained that 'Geraud Salat-Patagon, an inhabitant of the said village ... has taken it on himself, ... since he is rich and cock of the walk, to shut and

[43] Poullain du Parc, *Journal des audiences ... du Parlement de Bretagne*, ii, 1740, p. 256 ff.; J. Garnier, *Chartes de communes*, ii, Nos. ccclxxi and ccclxii; G. Lefebvre, *Les paysans du Nord*, p. 67, n. 1.

enclose the greater part of the commons pertaining to the said village and join them to his fields'.[44]

Encroachment was sometimes effected under more specious forms, legally almost above reproach. A prosperous *laboureur* might acquire the lease of part of the commons at too low a price. Or a lord might insist on partition (*cantonment*), a relatively harmless manoeuvre so long as the conditions were not too unfavourable to the community. But many lords demanded as much as a third of the land so divided; this was the right of *triage*, which with legal backing became widespread in post-medieval centuries and in 1669 received pusillanimous recognition from the Crown. Admittedly, in theory *triage* was held to apply only in certain circumstances, notably where the initial alleged concession had been gratuitous. In practice these qualifications, which in any case still left room for numerous claims, were not always scrupulously observed.

Finally, it must be noted that the peasants were often in debt, not only as individuals (we have already seen that loans were raised for the purchase of advantageous parcels by men who were extending their holdings) but also collectively. The debts, which might be heavy, were incurred by expenditure in the common interest, necessitated for example by reconstruction in the wake of war, and above all by the need to meet the pressing demands of royal and seigneurial taxation. How tempting it must have been to discharge this burden by selling all or part of the commons! The lords readily supported such moves, either because they saw themselves as prospective purchasers or else because they hoped, by invoking their right to *triage* as indemnity for the loss of their superior right over the soil, to take a share of the cake at no personal expense. The law and custom of Lorraine was so extreme on this point that it recognised the lord's right to a third of the purchase price obtained by the villagers. Official suspicion was sometimes aroused by these sales, either because the alleged reason appeared dubious—a royal ordinance of 1647 claimed that some persons setting out to 'fleece' the villages had saddled them with 'fictitious' debts—or else because of the conditions attached to fixing the price.

[44] Essuile, *Traité politique et économique des communes*, 1770, 178; C. Trapenard, *Le pâturage communal en Haute-Auvergne*, 1904, p. 57; cf. Arch. du Puy-de-Dôme, Inventaire, C. ii, n. 2051.

But the pressure of self-interested parties and the deplorable financial situation of many small rural groups (often also victims of mismanagement) combined to make such sales inevitable. Between 1590 and 1662 the village of Champdôtre in Burgundy sold its commons three times over: the first two transactions were cancelled as fraudulent or erroneous; the last —to the purchasers concerned in the second attempt—was final. The movement naturally encountered some fierce resistance. It is true that even where abuse was most flagrant, the peasants often hesitated to take on a struggle in which the odds were heavily against them. As the intendant of Dijon remarked in 1667 'since all commons have been usurped and are possessed either by the lords of the communities or by persons in authority, the poor peasants will not dream of complaining if they are ill-treated'. This opinion is corroborated by Fréminville, the great authority on estate management: 'will any villagers dare to incur the disfavour of a powerful lord' ?[45] But not all were so easily intimidated. Towards the beginning of the eighteenth century many Breton lords started leasing out heathlands to contractors in timber or for commercial farming. The limits of such appropriations were marked by sizeable earth embankments, thrown up round the portion of land withdrawn from communal use; and these irksome symbolic enclosures were often attacked by armed mobs. The Parlement was ready to take punitive measures, but it was impossible to find witnesses. After several embankments on Plourivo heath had been destroyed in this way, the lord published warning notices 'in order to bring the guilty parties to light'. But one fine day a gallows appeared on the boundary between the two parishes concerned; at its feet was a pit with the inscription 'anyone who surrenders will find himself in here'.[46]

The peasants were not alone in their efforts to check the movement. They had some support from the monarchy and its officials, who cherished rural groups as a source of taxes and soldiers. Starting in 1560 with the Ordinance of Orleans, which deprived lords of their judgment '*en souveraineté*' of suits relating to commons, a whole series of edicts was issued, some of general, some of local application, which prohibited alienations, annulled sales or *triages* concluded after a given date, and initi-

[45] *Pratique*, 2nd ed. ii, 254.      [46] Poullain du Parc, *loc. cit.*, 258.

ated enquiries into rights usurped from communities. The Parlements supported the lords in their aggressions; the intendants, their habitual enemies, in the seventeenth century embraced the opposite cause. At the time, this policy was so obviously the right one for any state at all mindful of its interests that it is no surprise to see it in action elsewhere, in the duchy of Lorraine for example. The shift in government sympathies— the concomitant of what amounted to a total reversal of ideas— came towards the middle of the eighteenth century, with the appearance of the 'Agricultural Revolution', whose whole nature, together with its effects on the common lands, will be considered in the next chapter.

Neither the monarchy nor the peasants were very effective in their resistance. The efforts of the monarchy were vitiated by fiscal preoccupations: the declarations of 1677 and 1702 authorise those who have seized common land to keep it, at least for the time being, provided they 'restore' (to the king, of course) the profits received over the past thirty years. The peasants were all too often content with fruitless 'popular demonstrations'. At this period the break-up of common lands for the benefit of the nobility and the wealthy was a European phenomenon. The operating causes were everywhere the same: the trend towards the reintegration of large estates; the increasing emphasis on production as a private undertaking, with an eye always on the market; and the crisis among the rural proletariat, painfully adjusting itself to an economic system based on money and exchange. The communities were no match for these forces; what is more, they were far from possessing that perfect inner coherence with which they are sometimes credited.

### 3. THE CLASSES OF MEN

Let us ignore the lords and burgesses, controlling their estates and collecting their rents from their city or small town residences. Strictly speaking, these people had no part in peasant society, which was composed of husbandmen living directly off the soil they cultivated. It is obvious that this was not an egalitarian society even in the eighteenth century; it certainly is not today. Some observers have imagined the different social strata to be the product of relatively recent changes. Fustel de Coulanges wrote: 'the village of the eighteenth century was no longer what it had been in the Middle Ages: inequality has made its appearance'.[47] But the indications seem to be that these small rural groups were at all periods divided into quite well-defined classes, although the lines of cleavage inevitably show some fluctuations.

It must be admitted that the word 'class' is among the most equivocal in the historian's vocabulary, so that it becomes important to define the precise sense it will carry here. We should be hammering at an already open door if we merely set out to prove that differences of legal status existed among villagers at various periods. The contrasts presented by the Frankish *villa*, although they soon became more apparent than real, were pointed enough while they lasted. On many medieval *seigneuries*, free villeins, whose numbers increased as enfranchisement advanced, and serfs lived side by side. If some scholars seek to argue, as they do, that peasant society was egalitarian in structure, it is not because they are blind to these undeniable contrasts. Their contention is that whatever differences of legal status may have existed, the peasants as a whole had enough in common, both as to their way of life and the extent of their resources, to exclude any conflict of interest. Loosely summed up, the kernel of the argument seems to be that while the existence of legal classes is admitted, that of social classes is denied. In fact, nothing could be further from the truth.

As we have seen, in the early Middle Ages there were often marked differences in size—which had either been present from the outset or were a symptom of decomposition—between *manses* of the same category on the same *seigneurie*. At Thiais the household of a *colonus* named Badilo held a free *manse* consisting of 16–17 hectares of arable, about 38 *ares* of vines and 34 *ares* of meadow. Another household of *coloni*, made up of Doon with his sister and of Demanche with his wife and son, between them held a free *manse* which consisted of just over three *hectares* of arable, 38 *ares* of vines and 10–11 *ares* of meadow. Are we really to believe that Badilo and his neighbours re-

[47] *Séances et travaux de l'Acad. des Sc. Morales,* cxii, 357.

garded themselves as social equals ? Again, there was normally a difference in size between *manses* of different categories. A servile *manse* might well be held by someone—a *colonus* for example—who was equal in law with his neighbour who held a free *manse*; but his *manse* would as a rule be considerably smaller. At the very bottom of the scale were those peasants whose snippets of land—*hospitia* or *accolae*—had not been raised to the dignity of a *manse*, squatters for the most part, who had been given permission to occupy a fragment of the waste they had cleared for themselves.

The dissolution of the *manse*, which often led to the break-up of tenures, could not fail to accentuate these distinctions. It is very difficult to form any idea of the size of peasant fortunes during the Middle Ages. Fortunately there are one or two records which permit us to take some soundings, however inadequate. In 1170 a tallage was imposed on the tenures belonging to three *seigneuries* in the Gâtinais, each tenure being assessed according to its value; we find that the payments range from 2 to 48 *deniers*. In the reign of St. Louis the royal serfs on the castellany of Pierrefonds purchased their freedom at the price of 5 per cent of the value of their property; translated into monetary terms, they appear to have been worth between 1 and 1920 pounds. Admittedly, the most affluent were probably not rustics at all. But the differences are still appreciable even among the more modest of these patrimonies, which one must assume belonged to farming people: while over a third amount to less than twenty pounds, over a seventh exceed forty.[48]

Over the centuries two main criteria came to distinguish certain groups of peasants from the rest. One was the eminence conferred by the power and dignity of service under the lord; the other, which had a more direct economic bearing, was the possession or lack of a plough team.

In the Middle Ages the master of the *seigneurie* had a representative who governed in his name. The title of this official varied with the region: he might be called 'provost' (*prévot*), 'mayor' (*maire*), 'bailiff' (*bayle*), or, in Limousin, 'judge', *juge*. In his personal status there was nothing to elevate him above

[48] M. Prou and A. Vidier, *Recueil des chartes de Saint-Bênoit sur Loire*, 1900 ff., No. cxciv (the text speaks of *masures* which must here mean '*exploitations*'); M. Bloch, *Rois et serfs*, 1920, p. 180.

those he governed. Indeed, he might well be the legal inferior of peasants who had retained their freedom. It was by no means unusual for him to be of servile condition, since originally dependent status might have been thought a guarantee of good behaviour. There were, however, numerous perquisites (legitimate and otherwise) attaching to his office; and above all he enjoyed the prestige which is always inseparable from the right to command, never more so than in periods of violent manners and unrefined passions. In his own modest sphere he was a leader of men, and when occasion arose a military commander, taking his place at the head of the village contingents in time of danger or for the prosecution of a vendetta. Sometimes, despite strict orders to the contrary, he even carried a sword and spear. In rare cases he achieved the dignity of an armed knight. He was set apart from the general ruck of peasants by his authority, wealth and way of life. From quite an early date this small world of seigneurial sergeants, some of whom were apt to become contumacious and tyrannical but who were in general loyally disposed, was held together by the operation of the hereditary principle which is well-nigh essential to the development of class solidarity. Although lords fearful for their authority did their best to prevent it, offices and their attached tenures ('fiefs') were handed down from father to son. In the twelfth and thirteenth centuries—as we know from records dealing with the exchange of serfs—the sons and daughters of bailiffs preferred to choose their marriage partners from among their opposite numbers on other *seigneuries*. When people are concerned to marry 'within their own circle', there is tangible proof that the 'circle' is on its way to becoming a class.

This particular class enjoyed only a transitory existence, and in France never received the ultimate accolade of a special legal status. In Germany, where from the thirteenth century the social hierarchy acquired numerous gradations, a place for it was found at the bottom of the aristocratic ladder. French society was also hierarchical, but after a simpler fashion. In France the nobility emerged as a well-defined class during the thirteenth century, but without any officially recognised subdivisions. Many seigneurial sergeants who achieved knighthood merged with the country gentry. They were then usually deprived of their offices, which were purchased back from them by lords now disinclined to retain the services of agents less tractable than formerly. These village tyrants had risen so far above the peasant community that they were no longer part of it. But there were others, less fortunate or less able, who never rose so high. Their offices became progressively less important as demesnes shrank, seigneurial authority declined, more and more revenues were farmed out and the lords lost confidence in their loyalty; from this time on their rank and way of life would be that of a wealthy villein, nothing more. After being so powerful in the eleventh and twelfth centuries, in the thirteenth century the sergeant class evaporated. There was no place for it in a crystallised society where everyone had to be either a peasant or a noble.

Hereditary officials were now less and less acceptable and those that remained were progressively stripped of their powers. In early modern times the lord came to be represented in the villages by his paid legal advisers or by men to whom he had farmed out his revenues or his demesne. The lawyer would be a townsman, and of no interest to us here. The leaseholder might also be a townsman; but he could as well be a rich peasant, in which case, he was no more than one *'laboureur'*— though in particularly easy circumstances—among many.

Voltaire tells us that Colin 'owed the light of day to a sturdy *laboureur'*. This word, which occurs frequently in eighteenth century literature, may strike the modern reader as merely a grander version of 'peasant' (*paysan*). To a contemporary, however, the word was full of meaning. Ever since the Middle Ages a careful distinction had been drawn between two categories of peasant: one group (clearly the wealthier) owned teams of draught-animals—horses, oxen, donkeys—the other had to rely on the strength of their own right arms. The antithesis was between *cultivateurs*, ploughmen who 'had horses to do their labouring' and manual workers, *laboureurs de bras*, *brassiers* or husbandmen *ménagers*. Medieval lists of labour services make a distinction between the two. At Varreddes during the thirteenth century ploughing and carting services were demanded only from anyone who could 'contribute a beast to the plough', whereas work in the bishop's close was incumbent on all peasants, 'whether or not they have a plough'. The name *brassier* is explicitly mentioned in a record of 1155 relating to Grisolles in the Toulouisain. Doubtless there was no strict equality even among *laboureurs*; when their dues were being assessed, the contents of their stables and stockyards were taken into account. The custom observed in the village of Curey in the Avranchin during the thirteenth century, by which the less prosperous were required to collaborate in yoking their beasts to the same plough, was more or less universal. In places where the soil was heavy probably as many as three or four pairs of oxen would be needed to trace the furrow. This in turn produced further distinctions: as at Varreddes, between villeins who could 'contribute' one, two, three, four (or even more) horses, or at Saint-Hilaire-sur-Autize in Poitou during the eleventh century, between the owners of two and four oxen. At much the same period we find the population of Marizy-Sainte-Geneviève ranging between miserable wretches who 'work without oxen' and peasants possessing a complete 'plough', with a middle group who could boast of only a 'half-plough'.[49] Notwithstanding these refinements, it is obvious that the essential cleavage was between *manouvriers*, manual workers, and *laboureurs*.

Was this then a distinction between the landed and the landless? Not altogether. The antithesis was economic rather than legal in nature. The manual worker often possessed a plot of his own—even if it was only his dwelling with its close—and possibly a few scrawny animals. We find men in this situation from a very early date. A memorandum concerning a contract concluded shortly before 1096 records that 'Amauri, son of Rahier, gave two *hospites*, whose land was only enough for their houses and closes, to the monks of Saint-Martin-des-Champs at Mondonville'.[50] The state of affairs revealed in eighteenth century records is very similar. As for the *laboureurs*, it may well be that they only held their holdings, or at least the greater part of them, on a temporary lease. In later centuries, with the growth of large estates which were rarely exploited by direct cultivation, this arrangement became increasingly common. The *laboureurs*, enjoying the benefit of their numerous

[49] Bibl. de Meaux, ms 64, p. 197 (Varreddes); C. Douais, *Cartulaire de l'abbaye de Saint-Sernin*, 1887, No. cvi (Grisolles); L. Delisle, *Etudes*, p. 135, n. 36 (Curey); L. Redet, in *Mém. de la Soc. des Antiquaires de l'Ouest*, xiv, No. LXXXV (St-Hilaire); F. Soehnée, *Catalogue des actes de Henri I*, 1907, No. 26 (Marizy).

[50] Depoin, *Liber testamentorum Sancti Martini*, No. lxxx.

fields and herds (they were the real capitalists of the village) and holding on lease lands which had been carefully amassed by noble or bourgeois landlords (or their ancestors), were often superior in wealth and prestige to the petty proprietors. It was no accident that from the eighteenth century *fermier* and *laboureur* became practically synonymous; even today, the word *ferme*, shorn of any precise legal content, is commonly applied to almost every agricultural holding of any size.

Since he had no draught-animals, how did the manual worker till his paltry fields? Sometimes—in earlier periods probably quite frequently—he must have done it without using a plough at all. A deed drawn up in 1210 for the monastery of La Cour-Dieu, in anticipation of a forest clearance, assumed that two categories of peasants will be involved: 'those who will till with oxen, those who will work with the hoe'. The map made of Vauquois in 1771 notes the existence of lands cultivated by hand.[51] Elsewhere, however, especially where the arable was more compact, it was necessary to borrow a team and plough from some more fortunate neighbour; although the loan was sometimes free—many rural communities honoured mutual aid as a social obligation—more often it had to be paid for, either in money or in kind, in the form of one of those manual services the poorer peasants were accustomed to perform for the richer. As it was impossible for the manual worker to subsist entirely off his own land, he usually ensured his livelihood by hiring himself out to a *laboureur*; he was a *manouvrier* or *journalier*. The two classes were thus brought together by a necessary collaboration, which did not exclude mutual hostility. At the end of the eighteenth century, the ploughmen of Artois, vexed to find *ménagers* taking leases of land for themselves instead of reserving their labour for the service of wealthier peasants, raised the hiring price of plough teams in punishment, a move which aroused such bitter resentment that the government was forced to intervene and fix an official rate.[52]

This definite distinction—and hence opposition—between

[51] R. de Maulde, *Etude sur la condition forestière de l'Orléanais*, p. 178, n. 6 and p. 114; Chantilly, reg. E 34.

[52] A. de Calonne, in *Mém. de la soc. des Antiquaires de Picardie*, 4th series, ix, 178-9. Cf. article 9 of the *cahier de doléances* presented jointly by the Lorraine villages of Bannay and Loutremange, Condé-Northen, Vaudoncourt and Varize, in *Quellen zur lothringischen Geschichte*, vol. ix.

the two groups existed at all periods. But the differences were greatly accentuated by the economic changes of more modern times. As we have seen, the entry of agriculture into the cycle of exchanges precipitated a genuine crisis in peasant affairs. The more prosperous and astute profited from it and became all the richer; but many *laboureurs*, because they fell into debt and were forced to sell part of their properties, came to swell the ranks of manual workers or at best to occupy a closely similar position. Even so, as long as the new masters exploited the land by leasing it out in small farms, there was opportunity (which was not neglected) for these socially displaced persons to acquire a small holding against a money rent or as a *métayage*. But the 'gathering in of leases', which took place on a large scale in many provinces during the eighteenth century, finally deposited a considerable number of them among the agricultural proletariat. There are many contemporary sources which echo the description of some Artois cantons written by the intendant of Lille in 1768: 'a single leaseholder has the monopoly of all the ploughs within a community, which makes him absolute master of the occupants' livelihood and does harm both to the population and to agriculture'.[53] On the eve of 1787 manual workers formed the majority in a large number of communities, for example in Lorraine, Picardy and perhaps Berry. When the 'agricultural revolution', which was at once economic and technical, started to transform the greater part of the French countryside around the year 1750, it was confronted, like the political revolution which was to overthrow the monarchy, by a peasant society deeply divided.

[53] Arch. Nat., H 1515, No. 15.

# CHAPTER SIX

## The Beginnings of the Agricultural Revolution

WE customarily use the term 'agricultural revolution' to describe that disruption of agrarian techniques and customs which, at different points of time in different countries, marked the advent of modern agricultural methods all over Europe. The expression is a useful one. It sets the metamorphosis in the countryside alongside the 'industrial revolution' which gave birth to large-scale capitalist industry; and this parallelism, whose accuracy none could contest, suggests links between the two revolutions which have a sound basis in fact. The term 'agricultural revolution' also helps to emphasise that the movement was one of great breadth and depth. By and large then, the expression seems fully entitled to a place in the historian's vocabulary. But on one condition only, namely that its ambiguities are recognised. For if we look at rural history over its whole sweep we can see that change has been a constant feature, and from the very earliest times. Consider only the purely technical aspects. What transformation could have been more decisive than the invention of the wheeled plough, or the substitution of settled courses of cultivation for temporary cropping, or the dramatic struggle waged by pioneers against the waste, the forests and the rights of commoners? The innovations we are about to consider may indeed amount to a 'revolution', if this is taken in the sense of 'a profound change'. But it was certainly not in the nature of an unexpected shock, interrupting centuries of impassivity. Nor was it an abrupt mutation. It spread itself out over many years, even centuries. And nowhere was this gradualness more evident than in France.

The revolution had two fundamental characteristics: the

progressive disappearance of collective obligations from regions where they had formerly been dominant, and the introduction of new techniques. These two movements were closely linked and when they coincided the revolution in its fullest sense had been born. But they were not completely contemporaneous: in France, as in most other countries (England for example), the attack on collective obligations antedated the more specifically agricultural changes to a quite appreciable extent.

### I. THE FIRST ATTACK ON COLLECTIVE OBLIGATIONS: PROVENCE AND NORMANDY

In Provence the practice of collective grazing on the arable had at one time been observed with almost as much rigour as in other unenclosed regions.[1] Although farmers were sometimes allowed to fence off part of their fallow, for example to provide grazing for their plough-animals, this permission applied only to a small fraction of their property (as at Grasse, after the ordinances of 1242).[2] The fourteenth century, however, saw the beginnings of a strong movement away from this ancient custom.

By the end of the Middle Ages the movement had gained so much momentum that attempts at legal reform could be contemplated. In 1469 the Estates of Provence, who were engaged on what amounted to a general codification of public law, presented the following petition to their sovereign of the moment, king René. 'Since all possessions belonging to individuals should be for their own advantage and not that of others, the Estates pray that all meadows, vineyards, closes and

---

[1] The agrarian history of Provence to a large extent still remains unwritten, although not for want of documents, of which there are plenty, especially relating to transhumance, in itself a subject likely to shed much interesting light on social structure. The following should be consulted: legal authorities of the *Ancien Régime*, especially J. Morgues, *Les Statuts*, 2nd ed., 1658, p. 301; the replies of the intendant and the Procurator-General to the enquiry into collective grazing of 1766, and the replies of the sub-prefects and mayors of Bouches-du-Rhône to the enquiries instituted in 1812 and 1814, Arch. B.-du-Rhône, M 13[6] and *Statistique agricole de 1814*, 1914; the printed local customs of Bouches-du-Rhône (C. Tavernier, 1859) and Var (Cauvin and Poulle, 1887, compiled from an enquiry of 1844); P. Masson, in *Les Bouches-du-Rhône, Encyclopédie départementale*, vii, *L'Agriculture*, 1928.

[2] F. Benoît, *Recueil des actes des comtes de Provence*, 1925, ii, p. 435, n. 355, c. VII.

other possessions, whatever they may be, which can be so treated shall put in defence\* throughout the year, under severe penalty and notwithstanding all custom to the contrary running in the places dependent on the king.' The king assented: 'seeing that it is just and equitable for everyone to dispose of and control his own property, let what has been asked be granted'.[3] Admittedly, the application of this statute (for such it became in virtue of the royal assent) to the arable was not entirely clear. However, the commentators were unanimous that it implied the complete abolition of collective grazing. As with most legislative acts of the period, its provisions were virtually ignored; its positive contribution was in revealing an attitude of mind. Effective change was introduced by other means, local decisions arrived at community by community. The process was drawn out over at least four centuries, from the fourteenth to the seventeenth. To chart its progress one would need to know the detailed history of nearly every small town and village in Provence. It will come as no surprise that I am forced—by lack of space and information—to offer only a sketchy survey.[4]

It often happened, especially in the earlier days of the movement, that collective grazing was restricted rather than totally abolished. In some places the protection traditionally enjoyed by certain crops was extended to new categories: as at Salon, in 1454, when the olive groves, almond orchards and even the meadows were included in the exemption hitherto exclusive to the vineyards.[5] Or again, grazing might be forbidden over a whole section of the village lands, usually the part nearest to the inhabited area or the most fertile fields; these were usually known as the *bolles*, a name taken from the delimiting boundary

---

\* Shut out all others but the owner or user from exercising rights of grazing etc. over the piece of land. (Translator's note.)

[3] Arch. B.-du-Rhône, B 49, fol. 301 v°.

[4] The nature of the documents, both printed and manuscript, makes it unusually easy for a researcher to study for himself the debates carried on in the more urbanised communities, even if he is unable to make investigations on the spot, village by village. These sources are quite useful, since all these Provençal *villes* (and Aix was no exception) were still more than semi-rural in aspect. The citizens of Aix were so attached to their grazing rights that in the fourteenth century they even produced a forgery on the subject: Benoît, *loc. cit.*, 57, n. 44 (earlier than 4 August 1351; cf. Arch. Aix, AA 3, fol. 139).

[5] R. Brun, *La ville de Salon*, 1924, p. 287, c. 9; p. 300, c. XX; p. 371, c. 27; cf. for Allemagne, at a later date, Arch. B.-du-Rhône, B 3356, fol. 154 (21 July 1647).

posts. This was the plan adopted in 1381 at Aix—with the proviso that in time of war the barriers should be removed, since it would then be dangerous for the flocks to roam too far from the town walls; we find these excepted areas in a number of places after 1390, for example Tarascon, Salon (from 1424), Malaucène, Carnoules, Pernes and Aubagne.[6]

But in other places more radical measures were taken right from the first. At Sénas all the village lands, including the seigneurial demesne, were by tradition open to collective grazing. The moment came when the lords realised that this custom was to their disadvantage; in 1322 they issued an order denying the village herds access during the current year to fields bearing stubble, wherever these might be, and claimed the right to reserve them for their own beasts. The peasants protested, not so much, it seems, on account of the prohibition itself but because of its unequal application. The problem was at once legal and technical: who had the right to lay down the law in agrarian matters? In the end recourse was had to the tribunal, where this always delicate problem of attribution received a rule of thumb solution: the lord had the right to exempt the stubble from collective grazing, on condition that he first consulted the villagers, and with the further proviso that he himself observed the prohibition; if these conditions were not met, the exemption could be ignored. The adjudicators obviously saw nothing unnatural in the overriding of ancient custom, which in this case was bound to lead to its eventual disappearance as the exemption was renewed year by year.[7] Other communities, at widely varying dates, abolished collective grazing at one fell swoop. Salon, having taken the preliminary measures already men-

---

[6] Arch. d'Aix, AA 2, fol. 42; 46; 45; E. Bondurand, *Les coutumes de Tarascon*, 1892, c. CXI; Arch. B.-du-Rhône, *Livre vert de l'archevêché d'Arles*, fol. 235; F. and A. Saurel, *Histoire de la ville de Malaucène*, ii, 1883, p. lv (4 June, 1500); Arch. B.-du-Rhône, B 3348, fol. 589 v° (28 September 1631); Giberti, *Histoire de la ville de Pernes*, 382; L. Barthélemy, *Histoire d'Aubagne*, ii, 1889, pp. 404 ff. (especially c. 29).

[7] Arch. B.-du-Rhône, B 3343, fol. 413 v° and 412 v° (5 Oct. 1322). There were further disturbances in 1442 (*ibid.*, fol. 323 v° ff.). This last text, which is in any case obscure, seems to suggest that the ban on grazing the stubble was not always strictly observed. Heated controversies also developed over the cultivation and collective grazing of the waste (the *herms*): in addition to the texts already cited (in this note and *supra*, 184, n. 41) see in the same register fol. 400 v° (5 December 1432, confirmed 6 August 1438) and 385 (29 December 1439). At Digne collective grazing on the stubble was also prohibited for a period of three years, in 1365: F. Guichard, *Essai historique sur le cominalat*, 1846, ii, No. cxxiii.

tioned, went the whole way shortly before 1463; at Avignon the decisive step was taken in 1458, at Riez in 1647, at Orange, further to the north, on July 5 1789.[8] The decisions in favour of abolition gradually mounted up. There were, too, many places where although collective grazing was not abolished in principle, it was recognised that men had the right to exclude the herd from their own fields; this exemption was either granted by an explicit deed or arose simply from usage, which quickly hardened into law. At times the right was restricted to a fraction of each property, a third for example, as at Valensolle in 1647.[9] But in other instances exemption was total. A simple mark, usually a heap of pebbles or turves (a *montjoie*), was all that was needed to warn off the herdsmen. In the end the compulsory observance of collective obligations vanished almost completely: but there were still a few communities, faithful to their old customs, who refused to permit any barriers, just as there were lords who thought their ancient privileges gave them the right to ignore the *montjoies*. If one made an agrarian map of Provence at the end of the *Ancien Régime*, it would show large blocks where individualism had triumphed interspersed with small dots marking the places where compulsory grazing on the arable was still practised. If we then joined these dots by an imaginary line (as geologists do with the 'outliers' of eroded strata or philologists with the survivals of ancient linguistic forms) we should see before us the whole extent of the area once occupied by communal practices.

Why did Provence abandon its 'primitive communism' at so early a date? It must first be recalled that the system was never so strong in Provence as it was in the northern plains. The supporting network of rules was less rigid, the looser field pattern made collective grazing less imperative—in Provence, where fields were almost as broad as they were long and were scattered almost at random over the village lands, there was little serious difficulty in achieving isolation. Yet this pattern is

[8] For Salon, see *infra*, 203, n. 12; J. Girard and P. Pansier, *La cour temporelle d'Avignon*, 1909, p. 149, c. 95 and p. 155, c. 124; Arch. B.-du-Rhône, B 3356, fol. 705 v°; Arch. d'Orange, BB 46, fol. 299 (listed in the inventory—I have been unable to find this document).

[9] Arch. B.-du-Rhône, B 3355, fol. 360 v° (the barrier-makers seem to have wanted more). At Allemagne in 1647 *devandudes* were permitted in proportion to the tax paid, B 3356, fol. 154.

also found in other regions (very close at hand in Languedoc and rather further off in Berry), which were much slower to discard their ancient practices. The field patterns of Provence are thus a sufficient but not a necessary cause for the transformation which took place there; and they cannot account for its early date.

Roman law had continued to be taught in Provence without interruption; Roman laws were officially recognised as fixing the legal norm, except where custom contained express stipulations to the contrary. Now, in the eyes of Roman law any restriction on individual ownership was 'heinous', as the ancient jurists put it. These Roman laws were thus both an argument in favour of agrarian reform and a stimulus to its implementation. Their influence is clearly visible in the statute of 1469 and also in more than one court judgment or community resolution, drafted by legal advisers. But although Roman laws lent support to the movement, they did not engender it. In Languedoc, also under their sway, the triumph of individualism was long postponed. The real key to the agrarian transformation of Provence is to be found in its economic and geographical make-up.

In Provence the nature of the soil prevented assarting on the same extensive scale as was possible in other regions. There was any amount of waste land which was destined to remain permanently uncultivated. Nearly every place had its patch of rock, its *garrigue* covered with aromatic scrub dotted here and there with trees. To this must be added stretches of arid land where the top-soil was too poor to bear a crop, though in a good year it might yield some precious herbage—la Crau is a good example. Admittedly, these uncroppable areas were used for grazing, sometimes free range, sometimes in the form of temporary enclosures or *cossouls*, to which some or all of the inhabitants were entitled to bring their beasts. These stony *'herms'* of Provence (the literal meaning of *herm* is desert) played a part similar to that of the heathlands in enclosed regions: with the *herms* to fall back on, the small Provencal farmer found it easier to give up collective grazing than did his counterparts in more thoroughly assarted territory.

In fact it was gradually becoming obvious that the small farmer or *laboureur* derived little benefit from the practice. It was the manual workers and the very small independent proprietors who had no wish to see the fields delivered from their ancient servitude; since they possessed little or no land of their own, they stood to lose important opportunities for grazing (in fact their only opportunity except where there was access to communal waste) without compensatory gain. It was often people who had suffered in this way who were behind attempts to bring back collective grazing at the time of the Revolution, when agrarian and political agitation went hand in hand.[10] There can be no doubt that they must have resented its disappearance, and some of the sporadic resistance offered by communities to the 'barrier makers' probably stemmed from this source.[11] But the real opposition to limitation of the old custom came from a far more powerful group, the commercial sheep-farmers or *nourriguiers*. At Salon, for example, where they were supported by the butchers who were their customers, they succeeded in holding up the total abolition of collective grazing for several years after the archbishop of Arles had given the township his consent to the reform.[12] Defeat on the main issue and two minor successes (permission for grazing to continue on isolated fields difficult to protect because of the surrounding waste, and the suppression of a *cossoul* set up by the community with the express object of excluding the sheep) did nothing to abate their hostility. Even in 1626, when fines for damaging vines and olive trees were increased, the *nourriguiers* are still found protesting against a ruling which might be prejudicial to

[10] For Alpes-Maritimes (the county of Nice, which was separated from Provence in 1388 seems to have followed the same lines of development as the rest of the region) see a report by the prefect, Arch. Nat., F[10] 337, Year XII, 10 frimaire). In Bouches-du-Rhône, it seems that the commune of Puyloubier had retained collective grazing, since we find the '*gros tenanciers*' anxious to abolish it during the Years IV and V: this was the 'cause of the rich against the poor', F[10] 336; cf. Arch. B.-du-Rhône, L 658.

[11] Cf. for the Digne region, Arch. B.-du-Rhône, B 158, fol. 65 and 66 (1345); and for Valensolle, *supra*, 201, n. 9.

[12] Arch. de Salon, *Copie du Livre Blanc* (eighteenth century), pp. 674 ff. See the piece published by R. Brun, *La ville de Salon* p. 379: the date is wrong (sinceit is addressed to archbishop Philip, the document must have been written between 11 February 1463 and 4 November 1475) and the account of the affair incomplete. The order forbidding grazing on the arable even when there had been no harvest dated from the time of Cardinal de Foix (9 October 1450—11 February 1463). The suit, which had its initial hearing before the royal court of the *juge mage*, was decided by the archbishop's officer and sentence delivered on 26 October 1476.

'individuals with a wish to feed their livestock'.[13] The new agrarian policy adopted by the communities was in fact deliberately aimed at damaging the stock-rearers, by putting a stop to their abuse of ancient customs to the detriment of other inhabitants.

Transhumance, or the seasonal migration of herds, had been practised in Provence from a very early date. The thirteenth century growth of the cloth industry and of towns, with their heavy demands for meat, only served to increase the economic importance of this time-honoured custom. The herds were usually assembled by wealthy personages who were owners of the animals or undertook responsibility for them. The route taken by the herds as they left for the mountains in spring lay along broad tracks left free among the fields by cultivators, under threat of dire penalties; as they went they raised clouds of dust, from which the toll known as *pulverage* took its picturesqe name. On their return in autumn the livestock spread out over the now denuded arable. The *nourriguiers* claimed that they had the right to profit by collective grazing, either as native-born inhabitants or by right of purchase, whether from a community which had run into debt or, more frequently and over the protests of the peasants, from a lord who was short of money.[14] Age-old rules, originally designed to ensure that each member of a small group had enough grazing for the beasts on whom his life depended, were thus being twisted to serve the interests of a few large-scale contractors—'noble and discreet persons' they called themselves at Salon—whose sheep devoured all. The small arable farmers, who thanks to the shape of their fields were well able to keep their animals in pasture on their own stubble and had access to the *herms* for an adequate supplement of herbage, were happy to abolish collective grazing altogether, now that it had become merely an excuse for subjecting their property to the depredations of the migrating herds. In Provence the destruction of the ancient system of collective grazing was one episode in the eternal conflict between arable and stock farming—one might almost say between the

[13] Arch. B.-Rhône, B 3347, fol. 607.

[14] Cf. an instructive complaint from the inhabitants of Sault dated 1543, in T. Gavot, *Titres de l'ancien comté de Sault*, ii, 1867, p. 137; and compare with the *bandites* of the county of Nice studied by L. Guyot, *Les droits de bandite*, 1884; J. Labarrière, *Le pâturage d'été*, 1923.

settler and the nomad—and between the small producer and the capitalist.

The change left no outward mark on the countryside. Few actual enclosures were erected, perhaps none. (The cypress hedges now so characteristic of the Provençal landscape were put up as wind-breaks, not to keep out livestock; most of them were introduced in the nineteenth century.)[15] There was no amalgamation of plots. In Provence the transition to individualist farming was made without disturbing the material framework erected by former generations.

In the open countryside of the north communities long retained their attachment to collective grazing, some of them down into our own day. But, especially in the sixteenth century and after, there were some individuals for whom it was a detestable imposition. These were the proprietors of the extensive and continuous parcels, formed by patient accumulation, which in many places were now starting to replace the traditional strip fields. The form of these properties made it possible for their owners to restrict grazing on the stubble to their own beasts. Considerations of rank made the thought of submission to rules binding on lesser folk intolerable. Lastly, the possession of well-filled stables which produced a good supply of manure made it possible, on some occasions at least, to dispense with the customary period of fallow. Instead of leaving their land completely idle for a year, these farmers preferred to sow a light cereal crop, such as millet, or an oil-producing crop, or best of all legumes, *fayoulx* or *porées*. This practice, known as 'stolen fallow' (was not the ground being robbed of its repose?) had had the blessing of classical agronomists and was probably never completely abandoned; but in the early Middle Ages it was rare and intermittent. As time went on, however, the custom of sowing the fallow was gradually reintroduced in provinces where urban markets offered producers an attractive outlet, in Flanders, for example, where it probably became widespread towards the end of the Middle Ages. When Provence was passing through the final stages of the movement against collective obligations, the advantages of 'stolen fallow'

[15] For an instance of enclosure, however, see H. Boniface, *Arrests notables*, iv, 1708, 3rd part, II, i, c. xxi.

may well have combined with the fear of the migratory herds to persuade the landowners of the virtues of reform. In Normandy the custom is attested from the beginning of the sixteenth century.[16]

In regions where the communal herd was still allowed free range over the stubble fields, that is in nearly all unenclosed regions with the exception of Provence, freedom to sow fallow fields would be useless without the protection of hedges or deep ditches. Here and there new barriers were in fact set up, despite the protests of village communities. In the majority of cases, however, these enclosures were not for the protection of arable. For reasons which will shortly be explained, fencing off was primarily used to preserve grassland, or to facilitate the conversion of arable into gardens or orchards, as in the case of the enclosure forbidden by the count of Montbéliard shortly after 1565.[17] Even at the end of the eighteenth century, the greater part of the arable was free of the type of 'Enclosure' which from Tudor times onward had been transforming the English countryside. If we look at early eighteenth-century field maps of the Beauce and Berry which show the broad patches assembled by men who had 'joined field to field',[18] we find that they are just as open as the narrow strips of the small peasants. Customary rules were too well established and the perpetual character of the tenures presented too many obstacles, for the movement towards integration of plots to result in enclosure on a vast scale, even if, as is doubtful, anyone had desired it. But there was one exception, namely Normandy.

The more recent history of the once open regions of Normandy has been dominated by three circumstances. One is of an agrarian nature: in the Pays de Caux at least, there were many places where the fields were arranged on the random pattern which, as in Provence, proved especially favourable to the abolition of collective obligations. The second circumstance

[16] Arch. B.-du-Rhône, B 3348, fol. 589 v° (Carnoules); *Le grand coustumier du pays et duché de Normandie . . . avec plusieurs additions . . . composées par . . . Guillaume le Rouille*, 1539, c. viii. From Burgundy there is evidence of the cultivation of *milot* on the fallow at Semur in the year 1370: B. Prost, *Inventaires mobiliers*, i, 1902–4, No. 1171 (noted by M. Deléage).

[17] *Mém. de la Soc. d'émulation de Montbéliard*, 1895, p. 218; further prohibitions on enclosure were issued in 1703 and 1748: Arch. Nat., K 2195 (6).

[18] Plates VII and XIV.

was of a legal nature. The duchy of Normandy was centralised at an early date and possessed a single legal code, which was first set out in due form during the thirteenth century in compilations which although private in origin were soon recognised by legal authority as sources of law, and served as the basis of the official version published in 1583. In its agrarian constitution, however, there was much less uniformity, since Normandy included both open plains and the wooded country, where enclosure had the sanction of tradition. The custumals of the thirteenth century, having to cater for both types and no doubt failing to distinguish between them, arrived at a hybrid solution whose interpretation is less than crystal-clear. They recognise collective grazing—*banon* they call it—on empty lands 'if they have not been enclosed from time immemorial'. But did this mean that people could enclose lands as they wished? It was probably intended that decision on this point should rest with local custom. But what an opportunity this text offered to self-interested interpretation by persons bent on enclosure, especially when we remember that the custumals had the authority of written law, while local usage was a matter of oral transmission! The last important fact about Normandy to be borne in mind is that from the twelfth century onwards the fields of Caux and Lower Normandy were the richest in all France. In these regions agriculture soon attained a peak of perfection. From the thirteenth century the practice of deep ploughing over fallow land had already induced the customary codes to limit collective grazing on unenclosed land to a shorter season, ending in mid-March.[19] The practice of sowing the fallow became respectable at a very early date. And since there was no lack of prosperous bourgeois landowners, there was a powerful trend towards large-scale ownership.

From the sixteenth century onwards the enclosure of arable on these fertile plains progressed to an extent undreamed of in other regions. The large arable plots so carefully pieced together at Bretteville l'Orgueielleuse by the Perrotte de Cairon were real Enclosures, '*parcs*'.[20] To look at them one might

[19] The prohibition was not strictly observed, at least in the Caux region; see *infra*, p. 209, n. 21.
[20] Plate XVI.

imagine one is looking at an Enclosure map from a volume on English agrarian history. In theory and practice alike the law favoured unrestricted recognition of the right to enclose fields which was admitted as early as 1539 by Guillaume la Rouille, one of the earliest commentators on the custumals, and given explicit sanction by the official code of 1583, which defined and amplified the provisions of the earlier collections. In the eighteenth century the plain of Caen was covered with growing hedges, at that time even more numerous than they are now, since a number were destroyed by Revolutionaries engaged in flushing out royalist supporters who had found shelter behind them, while others were demolished more pacifically by landowners during the nineteenth century, after the total abolition of collective grazing had made their continued existence pointless.

But the erection of enclosures was an expensive business. One might think it would be better simply to acknowledge that every landowner had the right, if he so desired, to keep his neighbour's livestock off his property, even if his fields were open. The earliest commentators on customary law never went as far as this; it was left to Basnage, writing in 1678, to take the plunge. The law long remained hesitant. In the seventeenth century we find the Parlement quashing the decision of a lower court which had admitted the claim of a lord to allow collective grazing on his land only if he were paid for it. In the following century the Parlement's judgments were more indulgent towards landowners, especially in the Caux region. In this area the rapid growth of the cloth industry in both towns and villages had produced the classic antagonism between arable and stock farming. In the words of a report written in 1786, 'it is by no means rare in these parts to see those who have no flocks contriving ways of preventing those who have from grazing their beasts during the *banon*, and what is more, there are even judges who connive at this system, so contrary to the public interest'. The enclosure movement was thus not allowed to proceed without protest from some quarters; characteristically, resistance was especially vigorous in villages such as Aliermont which had originated in medieval clearances and whose long narrow fields contrasted with the open plots of the ancient Scandinavian settlements. But despite such resistance, by the middle of the eighteenth century the introduction of enclosures or their equivalent had brought Normandy to a stage of agrarian development markedly different from that of regions like the Île de France and Lorraine, which still observed the collective customs relating to the arable in all their essential features.[21]

## 2. THE DECLINE OF COLLECTIVE RIGHTS OVER THE MEADOWS [22]

Where fallow land was still left unsown it was of small importance to a cultivator, if his arable was of the normal type, that the communal herd had access to it once the harvest was done —except, that is, in Provence, where the depredations of the

[21] The essential texts are as follows: *Summa de legibus*, ed. Tardif, VIII—in the sentence in c. 1 'nisi clause fuerint vel ex antiquitate defense' the word *vel* must mean 'that is to say . . .', an interpretation demanded by the words immediately following ('ut haie et hujusmodi) and still more by the content of c. 4; *Le grand coustumier . . . avec plusieurs additions composées par . . . maistre Guillaume le Rouille*, 1539, glosses on c. viii; G. Terrien, *Commentaire . . .*, 2nd ed. 1578, p. 120; Customs of 1583, c. lxxxiii; Basnage, *La coutume reformée*, 2nd ed., 1694, i, p. 126; judgment dismissing the claims of the lord of Agon to be paid for allowing collective grazing, 1 July 1616: Arch. Seine-Infr., register entitled *Audiences 1616, Costentin* (cf. Bibl. Rouen, ms. 869); judgment dated 19 December 1732, admittedly relating to land sown with young oaks but interesting for the characteristic marginal note 'No-one is obliged to set up a fence; the sown lands are protected without being enclosed'.; Arch. Seine-Infér., *Recueil d'arrets . . . depuis la Saint-Martin* 1732, 24–6; memorandum from the representative of the municipal assembly of Beaumont-le-Hareng, addressed to the *Commission intermédiaire*, Arch. Seine-Infr., C 2120—but it must be pointed out that while respecting the wishes of the proprietors in other respects, the judgment of 26 August 1734 for the county of Aliermont (*Recueil d'arrêts . . . depuis la Saint-Martin*, 1732, p. 204) prohibited collective grazing only during the close season from mid-March to 14 September, in keeping with written custom but contrary to usage: there was no doubt some change in the jurisprudence as a result of this decision. In the Caux region the villagers did not allow the communal herd to range over the whole parish but kept it within the limits of smaller *cantons* or *cueillettes*; always lukewarm in support of collective grazing, in the seventeenth century the courts became actively hostile: Basnage *op. cit.*, i, 127 (I have checked the judgments); at Verson in the thirteenth century villeins who wanted to enclose paid the lord a *porpresture* (L. Delisle, *Etudes*, 670, v. 103 ff.), but this relates obviously to changes in land use—probably the conversion of arable into a garden or orchard since this particular seigneurial right had its origin in a champart tenure.

[22] For this and the following section, and for Chapter VII, see my articles entitled 'La lutte pour l'individualisme agraire dans la France du XVIII siècle', published in *Annales d'histoire économique*, 1930. Here I shall mention only references not cited there. See also: H. Sée, *La vie économique . . . en France au XVIII siècle, 1924*; for the commons see G. Bourgin, *Nouvelle revue historique du droit*, 1908.

commercial flocks were a menace. The village herd might deprive him of a little of his stubble and a few weeds, but they left him the benefit of their dung; and his own beasts were among them. But where the meadows were concerned it was a different matter. It had long been recognised that in most places the meadows offered the opportunity of a second hay harvest. As a rule, however, this aftermath was either cropped by the communal herd or harvested by the community for its own profit. The proprietor, who gained nothing, was far from content at this dissipation of a valuable product, which he would have been glad to store as winter fodder for his stock or sell on his own account for a good price. What made it worse was that he had no compensatory benefit. Meadows were scarce and concentrated in the hands of just a few owners; many villagers who took advantage of collective grazing on another man's pasture had nothing to offer him in exchange.

Meadow owners were dangerous people to displease, since they were often in positions of power: they might be lords who, on the dissolution of their demesne, had relinquished their arable but retained the grasslands; or they might be one of the many types of land engrossers, who had purchased meadows in the course of their estate building. Such men were better placed than the village community when it came to imposing their will (even when what they wanted was illegal), and they were less likely to be deterred by fear of reprisals; they soon started looking for ways of exempting their meadows from collective grazing or at least of postponing the entry of the herd until after the second crop had been cut. They did not hesitate to protect their hay by putting up substantial barriers, which even in the thirteenth century provoked numerous lawsuits between lords and villagers. Their efforts met with considerable success. For when lords managed to exclude the communal herd, either completely or until after the second crop, for several successive years, their violation of custom itself became a tradition which the courts were almost bound to accept as a right. From the sixteenth century the judges in fact showed themselves very amenable on this point; in Champagne they accepted a proscription which had lasted for three years as effective, thus creating (like the Parlements of Dijon and Rouen), a jurisprudence favourable to this type of enclosure or exemption, except in cases where the law expressly forbade it.[23] In other instances we find the lord seizing the chance offered by the compilation of a terrier, the taking of recognisances or the conclusion of an agreement to secure his subjects' recognition of the privileged status of the seigneurial meadows.[24] Three classes of meadowland were gradually defined: those permanently closed; the somewhat larger category that lacked permanent enclosures but were only open to collective grazing after the second hay-harvest, *prés gaigneaux*, *prés de revivre*; and finally, by far the largest category, meadows still subject to the traditional obligation in all its rigour. The amount of grassland assigned to each category depended on the balance of local forces. As a rule the peasants offered some resistance. By very ancient tradition, which with the passage of time had acquired a distinctly emotional colouring, grass was held in higher regard than any other natural product and was regarded as the common birthright of all. A *cahier* from Lorraine drawn up in 1789 asserts that 'from the creation of the world up to the present time, the second crop' has always belonged to the communities.

But the time came when more powerful contenders entered the lists. The habit of allowing the aftermath to be squandered by collective use disquieted the authorities responsible for the general economy of the country: the governors, intendants and *Cours Souveraines*. Their concern was especially great in years when the first crop had been light and in frontier regions, where the interests of the Royal Cavalry, an important consumer of forage, were closely affected. In years when the spring was abnormally wet or dry it gradually became the custom to issue ordinances relating to the affected regions, which forbade or allowed the reservation of part or all of the second crop. These

[23] Taisand, *Coutumes générales des pays et duché de Bourgogne*, 1698, p. 748; I. Bouvot, *Noveau recueil des arrests*, ii, 1728, p. 764; P. J. Brillon, *Dictionnaire des Arrêts*, v, 1727, pp. 108 and 109. For judgments in the opposite sense, see Fréminville, *Pratique*, iii, pp. 430 ff. For Normandy, see Bibl. de Rouen, ms. 870, fol. 283; Arch. Seine-Infér. register of judgments, July-August 1588, judgment delivered 7 July; P. Duchemin, *Petit-Quevilly*, 1900, p. 59. The Parlement of Paris displayed a similar tendency in the sixteenth century: see the curious judgments in J. Imbert, *Enchiridion*, 1627, p. 194.
[24] Cf. (only a few examples from the many which could be cited), Saint-Ouen-en-Brie, Bibl. Nat., lat. 10943, fol. 297 (June 1266); A. Lacroix, *L'arrondissement de Montélimar*, v, 1877, pp. 24 and 183 (24 April 1415 and 27 January 1485); P. L. David, *Amance en Franche-Comté*, 1926, 458 (1603).

ordinances, which begin in the sixteenth century and become more frequent during the seventeenth, were at first issued very sparingly and only where the need was genuine. But the practice was habit-forming. The Parlements, which in many provinces claimed the right to exercise agrarian discipline in such matters, had a natural tendency to favour the rights of the landowners. Even the intendants, who had at first been disposed to protect the communities, in the seventeenth century came to be influenced by new economic theories which freely sacrificed the interests of small-holders and of established community rights to the necessities of production. About 1682 an attempt was made to abolish collective grazing on the aftermath in Alsace, one of the provinces most exposed to military attack. The attempt was premature; resisted by the communities, and with only tepid support from the courts, the regulation remained to all intents and purposes a dead letter. But in the eighteenth century edicts and judgments succeeded one another with increasing frequency and there were few parts of the kingdom unaffected by them; although in theory always of an emergency nature and limited to the current year, the edicts were issued on the slightest pretext, often without any real justification at all. In at least two provinces (in Béarn, from the beginning of the century, in Franche Comté from near its end) they were being automatically reissued year after year. 'The little folk' of the villages protested, not without violence; but also, in general, without success.

Even so, the victory of individual ownership was still not secure. It was easy to talk of reserving the aftermath. But who was to profit? It was here that difficulties arose, as the various claimants advanced their rights. At their head, naturally enough, were the proprietors. But the communities were also perfectly capable of undertaking the harvest and its distribution or sale on their own account; however, although their interest was sharply distinct from that of the tiny minority of owners, the villagers who had no grassland of their own included both *laboureurs* and manual workers, which meant that they were divided among themselves: whatever method of distribution was proposed seemed likely to affect these two groups in different ways. Finally, over and above the peasants was the lord, himself as a rule the proprietor of several meadows; and not infrequently the lord was armed with special privileges, for example the grazing right known as '*troupeau à part*' or *herbes mortes*, and any loss he suffered from reservation of the second crop might be made grounds for claiming an indemnity—in Lorraine a levy of a third of the community's produce. It is hardly surprising that these conflicting claims, symptomatic of a complex society caught in a tangled web of archaic survivals, were handled with indecision. Some Parlements, Metz for example, tended to oscillate from one extreme position to another. Where the law did achieve consistency, it was in a sense that varied greatly with the province. In regions such as Franche Comté and Béarn, where the annual prohibition on collective grazing on the meadows was coupled with a system allowing the proprietor to take the whole of the second crop for himself, all traces of the old obligations vanished. Elsewhere, in Burgundy and Lorraine for example, they were by no means completely dead, since there were still years when collective grazing on the aftermath was permitted; and, in seasons when this was not allowed, some or all of the forage thus withheld from the communal herd was returned to the community in another form. But since the amount of hay distributed to each man usually depended on the number of his cattle, the manual workers, foredoomed victims of the agricultural revolution, were inevitably among those who suffered considerably from the change. To sum up, the ancient communal practices disappeared from the meadows little by little, attacked by erosion from all sides, but never the object of wholesale reform.

### 3. THE TECHNICAL REVOLUTION

The essence of the technical revolution, which was to lend fresh vigour to the attack on collective obligations, can be summed up in a few words: the abolition of what was described by one agronomist, François de Neufchateau, as 'the disgrace of the fallows'. The land which under the straight fallow system had remained unsown for one out of every two or three years was henceforth to be allowed no repose. No greater contribution could have been made to the material well-being of mankind. It meant that agricultural production could be doubled or made to yield half as much again of its former value, so that a much larger population could be sustained; and since in practice the population increase did not keep pace exactly with the increase in yields, although there were now more people, they could be better fed than they had been in the past. Without this quite unprecedented avanced there could have been no large-scale industrial development based on huge urban populations divorced from direct contact with the soil, in a sense no 'nineteenth century', with all this expression implies for us of a time of human ferment and dramatically accelerated change.

But the older agrarian regimes worked as interlocking systems. It was difficult to take an axe to one part without destroying the whole. Several conditions had to be fulfilled before any radical changes in cultivation were possible.

What was to be sown in the course previously assigned to fallow? Corn, which was one suggestion, was obviously unsuitable. Observation proved that land perpetually sown with the same plant, or one of its near relatives, was doomed to produce only infinitesimal yields. What was needed was a crop whose roots spread through the humus at a level different from that reached by cereals. Vegetables, which come immediately to mind, were as a rule the starting point for experiment. But some places were unsuited to their cultivation, and there were limits to their consumption. The same is true of flax and rape. It was obviously not worth upsetting the whole of the ancient agrarian order on their count alone.

Nor was the correct choice of plant the only consideration. However suitable the alternative crop might be, there was still a danger of exhausting the soil by continuous cultivation; this could only be averted by an increased dose of fertiliser, and since chemical fertilisers had not been invented this in turn meant an increase in the supply of dung and so an increase in the number of livestock. But here was what seemed at first sight an insoluble problem. The fallow period had not only given the land a rest but had also provided grazing. During the seventeenth and eighteenth centuries the Parlement of Paris decreed through its judgments that certain villages round the capital should observe the traditional courses, including the fallow year; they were afraid that the new methods would interfere with the sheep-farming on which Paris depended for its meat supply.[25] It looked as though an attempt to abolish the fallow year while maintaining and actually intensifying animal husbandry was equivalent to trying to square the circle.

The solution of this twofold problem was provided by the cultivation of 'artificial' forage. The essential feature of the plan was to sow forage crops alternately with corn, thereby ensuring, as Saint-Laurent put it,

> From fields so lately harvested
> A tender blade for beasts astonishéd.[26]

The plants chosen were legumes such as clover, sainfoin or lucerne, whose roots penetrate deeper than those of cereals and absorb the chemical nutrients of the soil in widely differing proportions; or root crops such as the turnip—so ubiquitous in the writings of contemporary agronomists—which had the further advantage of making hoeing essential, so that the arable was periodically cleansed. The cultivation of these crops was not a complete innovation. Most of them had long been in use, but grown only in small quantities and never in fields. They had been regarded as garden vegetables: in a sense it might be said that the agricultural revolution was the triumph of horticulture over tillage, since it saw the invasion of the arable by garden produce, gardening methods (weeding and intensive manuring) and gardening conditions (no free grazing and fencing where necessary).[27] At the end of the eighteenth century the list of vegetable discoveries was augmented by the inclusion of the potato, which had been known since its introduction from America but whose cultivation had long remained on a small scale and restricted to the eastern provinces, where it was used primarily as fodder; its wider dissemination helped

---

[25] Cf. *supra*, p. 43, n. 27; the reasons are given in the summing up by d'Aguesseau, the Advocate-General, 28 February, 1722; *Journal des Audiences*, vii, 647.

[26] *Les Saisons, L'automne*, ed. of 1826, p. 161.

[27] In impoverished regions such as the Marche even wheat, more delicate than rye, was sometimes cultivated as a garden plant: G. Martin, *Mém. de la Soc. des sciènces naturelles de la Creuse*, viii, 109. The artificial meadows were sometimes made on the site of ancient oak plantations, which had always been free of collective obligations: Arch. Nat., H 1502, n⁰ 1, fol. 5 v°. We know from several instances that sainfoin was being cultivated in the region round Paris during the seventeenth century; it is equally clear, from records relating to tithes, that at this period sainfoin was sown in closes or orchards: *Recueil des édits ... rendus en faveurs des curez*, 1708, pp. 25, 73, 119, 135, 165, 183.

to exorcise the spectre of famine from a peasant population hitherto dependent on cereals. Later still came sugar beet, destined to partner corn in the most classical of all crop rotations. In its earliest phase, however, the 'new agriculture' (as it was described by its theoretical exponents) was linked in the public mind with the use of forage crops.

At first the innovators clung quite naturally to the old biennial or triennial system. But it was soon realised that many forage crops gave a better yield when they were left undisturbed to establish themselves on the same ground for several years. Then, when corn was sown again, the growth was all the thicker and the ears all the heavier. This discovery led to the creation of short-term 'artificial meadows' and the construction of longer and more flexible rotation cycles, to the total disruption of the former system.

There was one other condition which had to be met before a technical revolution could even be attempted (its presence was still no guarantee of success, since certain legal changes were necessary, which will be dealt with later): the realisation that a revolution was both possible and necessary. The main inspiration came from abroad. The agricultural revolution was a European event, whose filiations are very interesting to trace. In every country, fallow farming was first abandoned in the regions of densest settlement, especially where urban development was well advanced: in the areas immediately adjacent to certain German cities, in parts of Normandy and Provence, and above all in the two regions which since the Middle Ages had been the main centres of urban civilisation in Europe, northern Italy and Flanders. As early as the sixteenth century, a Venetian agronomist, the first of his tribe in the West, had recommended a course of cultivation including forage crops and omitting the fallow period;[28] but despite this contribution and despite references to Lombard practices in French writings of the seventeenth century, the Italians found few imitators north of the Alps. It was the farmers of Flanders and Brabant who made a vital contribution to our agricultural revolution, no doubt partly because their methods were better adapted to our climate. Yet if we ignore the part of Flanders which was

[28] C. Torello, *Ricordo d'agricoltora*; the date of the first and best edition is 1556— the edition in the Bibliothèque Nationale was published at Venice in 1567.

annexed to France in the time of Louis XIV and represented only an insignificant fraction of the whole kingdom, it must be admitted that the influence of these neighbours in the Low Countries reached us only by an indirect route, via England. The first book to be published in English which set out a clear-cut programme of rotation based on forage plants was entitled *'Discourse on agriculture as it is practised in Brabant and Flanders'*.[29] In an England which was giving birth to large-scale industry, where the demand for bread and meat was heavy and the land increasingly dominated by proprietors with a genuine interest in innovation, the 'new agriculture' found a receptive soil where it could flourish and be perfected. But few could deny that the pioneers took the essential features of their programme from what they had seen in the plains of Flanders. However, when the French theorists entered the field about 1760—the date of the publication of the *Eléments d'agriculture* by Duhamel du Monceau—it was from England that they received the torch.

The ideas and theories must be the first topic for our consideration. In 1766 an observer in Touraine could say 'there is no land-owner'—he is, of course, thinking of large landowners —'who does not reflect on what advantages may accrue to him'[30] Pessimists like Grimm mocked at these 'arm-chair farmers', sometimes with good reason. But reflection, reference to books as a guide to practice, attempts to apply reason to technical progress—all were significant features. None of the agricultural innovations of previous generations had been so intellectual in complexion. But it still remains true that the new learning only met with some success in France because it was launched in a society where all manner of propitious circumstances worked in its favour.

The population was increasing at a great rate, which made the public authorities realise that production of necessities had to be increased, to make the country as far as possible independent of imports whose flow was always unreliable and had on several occasions been threatened with interruption by the outbreak of war. The larger population was also a guarantee that proprietors who could make their estates more productive

[29] R. E. Prothero, *The Pioneers*, 1888, pp. 249 and 32; cf. *Dictionary of National Biography*, under R. Weston.

[30] G. Weulersse, *Le mouvement physiocratique*, 1910, ii, 152.

would find a steady market. A whole new school of economic theory developed which concentrated on production, if necessary to the exclusion of all other human interests. Further, the amassing of lands by the nobility and the bourgeoisie had led to the reconstitution of large estates, now ripe for technical improvement. Investors of capital turned readily from industry and commerce, where opportunities were limited and returns problematical, to the land—undoubtedly with the intention of extracting greater profit than was afforded merely by seigneurial rents. Lastly, this was the century of Enlightenment, in which thinkers were guided by two great principles. The first was that practice, like beliefs, must be submitted to reason, which meant that respect for tradition merely for its own sake was no longer valid; ancient agrarian habits, classed with Gothic buildings as barbarous, must be done away with if they had nothing but antiquity to commend them. Secondly, the rights of the individual were considered paramount, and in urgent need of liberation from the stranglehold of customary restrictions imposed by communities where enlightenment burned low. The craze for 'agronomy' which swept the salons has sometimes raised a smile; the physiocrat theory that all wealth derives from the land certainly appears strangely naive. We can agree that these were literary fashions, doctrinaire systems. But they were also and above all an emotional and intellectual indication of the presence of a mighty ground swell, the agricultural revolution.

The history of a technical development is the history of contacts between minds. The changes in agriculture, as with other changes of this order, were initiated by small groups of like-minded men: men in the offices of the central or local administration who had early been converted to the principles of reformed agronomy; agricultural societies, more than semi-official in character; and above all, less exalted but more effective, men up and down the country who were actually engaged in the intelligent exploitation of their estates. The initiative rarely came from the peasants. When we find peasants giving spontaneous support to the new methods it is usually because they had some personal or corporate contact with more progressive regions; the small producers of Perche, whose side-lines were cloth-peddling, cattle-droving and dealing in cask-hoops, learned the new techniques from travelling with their wares in Normandy and the Île de France.[31] More frequently the idea of creating artificial meadows was imitated from someone in the neighbourhood who had already introduced them: a gentleman who had learned of the new ideas from his reading or his travels, a country priest widely-read in the new authorities, an iron-master or post-master on the lookout for new inventions which would help to feed his teams of animals—towards the end of the century many post-masters found favour as tenant-farmers with proprietors eager to improve their land. Nor was it only ideas that travelled; Flemings, natives of the fatherland of agricultural progress, were introduced as tenant-farmers or labourers into Hainault, Normandy, the Gâtinais and Lorraine, just as somewhat later there was a move to attract men from the Caux region into Brie. Step by step, the cultivation of forage crops, accompanied by many other realised or attempted improvements—in equipment, in the selection of breeding animals, in the prevention of plant and animal diseases—spread from field to field. Fallow farming was on the wane, especially in regions of large estates and on fields directly adjacent to villages, where manuring was easier to carry out. Its disappearance was very gradual. Innate custom and economic difficulties were not the only bar to technical improvement. Over much of the country the innovators came up against the rugged obstacle presented by the legal system. Some revision of the law was essential if the technical revolution was to succeed, and it was to this problem that the authorities addressed themselves during the second half of the century.

4. THE TREND TOWARDS AGRARIAN INDIVIDUALISM:
COMMONS AND ENCLOSURES

In pre-Revolutionary France the heaths, marshes and woodlands were set aside for the collective enjoyment of the inhabitants; and even in enclosed regions where a man was fully master of his own ploughlands, this freedom was only made possible by the existence of the communal waste. Over much

[31] Dureau de la Malle, *Description du bocage percheron*, 1823, pp. 58 ff.

of the kingdom the use of the arable was itself strictly regulated in the interests of the group as a whole. Agronomists of the new school declared war on these communal practices. The commons, those 'vestiges of our ancient barbarism',[32] were condemned as a waste of much good land which with intelligent exploitation might be made to yield a rich harvest, or at least support a greater number of livestock than in the past. One notable expert, the Comte d'Essuile, exclaimed over 'the dearth of produce for consumption or sale among the masses'.[33] These gentlemen sometimes exaggerated the potentialities of the empty lands, which had often remained uncultivated simply because they were uncultivable. But they were not always mistaken. If productivity was to be the criterion, the Duc de Rohan was surely right when he complained of the Breton peasants, who by stripping the heaths of turves 'down to the bare rock' had made them 'permanently sterile'.[34] When they turned to collective grazing, the reformers could claim with some justice that the herds themselves derived little real benefit from a custom which made them toil over a wide expanse where blades of grass were so few and far between; what was worse, the existence of this system and its concomitant restrictions made the abolition of fallow farming and the introduction of forage crops impossible. These were all cogent arguments. But they could not, by themselves, have induced the real hatred displayed by the enemies of the traditional regime, who were motivated by deeper feelings of which they were only partially conscious. Many were themselves great land-owners, whose interests and pockets were directly damaged by these hampering customs; their indignation was increased by the fact that the existence of commons and grazing rights made it too easy for small-holders and manual labourers to eke out a meagre living, encouraged them to live in 'idleness' when they might have been hiring themselves out to work on the great estates. In the eyes of men with a keen appreciation of individual effort, such people were a disgrace to 'property'.

Towards the middle of the century the new ideas won some powerful supporters: provincial Estates, for example those of Béarn, which came out strongly in favour of agrarian changes

---

[32] Mémoire de la Soc. d'agriculture de Bourges, Arch. Nat., H 1495, No. 20.
[33] *Traité politique*, 1770, p. VI.      [34] Du Halgouët, *Le duché de Rohan*, 56.

in 1754, to be followed closely by those of Languedoc and Burgundy; intendants and their staffs; even some ministers and important government servants. Bertin, Controller-General between 1759 and 1763 and afterwards Secretary of State, with the support of his friend and most constant adviser, Daniel Trudaine, forwarded the cause of moderate reform in a spirit of cautious empiricism. But the man who exerted the greatest influence was d'Ormesson, intendant of finances in the department of the Controller-General, the office which until 1773 was in practice responsible for the direction of agricultural affairs; while ministers came and went, d'Ormesson remained at his post, firmly guiding government policy into what his exact and methodical mind conceived to be the path of true progress.

The theories were now translated into action. A series of legislative measures was issued, usually after an enquiry, and directed to each province in turn—France was never fully unified under the *Ancien Régime*. Between 1769 and 1781 edicts were issued authorising partition of the commons in the Three Bishoprics, in Lorraine, Alsace, the Cambrésis, Flanders, Artois, Burgundy, and the Generality of Auch and Pau. In other regions ordinances or judgments might be handed down by the *Conseil du Roi* or the regional authorities, authorising partition in expressly defined localities. In Brittany a wholesale leasing out of heathland was accomplished under the auspices of a legal code which favoured the landlords. The numerous benefits attaching to land clearance, especially those of a fiscal nature, were a further incentive to the exploitation of much land which by custom or sufferance had formerly been reserved for communal grazing; this was an open invitation to usurpation, to which both the wealthy and a throng of petty assarters responded.

The attack on collective obligations was just as vigorous. In 1766 the Estates of Languedoc obtained a judgment from the Parlement of Toulouse which in principle forbade compulsory collective grazing over much of the province, save where the communities expressly decided otherwise. The Parlement of Rouen prohibited collective grazing on some pastures without qualification, as did the *Conseil Souverain* of Roussillon and the Parlement of Paris in respect of certain sectors under its jurisdiction. In other places artificial meadows were given complete protection, by bailiwick courts, by intendants, or even by simple village communities, usually acting under the guidance of higher authorities. In 1767, at the instigation of d'Ormesson, the central government entered the fray. It seems that fear of popular demonstrations made outright suppression of collective grazing on the arable stubble too revolutionary and provocative a measure to contemplate. But the time was judged ripe for an attack on two ancient customs, the rules prohibiting enclosure and the practice of intercommoning. It was held that so long as he was willing to pay the cost of fences and ditches, a proprietor should be entitled to shut off his land and make himself master of his own fields, free to exclude his neighbours' livestock at all seasons of the year. Intercommoning was attacked, because where it existed any reform had to be agreed by all the villages concerned, so that in practice it was impossible for one group to break away and relax the grazing rules on their own land. Between 1767 and 1777 a series of edicts granted freedom to enclose in Lorraine, the Three Bishoprics, the Barrois, Hainault, Flanders, the Boulonnais, Champagne, Burgundy, Franche Comté, Roussillon, Béarn, Bigorre and Corsica. Between 1768 and 1771 intercommoning was officially abolished in Lorraine, the Three Bishoprics, the Barrois, Hainault, Champagne, Franche Comté, Roussillon, Béarn, Bigorre and Corsica.

The plan was an ambitious one and clearly owed much to what was being accomplished across the Channel by the English Parliament. Yet in France government action came somewhat abruptly to a halt, round about 1771; the last edict of enclosure, for the Boulonnais, was issued in 1777, but this was the fruit of negotiations started eight years earlier, and the only other measures taken after 1771 were purely local in application and few in number. A chill wind of timidity and discouragement seems to have assailed the official mind; when asked for their advice on reforms already accomplished or plans newly conceived, the administrators now counselled prudence, or even complete abstention from future undertakings. The essay in agrarian policy on the grand scale had encountered difficulties unforeseen by its original authors. French rural society under the *Ancien Régime* was so complex a structure that attempts to overthrow the ancient customs inevitably came up against a multiplicity of obstacles, all the more difficult to anticipate and overcome because their nature varied with the region.

Resistance came from many quarters. Some of it we may be inclined to leave on one side as being limited or temporary in its effects. Thus there were noblemen who opposed the erection of new barriers because they would spoil the hunting which was their pride and pleasure: on occasion, however, their objections carried weight—were not the lands lying within the royal hunting grounds strictly protected against enclosure by His Majesty's venerers? There were many administrators and still more magistrates who respected existing rights, including 'this form of property belonging to village communities as a body', to use the interpretation of collective grazing advanced by the Procurator-General of Paris; such men could not but regard the economists who saw property exclusively in terms of individual ownership as a revolutionary species. There were, too, plenty of people (often from the same circles) who feared that any disturbance to the established order would bring down the whole social edifice, including those seigneurial privileges which the bolder agronomists found just as reprehensidle as collective obligations. What we are left with as the hard core is the cult of tradition for its own sake. This 'sovereignty of habit', which resisted both technical innovation and reforms in agrarian law, operated at all levels of society. The setbacks encountered by certain innovators with more zeal than commonsense helped to confirm many wealthy and quite well-educated persons in their reluctance to dispense with tradition: hence the jeering attitude adopted by 'Nos Seigneurs' of the Parlement of Nancy towards the intendant of La Galaizière and his mania for agricultural reform. But nowhere was the grip of habit more powerful and widespread than among the peasants, where it was merged with an obscure sense of the dangers which the agricultural revolution held in store for the little man.

Even if we restrict our view to the level of elementary self-interest (although unavoidable, this simplification entails a distortion of what in reality was a shifting pattern), it is obvious that the technical and legal changes produced very diverse reactions from the different classes living directly or indirectly from the soil. These contrasts were still further accentuated by marked regional variations. It is true that the different classes had not always been fully conscious of their distinctive economic roles; indeed, there was often some uncertainty as to where the dividing lines between them lay. It was under the impact of the agricultural revolution itself that the sense of essential antagonism between the classes crystallised and strengthened, making them aware of their own identity. There was now scope for concerted class action, both by the lords, through the Provincial Estates or the Parlements, and by peasants of every degree, first through their community assemblies, and then, when the day of political revolution dawned in 1789, in the *cahiers*, whose resolutions often echo disputes of the preceding years.

There was nothing equivocal about the effect of the abolition of collective obligations, and of the more general abandonment of fallow farming with its threat to grazing, on the position of the manual workers and the smaller *laboureurs*, constantly in danger of slipping down into the proletariat. Possessing little or no land, cultivating whatever patches they had on a day to day basis, too uneducated to adapt themselves to the new methods, too poor to attempt improvements which demanded at least a modicum of capital, these people had not the slightest interest in a reform from which they could expect no benefit. On the contrary, they had everything to lose. Most of them owned a few animals, who subsisted entirely on the pasture offered by the common lands and the stubble fields subject to collective grazing. Theoretically, under the rules governing collective grazing the number of beasts contributed by each villager to the common herd depended on the size of his property, a system which favoured the more prosperous; but in practice it nearly always happened that even the poorest, without so much as a square inch of land to their name, were permitted to send a few cattle to graze on the stubble, a relaxation of principle which was either allowed for in the rules themselves or had become sanctioned by use—abuse, the agronomists preferred to call it.[35] Deprived of this resource, the humbler folk must either starve or fall into a much closer dependence on the *laboureurs* and greater landowners than any they had known in the past. Their position was only too clear, their protest unanimous. It was from this lowest group that shock-troops of

[35] Arch. Nat., H 1495, No. 33 (Soc. d'agriculture d'Angers) and *Annales d'histoire économique*, 1930, 523, n. 2.

rural resistance were being recruited all over the country, declaring war both on landlords who attempted improvements and on the enclosure edicts themselves. Their hand can be seen in the many breaches of enclosure expressing collective resentment at the actions of individual landlords in the Auvergne and Alsace, and at the legislation authorising enclosure in Hainault, Lorraine and Champagne.

Over the question of the commons they were much less united. It is true that any reduction in the extent of communal lands would inevitably restrict the grazing rights which were so vital to the poorer villagers. But division of the commons was not without its attraction for them, since by turning them into proprietors in their own right it might provide opportunity for the realisation of a long cherished dream. Clearly this would only happen if the division operated in a way which favoured the humbler inhabitants. The manual workers, in common with the majority of peasants, took their stand against piecemeal or outright usurpation of communal grazing by lords or village grandees who did nothing to compensate the poor for their loss, as also against the *afféagement* of the Breton heaths. They also resisted the arrangements, made in certain communities who were under the thumb of large landowners, by which the commons were shared out among existing properties in proportion to their size. The interests of the mass of the peasantry were better catered for under the royal edicts, which in keeping with their traditional concern for village populations (now giving way, however, to a growing administrative preoccupation with production) provided that the commons should be shared out by households rather than properties.[36] Except in mountainous regions, where a decrease in the alpine pasturage was in no-one's interest, the manual workers welcomed partition on these terms, since they were very willing to clear the land for their own use. In Lorraine, for example, they took advantage of their often commanding numerical position in the parochial assemblies to force assent to the laws of partition from the reluctant *laboureurs*.

Turning now to the other end of the social scale, the interests

[36] All the same, the edict dealing with Alsace allows the community a choice between partition and leasing to the highest bidder. I do not know how this system, so much more favourable to the rich, came into being.

of the lords were governed by a variety of considerations, some of them contradictory, which differed with the region. The lords filled a number of roles. They were great landowners, usually of extensive and homogeneous properties ripe for agricultural improvement, on which they were their own masters; in addition, they had a share in the collective rights, and in several provinces derived greater benefit from them than did the mass of the peasantry. Some of these privileges were precisely defined and recognised by custom, for example the *troupeau à part* of Lorraine and parts of Champagne, and the *herbes mortes* of Béarn; others were really abuses which had to all intents and purposes acquired the force of law, for example the practice prevalent in Franche Comté which allowed the lords to maintain almost unlimited numbers of beasts on the commons and fallows. The economic changes which opened up valuable markets for stock-raisers and set the stage for a capitalist mode of farming made these privileges all the more lucrative; in Lorraine the right of *troupeau à part*, farmed out to commercial sheepfarmers, was a means of keeping numerous cloth manufacturers in wool and Paris in meat. The declared policy of the landlords of Béarn, who dominated the Parlement and formed the majority in the Estates, provides the clearest possible expression of class egotism, presented with flawless logic: they said they were in favour of freedom of enclosure on the *coteaux* (the lands under intermittent cultivation), since the portions they possessed themselves were of fair size; but they were against enclosure on the *plaines*, where all the plots, their own included, were too small and hemmed in to be worth fencing off; lastly, they were determined to maintain their privilege of *herbes mortes*, no matter what barriers were erected or advances made on the sums offered in compensation. On this last point they were in fact forced to yield; but they carried the day over the two more important issues. No other group of landlords made any concrete objections to enclosure, since they realised that their well-rounded properties gave them a unique advantage. The suppression of intercommoning, however, which damaged their most cherished interests since it diminished the value of their grazing privileges, was nearly everywhere opposed; in Lorraine and Franche Comté, with support from the Parlements, the opposition was successful.

The lords had always cast covetous eyes over the commons, and their attempts at encroachment continued throughout the eighteenth century. The partitions sanctioned by law were not as a rule unfavourable to their interests; where an edict admitted the right of *triage* without laying down any precise conditions the adjudicators could accept all the claims advanced by lords. The chance of acquiring a third of the land without having to pay a penny for it was indeed tempting. In Lorraine, lords and manual workers were at one in bringing pressure to bear on the communities in favour of partition.[37]

The *laboureurs* could hardly be described as a united class. But there was one particularly sensitive issue on which they were nearly everywhere agreed, resistance to the division of common lands by households, with a third of the whole reserved to the lord. From their point of view, the extra land they acquired was insignificant when compared with the loss of grazing by the communal herd, in which their animals outnumbered the rest. Lastly, the transformation of manual workers into petty proprietors might deprive the *laboureurs* of an important source of labour, vital to the working of their holdings. The better-off peasants of Fenelle-la-Grande aired their feelings in the *cahier* they submitted in 1789: as they said, the lot of the manual worker was surely 'to work in the service of the *laboureur*'.[38] Characteristically, the Estates of Languedoc, to all practical purposes in control of agrarian policy in the province, were opposed to the division of common lands, preferring to see them leased out; in this way they satisfied both the lords, whose right to claim *cantonment* when they wished was carefully preserved, and also those peasants affluent enough to take up a lease.[39] The system was in fact an ingenious measure for creating solidarity among property owners. In Lorraine, where there was a different pattern of alliances and lords and manual workers sided together against the *laboureurs*, the struggle over the common lands took on the aspect of a genuine class conflict.

[37] The Parlement, however, was opposed to the partition edicts, perhaps because they were only prepared to concede rights of *triage* to persons holding higher jurisdictions, of whom there were very few in the duchy; but even when this is said, the point remains somewhat obscure.

[38] E. Martin, *Cahiers de doléances du bailliage de Mirecourt*, 1928, p. 90.

[39] *Annales d'histoire économique*, 1930, p. 349.

Over everything else, however, the *laboureurs* were sharply divided. The interests of the more prosperous, who tended to be tenant-farmers rather than proprietors, were almost identical with those of the landed bourgeoisie. Some made efforts to acquire part of the commons for themselves, and were agreeable to partition so long as the communities accepted a division which allocated the land in a ratio based on the value of property already held or the amount of taxes paid. As the owners or cultivators of fair-sized fields, formed from the amalgamation of a number of separate parcels, these *laboureurs* were easily converted to the cause of continuous cultivation and the use of forage crops. All they asked was to be allowed to enclose their fields, a privilege all the more valuable since with astonishing complaisance the edicts permitted enclosers to continue to exercise collective grazing rights on those parts of the arable left open, so that the encloser had everything to gain and nothing to lose; it was only in Flanders and Hainault that this system did not apply.

But *laboureurs* prepared to innovate in this way were the exception; the mass of the peasant proprietors, as of the peasants as a whole, were still wedded to their old ways. No doubt this was partly from force of habit; but it may also have been due to an instinctive and justifiable feeling that there was danger in the air. Whichever way one looks at it, adaptation to a new economic regime would have been no light matter for men of modest means with awkwardly placed fields, their shape and position dictated by an outmoded design. The specific threats represented by the reforms themselves, conceived to serve quite different interests, were further grounds for uneasiness. The rich tenant-farmers or peasant proprietors usually had meadows to make up for their loss of communal pasturage; freedom to enclose gave them the chance to conserve their precious hay for the use of their own animals. The less prosperous *laboureurs* had little or no pasturage of their own; they relied on communal grazing grounds, collective grazing on the arable stubble and the use of other people's meadows. Admittedly, they might have sown their fields with forage crops. But an innovation of this kind presented its own difficulties, especially in regions of strip fields. Any alteration in the cycle of cultivation would have to apply to the *quartiers* as a whole, and this could only be achieved by mutual agreement. Such agreement was not wholly unattainable. Towards the end of the eighteenth century we find that several communities in Lorraine had managed to set aside tracts of land, usually at the extreme edge of the main fields, to be regularly maintained as artificial meadows. But in places where there was still support for the age-old customs of collective grazing, not merely from among the manual workers but also from lords enjoying the privilege of *troupeau à part*, and where enclosing proprietors still looked to their neighbours for pasturage, it was difficult to see how these sacrosanct corners could be protected in years when the rest of the field was fallow and therefore open to the herds. One solution was to make all lands bearing forage exempt from collective obligations, and as we have seen, there were provinces which sought to impose this rule through edicts or judgments; elsewhere, village communities themselves made regulations in this sense, which in the Cambrésis and Soissonnais were usually respected. But in other regions, particularly those affected by enclosure edicts, these bye-laws were often contested in the courts and frequently quashed.[40] In fact the mere decision to exclude the herds was hollow unless there was a physical barrier to back it up. But this was precisely where the *laboureurs* of moderate means were most vulnerable. Enclosure, always an expensive matter, was especially so at a time when the shortage of timber was giving rise to innumerable complaints; it became still more costly, indeed utterly impracticable, when the plots to be enclosed were long and narrow and their boundaries excessively lengthy by comparison with the very modest area contained within them. The fact that liberty to enclose made enclosure a necessity if the fields were to be protected meant that enclosure virtually became a monopoly of the rich. Enclosure made it impossible for other cultivators to avail themselves of the improved techniques, which some of the more progressive would have been glad to employ. Had the transition been easier, the *laboureurs* as a group would no doubt gradually have abandoned their former ways; as it was, it is hardly surprising

---

[40] In Alsace the edict dealing with the commons, dated 15 April 1774, made it legal to protect one *arpent* of artificial meadow for each head of cattle employed in cultivation. This is the only measure of this sort issued by the central government under the *Ancien Régime*.

that in nearly every part of the country we find them making common cause with the manual workers whose only concern was the preservation of the traditional order, and joining with them in protests against the agrarian policy of the crown.

Basically speaking, what the reformers were attempting was not a transformation of the social order but a wholesale alteration in what the Parlement of Nancy described as the traditional 'rural economy'. It would be wrong, however, to conclude that they were blind to the far-reaching implications of the changes they advocated. Certainly, they failed to attach sufficient weight to the resistance offered by the majority of the *laboureurs*. But they were very well aware that the poorer peasants, especially the day workers, were in danger of being crushed. Despite his conversion to the new agronomy, the Archbishop of Toulouse could still declare before the Estates of Languedoc in 1766 that collective grazing was to be 'regarded as a consequence of society, a necessity among villagers belonging to the same community and the embodiment of an equality at all times just'. There were some agronomists at least who viewed the serious consequences of the agrarian revolution with misgiving. It was fears of this nature that gave Bertin and his adviser Trudaine grounds for hesitation. One intelligent observer, Musac, who was President of the Parlement of Metz, predicted the possibility of an exodus from the countryside, which would at one blow deprive large landowners of their labour force and consumers everywhere of their necessities.[41] The more ruthless, however, were left unmoved by the element of tragedy inseparable from improvements in the human condition. They were on the side of progress, and knew that progress must have its victims. Nor were they ill-disposed towards a form of economic organisation which would bring the proletariat into stricter dependence on the principal producers than it had been in the past. A distinctly callous note is often sounded. In 1784, at a time when the scarcity and high price of labour was causing concern, the Agricultural Society of Orleans

---

[41] It seems however that this exodus was already noticeable in the eighteenth century: cf. a memorandum (which must have been written by Essuile) on the partition of the commons, Arch. Nat., H 1495, No. 161 (the need to arrest the emigration to the towns and the 'vagabondage' of the 'poor people' is given as one of the reasons in favour of partition, and of partition by force); see also, for Hainault, *Annales d'histoire économique*, 1930, pp. 531.

put forward proposals for meeting the shortage: whilst rejecting the idea that artisans should be made to hire themselves out as harvesters 'because most of them are unaccustomed to heavy work', they suggest that the problem could be solved by forbidding village women and girls to go out gleaning, so that for want of other resources they would be forced to work as harvesters—and very good ones they would make, since their gleaning had accustomed them to walk with bent backs. The administrators were clearly determined to see in poverty nothing but the fruit of culpable 'indolence'.[42]

Sensitive men could hardly fail to be revolted by such obvious inhumanity. But they could take some comfort from that superb optimism which was to be handed down as the legacy of the reigning economic theory, close cousin to Dr. Pangloss, to the 'classical' school of the following century. In 1766 the subdelegate of Montier-en-Der invited general assent to the proposition that 'what is good for the public is necessarily good for the poor'; in other words, the happiness of the poor, whose whole ambition should be to find work and remain a stranger to famine, depends in the last resort on the prosperity of the rich. Calonne, when he was still the young intendant of Metz, wrote: 'since in general the manual workers and day labourers stand in relation to the cultivators as an accessory does to his principal, there is no need to fear for their lot if improvements are effected for the benefit of the producers; we can take it as constant, that when production and supplies are increased in any *canton*, the standard of living is improved for everyone, of whatever degree and condition; from this it follows that the converse must be true, and anyone who entertains the least doubts on the matter evinces a poor understanding of the natural order'. In France, as in England, it was agriculture rather than industry that first provided a platform on which capitalism (for want of a better word) could display

---

[42] Arch. Nat., K 906, No. 16 (Soc. d'Orleans). In 1765, writing of the dearth of corn, the intendant of Bordeaux said: 'This dearness, which will infallibly produce a greater abundance in future, since men hope to profit from it, will most likely excite complaints from persons among the common folk who are in poverty on account of their idleness; complaints of this kind deserve to be greeted with nothing but contempt.' Arch. de la Gironde, C 428. It is by no means difficult—I have in fact done so in another place—to collect a number of texts of this kind dealing with commons or with enclosure laws.

the disingenuous illusions and cruelty of its admirable and creative genius, decked out in the naivety of youth.

Neither the reforms introduced during the last three decades of the century nor the advance of technical innovation appreciably affected the appearance of the countryside. The only regions whose outward aspect was radically transformed were those where the advent of the agricultural revolution had coincided with a changeover from arable to grass, that is to say the eastern fringes of Hainault and the Boulonnais. This is a region where soil and climate are especially suitable for stock and dairy farming; in the eighteenth century, as communications improved and the circulation of commodities increased, its potentialities could at last be fully exploited and the old predominance of corn shaken off, especially since there were extensive corn-growing areas close at hand to supply the graziers with food. The conversion was effected by large landowners, the only people who could profit from the introduction of a new economic system. They took advantage of the freedom to enclose, which they claimed as a right, to plant stout hedges round their grasslands, whether old or new, to protect them against any exercise of collective rights which were so wasteful of hay. And while these vistas of unencumbered arable were being replaced by green hedges, the erection of barriers was going forward in other provinces, usually on seigneurial or bourgeois estates and mostly for the enclosure of meadowlands. It was grass, not arable, that stood most in need of protection. The same unevenness characterised progress in matters more strictly related to tillage; with the exception of unusually advanced provinces such as Normandy, the end of the eighteenth century saw fallow farming still generally practised on the vast majority of peasant holdings and even on many larger properties. The improvements were certainly making some headway, but at no overwhelming speed. The fact was that over much of the kingdom, above all in the regions of strip fields, much more fundamental upheavals than any so far envisaged by agrarian reformers would be needed if the new techniques were to carry the day—what was needed, in fact, was a complete redistribution of the land, such as had already been effected in England and in various parts of Germany.

There was one great obstacle still to be surmounted. The

*laboureur* who was anxious to fence off his land or free his fields from each and every extraneous obligation was often foiled by the existence of laws making the division of small properties obligatory, and from which, despite their successes in amalgamating plots, even the larger and richer proprietors were not fully exempt. The construction of several large continuous fields. each with independent access, from the tiny awkwardly-shaped plots scattered over the terrain seemed simple enough—on paper. England had already shown how it could be done; there every deed of enclosure prescribed a redistribution of properties, and the farmers had no choice but to submit. This procedure was natural enough in a country where very few tenures had achieved perpetuity; but in France any such coercion was quite inconceivable. The economists and administrators never for a moment considered even the possibility of an imposed redistribution, remaining content to recommend that exchanges be viewed with approval. This was a resort to persuasion. But even in provinces such as Burgundy where the law tried to encourage exchanges by grants of fiscal exemption, the peasants rarely co-operated; it was even more exceptional for them to take advantage of the redistributions of land proposed on generous terms by some of the higher-minded agronomists. Their reluctance is understandable; they were attached to their old habits, unwilling to exchange land whose ways they knew for the unfamiliar and possibly inferior plots belonging to a neighbour; they were concerned to reduce exposure to agrarian accidents (*orvales* as they were called in Franche Comté) to a minimum by working plots scattered over the whole terrain; and finally, with some justice, they were suspicious of a plan whose implementation would naturally have rested with the lords and the wealthy. Peasant proprietorship, born of custom in a period when land was more plentiful than men and subsequently consolidated with the help of royal patronage, had already declared its strength by acting as a brake on the progress of rural capitalism. Peasant proprietorship was now to be an obstacle to the agricultural revolution, not least because it helped to cushion the peasantry against the cruellest and most immediate of its effects. The manual workers who had lost what land they had or perhaps had never possessed any, were foredoomed victims of any radical alterations in techniques or in the economic system. The *laboureurs*, on the other hand, could reasonably hope that if they gradually adapted themselves to the new conditions they would one day reap the benefit.

# CHAPTER SEVEN

# Lines of Continuity: Past and Present

IF all the nuances are to be appreciated, the rural history of the French Revolution needs constantly to be related to the course of the political revolution as it passed through its different phases. Despite some excellent regional monographs, the general pattern of agrarian development in the nineteenth and early twentieth centuries is still too little understood for it to be summarised without risk of distortion. We must therefore be content to stop in 1789. But before leaving our subject, it is important to notice the repercussions on the recent past, and even on the present, of the development which has been the subject of this book.[1]

When the Revolutionary Assemblies tackled the agrarian question they were not faced with a completely blank sheet. The problems had already been ventilated under the monarchy, which had also made some tentative efforts at a solution. The new regime carried on where the old had left off, and in very much the same spirit. But this was no slavish imitation. The new men were able to profit from the lessons of past failures; they were moved by a noticeably different set of class considerations; and many obstacles to progress had already been removed.

Had they been left to themselves there can be no doubt that the majority of country people would simply have returned to their former communal practices, as was in fact predicted by a foreign observer, Arthur Young, in 1789. The peasants in a number of regions affected by the enclosure edicts, and by changes introduced even earlier, made some attempt in the

---

[1] Cf. for the Revolution, G. Lefebvre, in *Annales d'histoire économique*, 1929 (with a bibliography which makes it unnecessary to provide references here); G. Bourgin, in *Revue d'histoire des doctrines économiques*, 1911.

early days of the Revolution to reimpose the observance of collective obligations, sometimes by force. Demands of this kind were included in many of the *cahiers* submitted by parochial assemblies and were later pressed by rural townships and popular associations in the villages. The sans-culottes of Parly (Yonne) said of the enclosure law that it 'could only have been made by the rich for the rich, at a time when liberty was still but a word and equality but a dream'. And there were many *cahiers* and clubs to echo the denunciations of the Société Populaire of Autun, for whom the 'egotistical agriculturalists', 'miserly landowners' and 'greedy tenant farmers' were a league of parricides, whose artificial meadows, which took up so much of their estates, robbed the people of bread.[2] But the men of the Assemblies were neither *manouvriers* nor small *laboureurs*; nor did they represent their views. They were educated and prosperous bourgeois who believed in the sanctity of private property: did not one member of the Constituent Assembly, Heurtault-Lauerville, propose to make the 'independence of the soil' an article of the constitution? At the height of their power, the more ruthless members of the Convention found it easy enough to compromise these principles, when faced with external and internal attack from enemies of the Revolution; but the majority remained loyal to them at heart. In any case, these men were so imbued with the philosophy currently in fashion that they equated economic progress (for them an article of faith) with production and agricultural progress with the cultivation of forage crops. 'Without dung there can be no harvest; without livestock, no dung'; such was the curt rejoinder made by the Agricultural Commission set up by the Convention to the Société Populaire of Nogent-le-Républicain, who had called for a law making observance of a fallow period obligatory.[3] The traditional routines were clearly despised as an irksome legacy of 'feudal' barbarism: writing in the Year II, the administrators of the department of Eure-et-Loir declared 'fallows are to agriculture as tyrants are to liberty'.[4]

Many obstacles which had frustrated the agrarian policy of the crown had disappeared. There were no longer any Parlements, which had so often in the past blocked measures which

[2] Arch. Nat., F$^{10}$ 284 (29 August 1793).    [3] Arch. Nat., F$^{10}$ 212$^{13}$.
[4] (L. Merlet), *L'agriculture dans la Beauce en l'an II*, 1859, p. 37.

were injurious to seigneurial interests or a menace to the established order; there were no longer any Provincial Estates. Privileged interests had been swept away: there was no more *troupeau à part*, no more *herbe morte*, no more *triage*. There was no further need to tailor reforms to suit the interests of very large landowners. While the Revolution paid little attention to the *manouvriers*, there was, however, a general attempt to satisfy the demands of the more forward-looking *laboureurs* of the middling sort. Lastly, now that the nation was one and indivisible, there was no longer any need for legislation to be provincial in its application. The 'general law' which d'Ormesson had dreamed of in the heyday of pre-Revolutionary reform, but had never dared to clothe in concrete form, could now become a reality.

But caution was still to be the guiding principle. It is true that the compulsory rotation of crops was too repugnant to the new and totally individualistic notion of liberty for anyone to want to retain it. By proclaiming the right of proprietors to 'vary the cropping and exploitation of their land as they wished', the Constituent Assembly damned compulsory rotation as illegal. There was even a project for the total abolition of compulsory collective grazing on the arable, although this was never taken seriously. The Constituent Assembly was content to follow and enlarge upon the policy adumbrated by the enclosure edicts, by proclaiming absolute liberty of enclosure over the whole country. But they inserted two new provisions, which removed the most serious disabilities suffered by the peasants under earlier edicts. The right of proprietors to participate in collective grazing was either abolished or restricted, depending on how much land they had enclosed. Secondly, artificial meadows were to be closed to grazing at all seasons of the year, a measure frequently advocated during the last years of the *Ancien Régime* and which might in fact have been implemented if ministers and officials had been able to conquer their timidity.[5] This law made the benefits of agricultural progress available to the mass of petty cultivators. The simultaneous abolition of seigneurial rents and dues freed them from the anguish of increasing production only to find the fruits

[5] Officially at least, the reform was partly carried through in Alsace, cf. *supra*, p. 229, n. 40.

of their labour swelling the pockets of the *dîmeur* and the *terrager*, as had deen liable to happen in the past.[6]

There remained the problem of the natural meadows, or more precisely that of the aftermath. This might also have seemed a suitable case for a general law which forbade collective grazing before the second crop had been cut, and the idea was in fact briefly entertained by the Commission appointed by the Constituent Assembly to work out details of the Rural Code. Nothing came of it; in the face of so many competing interests, the only course was to maintain the policy of gradualness initiated under the *Ancien Régime*. For a long time to come, the system adopted for the apportionment of the second crop was governed by local regulations issued by municipalities, districts, or departments and even by representatives seconded to the armies—when it came to fodder the demands of the Republican cavalry were as imperious as those of the Royal squadrons. There were two main systems for apportioning the hay: some places allowed the proprietors a share, others reserved it all for the community. There were also probably places where the proprietors were allowed to keep the whole of the aftermath for themselves, but the Jacobin Convention, mindful of the grievances of small peasants with no meadows of their own, made it plain that such decisions were regarded as inequitable. The men ot Thermidor thought otherwise. In 1795 the reconstituted Committee of Public Safety passed a measure of unusually wide application, which enjoined protection of the aftermath over the whole country and declared that the second crop should be the property of the meadow owner. But in the following year there was a return to the principle of local decision, and this habit has persisted into our own day. In principle, the only individual whose claim to the whole of second crop could be allowed was the proprietor, though there might be one or two exceptional instances where local custom decreed otherwise. The whole affair brings out in bold relief both the continuity in development and the fluctuations in the curve. Responsibility for agrarian discipline passed at the Revolution from the intend-

---

[6] Letter from the intendant of Soissons, 1760, printed *Vierteljahrschrift für Sozial- und Wirtschaftsgeschichte*, 1906, p. 641. The question whether newly cultivated lands were subject to tithe was often ventilated during the eighteenth century; in general it seems to have been answered in a sense favourable to the tithe collectors.

ant to the prefect. The ancient custom of grazing on the second crop, which had been under piecemeal attack during the last three centuries of the monarchy, was in many places finally brought down by a repetition of the same methods, without ever being made the subject of general legislation. Yet the Revolutionary governments were more daring than their predecessors; after some wavering, they abolished all collective rights over the second hay harvest (except where they took the form of pasturage) thus diverting all the profits from the changed law into the pockets of a few individuals. Indeed they make it plain that this was their intention. The decree of 1795 refers expressly to the 'sacred character' of property, threatened by systems which encourage 'immorality and idleness'. It is significant that this decisive act emanated from the reconstituted assembly which had recently shown such ferocity in suppressing the hunger riots and had once again made the franchise exclusive to property-owners.

Collective grazing on the meadows, although not abolished, was now restricted to a briefer period in the year; the custom of collective grazing on the harvested arable long survived in regions where it was traditionally obligatory and where fields were still unenclosed or had not been converted into artificial meadows. After 1789 each successive political regime had dreams of abolishing the practice, but however sympathetic towards private property, none was bold enough to face the certain discontent such a measure would arouse among the mass of the peasantry. In the end the Third Republic adopted the compromise solution which the Estates of Languedoc had brought into operation in 1766. Under this, the obligation was abolished in principle, but each municipality had the right to ask for its continuance. This ancient communal practice is thus still written into our laws.

If legislation was hesitant and slow-moving, it was because it followed the curve of technical improvement.

Peasant communities, especially in open-field regions, long retained an obstinate attachment to their old habits. It was not enough for one man to enclose his field; he still had to persuade his neighbours to respect his fences. Breach of enclosure, the classic punishment meted out by the injured community, was by no means a dead letter in the time of the July Monarchy. The adequate protection of unenclosed artificial meadows would have meant stationing 'a guard over each furrow', as was remarked in Haute-Saône in 1813. During the first half of the nineteenth century the lower courts sometimes refused to sanction the protection of forage crops, basing themselves on local custom. Gradually, however, as technical improvements became more widespread, the rights of the individual secured more general recognition. Enclosures were still a rarity, except in those regions where arable was being replaced by grass. Most of the regions which were anciently open country have remained so into our own day; the striking contrast between 'plains' and 'woodland' is as evident to the modern traveller as it was to the poet Wace. Collective grazing on the arable waste has certainly lost some ground; but in regions of open fields, especially where the fields are long, it survived for many years and in many places is still practised today. Collective grazing on meadows was completely abolished by the Chambers in 1889. But in the following year it was once again made legal, in consequence of strong peasant protests. In Lorraine, Champagne, and Franche Comté, as in other places, many communes retained the practice of collective grazing on both the arable and the meadows, taking advantage of the permission accorded them under the law. The English historian Seebohm, whose researches into the long-vanished collective practices of his own country had to be based on ancient records, was astonished when he came to the Beauce to see herds actually at large on the stubble. The abolition of compulsory rotation by law, which took place under the First Empire, aroused considerable regret even at that late date. In practice it survived much longer, applied with almost as much rigour as in the past; in regions of long-furlong fields it can still be observed today, kept alive by the shape of the plots and a sense of moral compulsion. Springtime on the plateaux of Lorraine and in the plains of Alsace and Burgundy is still marked in the fields by the appearance of the three contrasting hues, corresponding to the three 'courses'.[7] The only difference now is that the lands formerly

[7] In the same way, regulations about the hay, corn and grape harvests have remained in force, although it seems they are of practical importance only in the case of the vintage.

fallow are nearly everywhere planted with the new crops, instead of being left to the scanty herbage produced by land in repose.

The full story of man's liberation from fallow farming—an achievement just as dramatic in its way as the great clearances of the Middle Ages—has yet to be written. At present the materials are lacking. However, it is possible to point to some of the factors whose presence helped the movement on its way: the cultivation of industrial crops; the appearance of chemical fertilisers which solved the problem of manure, relaxed the age-old association between corn and cattle, and freed agronomy from its obsession with the forage crops whose large-scale cultivation had at first seemed the necessary if somewhat irksome condition of any agricultural improvement; the advent of rational specialisation in the use of different types of soil, which was fostered by the development first of European and later of global trade; and finally, the growing commerce in ideas, which brought small rural groups into contact with better informed and more adventurous circles. One thing at least is certain; the rhythm of change, which naturally varied with the region, was nowhere rapid. Until the second half of the nineteenth century there were districts—especially in the east— where the empty *sombres* or *somarts* were abandoned to herdsmen and hunters. In the end, however, men gradually became accustomed to the idea that, except in regions condemned by nature to irremediable sterility, the land should be made to work almost without interruption. Even so, average yields continued below the level achieved in many other countries. Nearly everywhere else in Europe, and in other parts of the world under European influence, agriculture showed a tendency to become more rational and more scientific, using technical and financial procedures akin in many respects to those of industry. In France the course of this evolution, one of the most distinctive features of our modern economy, has been more wavering, and the total achievement somewhat inferior to that of most of her neighbours. Even where, as in wine-growing and exclusively pastoral regions, concentration on a single type of farming—one of the improvements made possible by better trade and communications—has proved successful, the French peasant, unlike let us say the American small farmer, still relies in part on produce from his cottage garden and poultry yard, and may even have stables and pig-sties as well.

Some of the reasons for this attachment to past habits are obvious enough. Material considerations play an important part. In some regions, especially of long-furlong fields, which happen to be among the most fertile, the ancient lay-out of the fields has scarcely altered and dictates the continuation of agrarian habits for which it was originally designed. Plans for a general distribution of plots have often been mooted; to succeed, any such programme would have to be imposed from above. The dictatorial Marat saw no objection to the use of force. But the Constituent Assembly, the Conventions, the economists and governments of later generations were all inhibited from following his example by the respect for the independence of the property-owner which underlay their whole social philosophy. The enforced surrender of his hereditary fields was surely the greatest injury a master of the soil could suffer. What was more, the mass of the peasantry would certainly jib at an upheaval on this scale, and even before the days of universal suffrage, governments could not fail to be sensitive to the reactions of these non-voting citizens. One might think that amalgamation of strips could have been effected by persuasion, but instances of this are in fact very rare. It is one of the paradoxes of history that the very cult of private ownership which had led reformers to reject the old communal principles also blocked the one decisive measure which could have freed property from its hampering restrictions and cleared a free path for technical progress.

The truth is that redistribution would follow automatically in the wake of any purely economic revolution in which the small holdings were sacrificed. No such revolution has so far taken place.

The great crisis which broke in 1789 had not meant the destruction of the large landed property as reconstituted in the immediately preceding centuries. Such noble and bourgeois proprietors as did not emigrate—far more numerous, even among the nobility, than is sometimes imagined—hung on to their possessions. Some émigrés were able to arrange for their properties to be bought back by relations, or had them restored by the Consulate or Empire. The survival of aristocratic fortunes in certain parts of the country, particularly the east, is at once one of the least studied and least disputable facts of our recent social history. Even the sale of national property—lands belonging to the Church and to émigrés—did not inflict a really damaging blow. The procedure followed made it possible for the land to be sold in blocks, or even as complete estates; big tenant farmers became big proprietors, the bourgeoisie continued the patient and fruitful work put into the land by their predecessors, prosperous *laboureurs* added to their patrimony and made their decisive entry into the ranks of rural capitalists.

Nevertheless, in releasing a considerable number of properties onto the market, the Revolution brought some reinforcement to small ownership. Many peasants of only modest means, notably in areas where the communal way of life was strong and community pressures could make themselves felt in conditions of sale, were able to acquire plots for themselves, which gave some stability to their economic position. There were even some lowly manual workers who secured a share of the spoils and hoisted themselves into the land-owning class. The partition of the commons produced a similar effect. This measure (from which woods were exempt) was passed by the Legislative after the Tenth of August 1792, together with others designed, as one deputy (François de Neufchateau) put it, to 'attach the inhabitants of the countryside to the Revolution'. If it was to achieve its avowed purpose, the distribution would certainly have to be made by households. And this was in fact the plan adopted by the Convention when it came to ratify the measure shortly afterwards, at the same time reducing it from a mandate to an authorisation. There was to be no more *triage*—naturally enough, since there were no longer any lords; in this August of 1792 they even went so far as to revoke in principle all *triages* effected since 1669. In addition, the communities were accorded some presumption of ownership over the waste. To sum up, the assemblies indulged in the luxury of satisfying both the individualism vaunted by the economists (hence the partition of the commons, which gradually put an end to all collective enjoyment of them) and the demands of small country people whose support was necessary to the new regime and who were pleased at the manner in which the partitioning was conducted. The bourgeois governments of the last years of the Revolution, the Directory and the Consulate, put an end to forms of partition which favoured poorer villagers, thus repeating the pattern of events familiar to us from the history of the aftermath. What was still worse, some partitions which had been effected without necessary legal safeguards were actually annulled, often with the support of municipal governments which from now on would be in the hands of the rich: some of the partitions cancelled in the north even dated back to the time of the monarchy. In future, alienation of commons (except where it was a question merely of the right to use them) could be made only against payment; and although the law itself at first forbade this practice it soon decame re-established and was recognised by the courts. Once this had happened, the way was clear in certain regions, especially in Central France, for progressive attrition of the commons, leading in some places to their virtual disappearance. This is a subject which still awaits detailed investigation; it is obvious, however, that few new properties were likely to be created in the process. Yet despite this retrograde step, and despite our ignorance of the way in which the decrees of the Legislative and Convention were carried out, there can be no doubt that while it lasted partitioning of the commons provided many poorer people with the chance they had long been waiting for, the chance to acquire land for themselves. The last great boon conferred on the peasants by the Revolutionary Assemblies was the abolition of seigneurial charges, which removed one of the main causes of the indebtedness which from the sixteenth century onward had made their grip on the land so precarious. If we take the larger view and ignore the nuances, which although interesting enough in themselves deserve a separate study, we can fairly say that the co-existence of the large capitalist-run estate with small peasant proprietorship, evolved under the *Ancien Régime*, was carried over into this new era of French history.

Except at those moments when the Revolution was struggling for its life and some men perceived the need for support from the common people, the Revolutionaries were as cavalier of the interests of the *manouvriers* as the reformers of the eighteenth century had been. Delacroix, who was a member of the Convention, thought that industry and even agriculture itself might be starved of labour if manual workers were given land of their own. The Committee of Public Safety set up after Thermidor deprived landless workers of all their rights over the aftermath and advised them to seek work from meadow owners if they needed forage for their animals. Like some of the more insensitive members of the governing class under the *Ancien Régime*, they even allowed themselves to doubt whether genuine poverty existed in the countryside: 'even indigent villagers (if any still exist). . . .' The truth is that the disappearance of collective obligations struck a blow at the rural proletariat from which it has never recovered. Both the edicts issued under the *Ancien Régime* and the Revolutionary legislation admittedly had their good effects, since they allowed the landless some share in the partition of common lands and in the acquisition of scattered fragments of national properties. But these benefits were often illusory; there were plenty of disappointments in store for peasants who toiled at clearing these indifferent patches of ground and working the wretchedly small holdings. The *laboureurs* of Frenelle-la-Grande who predicted in 1789 that partition of the commons would give rise to a temporary surplus of births, to be followed by a crisis of poverty, were not entirely unjustified in the event. And this was only one of the reasons for the exodus of day labourers and small holders from the countryside, which came to pass just as Musac had foretold. The others were various: the attraction of urban wages, the decline of the cottage industries which had helped agricultural workers to eke out a living, the difficulties of adapting to a new economic regime, the flagging of the communal spirit, which showed decreasing zest for communal works, and the growth of a new taste for comfort, which made the harsh conditions of life as a farm worker seem more than ever repugnant. It was the landless who largely contributed to this oft-deplored exodus, which was already noticeable in the time of the July Monarchy and which from the middle of the nineteenth century accelerated in an almost uniform rhythm. The resulting scarcity of labour (further increased by the dramatic decline in the birthrate which set in at much the same time, and later by the horrifying loss of life in the Great War) was itself an incentive to further technical innovation, for example the mechanisation of agriculture and the substitution of grasslands for arable. The congested countrysides typical of the later eighteenth century and still more of the first half of the nineteenth have given place to great half-empty spaces. No doubt the swing has gone too far the other way; here and there land has actually fallen out of cultivation. But the rural France which has emerged is perhaps in better trim for pursuing an economy untrammelled by respect for tradition and relieved of that perpetual fear of starvation, whose oppressive weight for so long dictated modes of cultivation.

It is much more delicate—in the present state of our knowledge in fact virtually impossible—to give an accurate account of the lot of peasant farmers—whether owners, tenants or *métayers*—under modern conditions. Peasant farming has certainly passed through critical times, some of them very threatening: there have been constant difficulties over credit, competition from imported food-stuffs (in particular the entry of Russian and American grain from about 1880), problems of labour shortage brought about by the flight of landless peasants and the decline of the birth-rate and, at present, the higher prices of manufactured goods, which the peasant now finds more than ever essential. In certain regions, where the small producers are mostly tenant-farmers or *métayers*, the great estate is still a dominant influence; few peasants anywhere can avoid being dependent on external sources for capital and loans; lastly, small growers find that prices for their produce are dictated by the dealers, who are in a better position to take advantage of market contingencies. The economic position of the small and medium peasant holding is thus in many respects unstable. All the same, it must be admitted that none of the essential features of small peasant farming have disappeared in the course of the nineteenth and early twentieth centuries. Peasant proprietorship, in the full legal sense of the term, has been conspicuously successful in maintaining its ascendancy over much of the soil, and has even some noticeable conquests to its credit; in recent years it has reaped some profit from the crisis in food production accompanying the Great War and the immediate post-war years, and also from the monetary crisis, just as in the time of the Hundred Years' War. It is trite but true to observe that today peasant farming is still a great economic and social force. The small holding is still landlocked in its antiquated lay-out of fields, still stubbornly resistant to change; there is little inclination toward sudden innovation—as Olivier de Serres remarked long ago, 'what majesty resides in the old style of land disposition'—and ancestral habits are abandoned only with difficulty; technical improvements have made little headway. Despite the latest revolution in general attitudes which has followed from a growing familiarity with machinery in all its forms and will doubtless accomplish much more in the future, actual progress has been slow. But it can at least be said that peasant farming has not succumbed under the pressure of agricultural change. France is still a country where the land is in many different hands.

And so the past continues to dominate the present. If we seek to explain the physiognomy of modern rural France, we shall find that the antecedents of nearly every feature recede into the mists of time. The exodus of the rural proletariat is the outcome of an age-old antagonism between *manouvriers* and *laboureurs*, the end of a story whose earlier chapters are written in medieval parchments which set manual and ploughing services in opposition to one another. And what of peasant proprietorship, whose tenacious strength has in turn been responsible for the continuing conservatism of field patterns, for the long drawn-out resistance offered by communal practices to new brooms and for the slow-moving pace of technical progress ? The fact is that peasant proprietorship had a legal basis—the custom of the *seigneuries*—an and economic justification—abundance of land and scarcity of men—well before the royal courts finally set the seal of their authority on tenants' rights. But the small peasant was not the only occupant of the soil; he has had to contend, as he still must, with fierce competition from huge estates created by seigneurial and bourgeois capitalism, the estates where the agricultural revolution had its first beginnings and without which it might have been impossible. In regions of long-furlong fields fragmentation goes back to the earliest days of our agrarian civilisation; the stages in its development reflect the vicissitudes of the family on its passage from the patriarchal *manse* to the implicit community established during the centuries which followed; temporary checks to the progress of fragmentation are to be explained by the introduction of a new economic system, in which amalgamation of plots was a cardinal feature. The key to the most fundamental of all agrarian contrasts, namely the existence of three major field systems—long and open, irregular and open, and enclosed—and of contrasting ways of life with which they are associated (for example the great strength of collective feeling in the north and east as compared with the villages of the Midi and the western hamlets) must lie, if anywhere, in events which attended the occupation of the soil and in characteristics of a social structure now lost in the mists of a past without written records. To anyone of a reflective turn of mind, it is these observations which give rural history its intense appeal. Indeed, what discipline is more imperious in forcing its practitioners to come to grips with history as it really is? In the continuum of human societies, the vibrations between molecule and molecule spread out over so great a span that understanding of a single moment, no matter what its place in the chain of development, can never be attained merely by contemplation of its immediate predecessor.

# Index

249

# Index

# Index